BRIDGE TO THE SUN

by GWEN TERASAKI

BRIDGE
TO THE SUN

Newport, Tennessee

WAKESTONE BOOKS

To Terry

Two things greater than all things are,
The first is Love, and the second War.
And since we know not how War may prove,
Heart of my heart, let us talk of Love!

Kipling

INTRODUCTION

I can just imagine the tall woman - proud in the way of Tennessee mountain people - towering above a sea of Japanese who are trudging up the mountain roads, escaping from their burning Tokyo homes.

"The Japanese never touched me," she told me forty years later.

"We buried our household goods with them in Tokyo, shared fish if we could find it, grew a few precious vegetables and flowers and waited together for the war to end."

Gwen Harold of Johnson City, Tennessee, had married Hidenari Terasaki, an ambitious young Japanese diplomat, at her aunt's home in Washington in 1931.

Gwen and Terry had a dream: to build a bridge to the sun. They were two young people of different nationalities and different races who hoped to bring their countries together in peace. The Japanese Ambassador warned Terry it was a reckless thing for them to do, that their countries might instead go to war.

When Pearl Harbor was bombed, Gwen was at Sunday lunch. Later at their Washington apartment Terry asked her what she wanted to do. "I made that decision ten years ago," she shot back. She and Terry, and their only daughter, Mariko, were deported to Japan.

Gwen's book is a love story about her dream with Terry. "It came from the heart," she told me. It has been translated into six languages and has had twelve printings.

In 1983, Japanese television made a film about Mariko. Its tender story in the midst of fire, hunger and death so touched the Japanese that it showed a second time. Today, Gwen and Mariko are two of the best known Americans in Japan.

Gwen's friend, Martha Ragland, gave me the book in 1982. I read it in one sitting. Then, finally, I met Gwen at her home in Johnson City one day in February, 1985.

We talked about Terry, especially about his preference for southern Americans. She was surprised to learn that during the last few years 30 Japanese companies had invested more than a billion dollars in Tennessee. After forty years, the bridge that she and Terry had dreamed about was being built.

I'm glad that Dykeman Stokely - the son of our State Historian, Wilma Dykeman - is reprinting the book. I am especially glad that Nissan Motor Manufacturing Company - the largest of our new Japanese companies - is presenting a copy of the book to every one of the 1,700 public school libraries in the state.

Nissan is making this gesture in response to the publication of the book, *Friends*, which I wrote and which includes stunning photographs by Robin Hood. All of this is part of a week-long Salute To Japan during a year when Japan is being Honored at Memphis in May and when the Smithsonian Folk Arts Festival in Washington honors both Tennessee and Japan.

In 1979 I began my visits to Japan in order to help bring new jobs to Tennessee. During eight visits since then, I've become convinced that the Japan/U.S. relationship is the most important two-country relationship in the world, central to the struggle in the United States to maintain our standard of living in an increasingly competitive world market.

Our success depends upon our ability to understand Japan. But one cannot understand Japan simply by wallowing through the bog of statistics and brochures and figures that are available everywhere. It is much better to read Gwen Terasaki's love story and to imagine the tall woman among the Japanese moving into the mountains, leaving behind their burning homes in the city.

Lamar Alexander
Governor of Tennessee
February,1986

FOREWORD

I STARTED WRITING *Bridge to the Sun* shortly after we returned from Japan. Writing it helped me overcome the deep sadness I had felt when we landed at San Francisco to journey across the continent, leaving the Pacific and the Japanese islands so very far behind.

Three years later, our daughter, Mariko, was married and the new member of the family read what I had written. Thus it was that a certain continuity with the past was evolved, for my son-in-law, Mayne Miller, believed in the story and felt that it should be published. He furnished the impetus and the necessary work on the revision and completion of the manuscript. My husband was proud of Mariko for carrying on "what I meant to do" in this country; it would be a great happiness to him that he is so well understood by the son-in-law he never knew.

Johnson City, Tennessee
December 10, 1956

CONTENTS

BRIDGE TO THE SUN

1

PEARL HARBOR

SUNDAY, the seventh of December, 1941, began as an ordinary holiday. Mother was visiting us—my husband, Terry, our nine-year-old daughter, Mariko, and me—in our Woodley Park Towers apartment in Washington. We arose late and had coffee while Mariko read the comics. Since it was a mild day, I suggested we take our Sunday dinner out. It would be a pleasant drive if we went out to Collingwood, an excellent restaurant several miles from the city. Living in diplomatic circles in Washington, one does not get much simple American food, and I looked forward to the fried chicken and sweet potatoes I knew were on the menu at Collingwood: the kind of Sunday dinner I had been accustomed to at home in Tennessee before I had met and married Hidenari Terasaki of the Japanese Foreign Office.

Terry had been working too hard, eighteen to twenty hours a day, for the past several weeks. I was glad he could be away from the Embassy for awhile and enjoy the relaxation of a holiday. He drove fast as always and made sport of the trip to the restaurant, all the while extolling the prowess of his new convertible Buick to his daughter in the front seat. If Mother was frightened at the way he drove, she did not show it. We were gay and animated that pleasant December day.

When we arrived at the restaurant, Terry went in to inform the headwaiter that we were awaiting our turn for a table. There were several people ahead of us and the suggestion was made that we stroll through the gardens until our table was ready. While we were visiting the gardens, Terry's manner changed. He left off bantering with us and walked to the far corner of the garden while Mother and I engaged in guessing the name of a certain shrub that had caught our attention. I feared that Terry would lapse again into the preoccupation which had made him somewhat remote in recent months. But he returned to us in a minute or so and we soon went in to have dinner.

Afterwards we drove leisurely along the Potomac. Terry wished to drop in at the Embassy to look over the late dispatches, so Mother, Mako, and I decided to go to the Uptown Theater to see a movie. Terry dropped us off there and waved goodbye. It was ten days before I saw him again.

We entered the theater and found the movie mildly enjoyable. It seems a trivial thing to remember, but it was "Unfinished Business," with Robert Montgomery and Irene Dunne. When the movie was over and we had consumed two boxes of popcorn, we left the theater and strolled to the apartment, only a few blocks away. We entered the lobby of the Woodley Park Towers.

The groups of people standing around were speaking in hushed tones. There was a strange tenseness in the air. Instantly I felt something was wrong. When I went to the desk to get my key, the telephone operator informed me, "Madame Terasaki, Mr. Terasaki has called you many times from the Embassy and asked me to have you ring him up as soon as you came in." She added, "I think he's very worried about you."

Alarmed and puzzled, we went up immediately to our apartment amid the curious stares of the people around, stares that were not unfriendly, just blank and wondering. I was uneasy and

2

rushed to the telephone at once. At first I could not get connected with the Embassy but finally got through to my husband's secretary.

"Mrs. Terasaki, Mr. Terasaki is so worried about you. He's busy now and can't come to the telephone. He'll call you again in a few minutes."

I asked quickly, "What's wrong?"

The answer came back, "Don't you know? Then turn on your radio!"

I hung up and dashed to the radio.

All I can remember of that hour of horror, grief, and tears, there with my mother and my frightened little Mako, was my concentration upon comforting Mako. She was crying over leaving her school. Thinking of her sorrow at having to leave it gave me something commonplace and natural to hold on to. I saw rows of school desks, lines of American boys and girls, and could almost hear them saying, "I pledge allegiance to the flag of the United States of America. . . ." Anything to wipe out the sound of the newscaster and thoughts of the fearful unknown future.

Mother suggested coffee, as she is prone to do in any emergency. I remember a favorite expression of hers, "There's no crisis in life that a cup of coffee won't help."

At last the telephone rang and I heard Terry's voice, fuzzy with fatigue and emotion.

"Oh, it's terrible! Why did they do such a terrible thing? Japan is doomed. I won't be able to call you again because the telephones are to be disconnected. Be strong, darling, and say goodbye to your mother for me. I'm sure I can't see her again."

That night my telephone rang constantly. Old friends called up to express their sorrow. Knowing he had worked hard for peace and that the war was a personal defeat for him, they were especially solicitous about Terry. They pledged their love and friendship regardless of the war between America and Japan.

2

"TERASAKI'S FOLLY"

ALONE in the double bed that night I could not sleep.

The years kept coming through my mind as if, by recalling them, I could escape into the past. I dwelt on each detail of our life together, our attempt to "bridge" our beloved countries, searching to find how this disaster had come about.

It had been almost exactly ten years since we met, years devoted to preventing the calamity which had overtaken us, years of joy and hope which might never return.

I was twenty-three the winter of 1930 when I went from Johnson City, the little town in the blue mountains of eastern Tennessee where I had grown up, to Washington to spend several months visiting my aunt. One afternoon not long after my arrival, she told me that we had been invited to two embassy functions; the French Embassy was entertaining, and Ambassador Debuchi was having a reception at the Japanese Embassy. My aunt felt that I should see what a Japanese party was like— the floral arrangements, the kimonos, and the oriental furnishings—

4

and that this would be more of a novelty for me than the French gathering. So we chose the Japanese.

When we started through the long receiving line, I noticed particularly the two handsome Japanese standing near Ambassador Debuchi. They were tall, even by American standards, and seemed to tower over the diminutive Ambassador. My aunt identified the older man as Sotomatsu Kato, the counsellor, a man famous in Washington society for his good looks. The younger man was handsome, too, as he stood erect and slim by Mr. Kato's side, watching us approach. His large eyes were very black and luminous, and I was aware that he kept them on me. We spoke to Ambassador Debuchi, who greeted us warmly, and moved on toward the punch bowl. In a moment the young Japanese approached and spoke to my aunt. They exchanged pleasantries and then Hidenari Terasaki was introduced to me.

He spoke English fluently and I learned, as we talked on, that he had studied the year before in the graduate school at Brown University and that he was now the private secretary to the Ambassador. He told me, with less diplomacy than he might have, that he was tired of escorting middle-aged matrons and answering frivolous questions about his country, and that I was the first young person to attend a Japanese party in weeks. As I had never known a Japanese before and knew nothing of Japan, I found myself asking him about his country—and apparently he did not consider my questions frivolous, for he answered them with enthusiasm. I left the Embassy, and Mr. Terasaki, reluctantly.

The next day I received a package of Japanese books and pictures, a fan, a small container of green tea—and a bouquet of yellow roses. It appeared my wish to know things Japanese was to be fulfilled. I told my aunt that I felt I really must do something for this Mr. Terasaki who had been so overwhelmingly kind to me. She invited him to tea. He arrived with more literature and pictures and prepared to lecture on his native

5

land. Then he asked me to have dinner and included my aunt in the invitation as a matter of course. Later, realizing that a chaperone was not essential, he began calling often, always bringing a picture or a book he hoped I would enjoy. One afternoon I opened a parcel to find a daguerreotype of General Robert E. Lee, whom Mr. Terasaki admired. He had obtained the photograph through Ralph Pollio, the manager of the Mayflower Hotel and an old friend. Accompanying the picture was a copy of Edgar Lee Master's poem, "Lee."

We often walked in Rock Creek Park and once or twice he tried futilely to teach me golf—thereafter I just followed him around the course. He had two names, Hidenari and Eisei, because the characters in Japanese could be pronounced either way, but he permitted me to call him Terry although it is considered bad luck in Japan to shorten one's last name.

I learned that his father had been in the export-import business in Yokohama, and that he had an older brother, Taro, then Consul in New York, and a younger brother, Taira, who was still in school in Japan. Although the father was a Buddhist, he had thought the discipline and high scholastic standards of the Catholic school system would be good for his sons, and Terry had attended the Catholic school Morning Star, where he was prepared well for his college work at Ichiko.

I discovered later that after finishing at Ichiko he spent four years at the Imperial University and earned a law degree. At the University aspirants to the Foreign Office must choose the language in which they intend to become most proficient, and the choice, of course, has a large bearing upon where they are later sent for duty. Everyone was expected to study China but in addition it was required that a Western country be chosen for special consideration. Taro had chosen France and, being of scholarly inclination, had attended the Sorbonne and received his doctorate there. Terry had chosen English-speaking countries and the Foreign Office had sent him to Washington, where, as a matter of routine, he was required to attend an American

6

college during his first year in the new country. At Brown he had studied English language and literature.

Terry played eighteen holes of golf each morning before breakfast. He had won the Debuchi Cup several times at the Burning Tree course. I should have thought, having done that, he would be content to sleep in the mornings, but he explained that golf is something that gets in the blood, like the desire to gamble, and he had an urge to improve which he was pleased to satisfy even at six o'clock in the morning. His love of sports was not limited to golf; he was an excellent swimmer, and he took special delight in scaring me out of my wits in his convertible roadster.

I was occasionally going out with other men, and this made Terry furious. To him this was as strange and incredible as if I had taken to pole-sitting. His attitude ranged from wonder to muted rage. I did not stop going out with other men, but I realized that whoever married Terry would have to get her way by indirect means; he was a forceful, dominating person. I felt the magnetism of his dark, intelligent eyes and was a little disturbed.

His zest for Japan was contagious and I found myself reading the books he had given me so that I could converse with him intelligently. What I could not readily understand I referred to my delighted teacher, who would launch into rapturous and intense lectures, answering my questions but digressing happily into much more that I could not grasp.

I became greatly interested in the reaction of the *samurai* class to the coming of Western civilization after Commodore Perry visited Japan in the 1850's. The *samurai* were violently opposed to change and, in an attempt to "expel the barbarians," fired upon the foreign ships. The combined fleets of the powers soon appeared, shelled the seacoast cities, and the Japanese were forced to pay a huge indemnity. The *samurai* then saw that their future independence required the acceptance of the Westerners and the development of an industrial society. Soon, they decided

to create a strong central government for their islands and over-
threw the Shogunate, abolished feudalism, and restored the Emperor to supreme power. The capital was then moved from Kyoto
to Tokyo.

Terry had many heroes among the early *samurai;* most of them
were the architects of the new Japan, but some opposed the
Western movement. The great *samurai*, Saigo, had resisted
change, thinking Japan would lose tradition and identity in the
process. As there were others who shared this belief, a resistance
movement was begun. Saigo was reluctant to see civil war but
found himself thrust to the head of the revolution. In 1877 the
two forces fought a great battle to decide the future course of
the country, a battle which proved that the sword-wielding
samurai of the south of Japan were no match for the guns of the
new army of the central government. As Terry related Saigo's
"lost cause," I saw some parallel in the careers of Saigo and Terry's
American hero, Robert E. Lee.

The man of whom Terry talked most often was Prince
Saionji, the one surviving elder statesman who had advised the
Meiji from 1867 until the Emperor's death in 1912. Still holding
great power in Japan, Saionji was of a noble family which had
been a part of the Emperor's court at Kyoto before the Restora-
tion. When he spoke of this venerable statesman, Terry became
solemn.

When the *Washington Post* carried a story of the clash in
Manchuria between the Japanese and the Russians, I found myself
reading it with great interest. I asked Terry about it when he
came for me one Saturday afternoon. He explained that there
was great competition in Manchuria between the Russians and
the Japanese. His country had once called Russia "the sleeping
colossus," but she was sleeping no longer. Her activity in China
was obviously quite dangerous for Japan—and the world. Terry
felt that this problem could be solved by wise leadership on the
part of the Japanese statesmen. His country did not want a war
with Russia, and he felt that the United States and Great Britain
would help avert it. Japanese friendship with the United States

must be an immutable policy—that was the primary reason Terry had wanted to be stationed in America.

When Terry asked me to marry him, as I *thought* I hoped he would, I could only ask him to give me time to consider. He said I was wise to weigh carefully the great adjustments we would have to make. He pointed out that there would be many who would not understand, both Americans and Japanese—and that it would be difficult for my parents also. We would be constantly surrounded by strange people and strange customs in various parts of the world. He urged me to say "yes" and added,

"We would have much to endure, but we would walk through a few doors and open a few windows together—and that would be our compensation."

Spring came and it was time for me to return to Johnson City. Terry repeated his proposal more and more frequently as time came for me to leave, but I was still undecided. I wanted to be with him, I hated to leave him, but did I want to marry him? I kept postponing the decision. How odd it would sound to be called Gwen Terasaki!

On the evening of my departure, I was still confused. Terry arrived to take me to the train, and I said goodbye to my aunt, who had been so kind and understanding. Feeling very tense, I walked to the car with him, keeping my eyes averted from the question I knew appeared in his dark eyes. As he opened the trunk for my luggage, my aunt called out to remind me that I had forgotten a package for my mother. I ran back to my room and found the package where I had left it on a chair by the open window. As I picked it up, I looked out toward the street where Terry stood by the door of the car, the moonlight reflected on his face. The scent of the spirea blossoms in the yard swept through the open window and in that instant I knew I would be his wife. Perhaps my decision had already been made, but in that moment my doubts vanished and my future was determined.

Since my acceptance of Terry's proposal had been made just

9

before boarding the train for Johnson City, we had to make our plans by mail. There were many matters to be settled. I wanted my parents to understand and approve, and Terry must have permission from the Foreign Office. And what about Terry's family?

Every nation is dubious of marriages between Foreign Service personnel and nationals of the countries in which they serve. Taro had been in the Japanese Foreign Office considerably longer than Terry had. He had been first secretary to the important Embassy in London, had attended the Washington Disarmament Conference in 1921, and had been with the Japanese delegation to the League of Nations. He, I feared, would oppose an international marriage because it was against the policy of the Foreign Office. I knew also that he had a famous temper. Terry told me, however, that Taro was pro-American and pro-British and that his temper was exercised only in favor of the measures which would promote amity among the three countries. I did not know how this elder brother would react.

Ambassador Debuchi, a small, chubby, thoroughly delightful person much loved by the Americans, was opposed to another marriage by any of his staff. Five Japanese had married foreigners while serving with him, and it had become a ticklish point. There was a saying in the Foreign Office, "If you want to marry a *gaijin* (foreigner), go out with Debuchi."

To make matters worse, a Japanese diplomat in London had recently become engaged to an Englishwoman without so much as notifying the Foreign Office. The first knowledge his superiors had of the engagement was acquired from the society section of the newspapers. This incident had caused considerable comment in Japanese circles.

Terry called me frequently that summer (always at midnight because of the lower rates and my father growled at me, "Confound it, doesn't he know people sleep at night?"), and I sent him a telegram containing the grotesque indiscretion of *"koi shimasu* (I love you)." This proved quite embarrassing because

Terry's colleagues in the Embassy learned of the wire through the telegraphers handling it.

"Who is this *gaijin* who says '*koi shimasu*,' Terasaki-san?" was their mockingly solicitous inquiry.

Mr. Kato, Terry's handsome friend and superior, remarked to Debuchi that our romance pleased him and he hoped the Foreign Office would permit us to marry. Debuchi frowned on the suggestion and became cool toward Kato for mentioning it. Terry approached the Ambassador with some hesitance. As he had anticipated, Debuchi told him that marriage to a Westerner would put unneccessary troubles in his path, and he urged Terry to consider carefully the double life he would have to lead. The Ambassador even suggested the possibility that the two countries might go to war sometime in the future, and then what? Terry's response to this was filled with conviction—such a thing was impossible and unthinkable, our countries were friends and needed each other. Finally, Debuchi invited Terry to play golf the following Friday and asked that he weigh the matter seriously in the meantime.

But before Friday Terry went to New York to speak to his elder brother. After he and Taro had talked it out, both wrote out their resignations, mutually agreeing to protest in that way if permission was not granted by the Foreign Office.

On Friday things were solemn at the golf course. Terry would have been respectful of any superior and he admired Ambassador Debuchi deeply. He tried to concentrate on his game but his game was not very good. They went the first few holes almost in silence. Then, as they stood on a tee ready to drive toward one of the more distant holes, the Ambassador spoke of the subject which neither had mentioned. "Well, Terasaki, have you reached a decision?"

Not answering at once, Terry carefully teed his ball and made his drive. The club head made a resounding "smack" against the ball, which rose beautifully in the air. The two men watched and, when it had fallen and finally rolled to a stop, Terry was heartened to reply. "Yes! I have shot the ball down the fairway!"

Masking his disappointment as best he could, Debuchi said, "In that case I will see what can be done."

Mother came to Washington with me to meet Terry and, I suspected, to see if she and Taro could do something to avert our marriage. However, she agreed that the decision was mine and promised to stand by me. Her hope that she and Taro might find a means of impressing the unwisdom of marriage upon us was short-lived. When she came down the steps to greet the two boys who had come to my aunt's to call, she could see from their glowing faces that Taro was in league with Terry.

Taro had already discussed our marriage with Debuchi and had proved an equal disappointment to the Ambassador. Debuchi had told him,

"Taro-san, you know that Eisei is going to be a great statesman. You know it. It is in him, in his face, and you know that a Western wife is going to be a handicap. We don't want anything to stop your brother."

Taro had replied, "Yes, I know—but he loves that girl, and I know my brother. If he ever wanted anything in his life, this is it. I don't know what he might do. He might never succeed without her."

"Ah, so," the Ambassador had muttered, "you're the elder Terasaki—what can I say?"

Taro pleaded Terry's case with Mother in much the same fashion and assured her that his brother would do everything in his power to make me happy. Although Taro supported us all the way, he had reservations concerning Terry's extravagance. He had objected to the stationery Terry had ordered for writing to me, engraved "Deeper than the Pacific Ocean, higher than Fujiyama."

"*Baka da yo,*" he would say. "Stupid idiot."

The Manchurian Incident of 1931 had occurred during our courtship. American-Japanese relations were strained and officials in Tokyo were busy. For some ten days Tokyo delayed answering Debuchi's request that permission for the marriage be granted. I had told Terry that if we did not receive permission

I could not marry him—I would not destroy two careers. But permission was granted! Debuchi had wired that ours was a special case.

When the Washington papers carried the story of our engagement, they used, through some mistake, a picture of Mr. Kato instead of Terry. How embarrassed Terry was to appear at the Embassy the next morning! Kato told me in a fatherly way that Terry must treat me well or answer to him—after all, I had been engaged to him first.

Fearing the "East meets West" publicity, Terry and I planned to announce one date for our wedding to the papers and to be married a few days earlier. First we decided on a Friday, but changed the date when we realized it was the thirteenth of the month. We settled on the following Wednesday and were married at my aunt's home in Washington. I remember that when I entered the room to approach the altar where Terry stood with the minister, Terry turned and caught the attention of all by the manner in which he watched me as I went to him. He explained later that he had simply wanted to see how I looked as a bride, that I would never look exactly that way again. The papers learned of the wedding some time later, on the date they had been told it would take place. The stories of the wedding appeared in the same issues of the papers which spoke of ominous occurrences in Manchuria.

We honeymooned briefly in New York and then returned to Washington where we were entertained at the Mayflower by the Pollios. We did not have long to stay in the United States. The Foreign Office had decided to recall Terry to Tokyo, whether because it had real need for him or to test his American wife, I do not know. At any rate, after only a few short weeks, we sailed from San Francisco and arrived in Yokohama on Christmas Eve, 1931.

We were met at Yokohama by the parents of Taro's wife, Sugako. They knew about as much of Westerners as I had known of Japan when I first went to Washington. Sugako's mother had almost fainted once when kissed on the hand by the Turkish Ambassador, thinking, perhaps, that he was about to bite her; it was an unheard-of custom, a personal offense, and it did not matter to her that it was considered polite elsewhere. She had jerked her hand back, saying, "He shouldn't do that! Why did he kiss my hand?" She was told he kissed only the hands of married women, not young girls' hands; but she thought that made matters even worse. I came to know her as *obāsan* (grandmother) and the father as *ojiisan* (grandfather). *Ojiisan* was good to us and allowed us to live in the teahouse the entire time we stayed in Tokyo.

Taira was with them when they met us at the dock. He had read much about Westerners and was in love with Anne Lindbergh. Her *North to the Orient* had made her a favorite of all Japanese by capturing the essence of their islands, especially in the passages about the singing sailors and Japanese poetry. Taira thought I should look like Mrs. Lindbergh. When he saw me at the porthole as the ship was being tied up, he remarked to *obāsan,*

"I hope the girl looking out of the porthole is my new sister, but Eisei couldn't get anyone as pretty as that." Then when we disembarked, he shouted, "It *is* the girl at the porthole!"

He asked Terry what he should say to me, and Terry told him to say, "How do you do," and shake hands. I told him he was not going to get away so easily and held him and kissed him. He froze and stood stiffly at attention, and I began to learn how wrong it is to show affection in public in Japan.

My first impression of our new home, the teahouse, was that it was chilly. Nor did the quantities of tomato juice or the canned asparagus sent over by Sugako's family do much to warm me— somewhere they had gotten the idea that Westerners loved tomato juice and they sent over tray after tray of it. Terry handed me a *dotera*, a heavy quilt in the shape of a kimono that is worn at bedtime, and told me to put it on. It was very cozy but I asked him, "What about the heat?" He demonstrated the heating apparatus, a *kotatsu*, he called it; it was no more than

14

a sunken fireplace used to hold charcoal, but he explained that if one held the *futon* (blanket) over the wooden framework around the fireplace, the heat from the charcoal would be held inside and warm my legs. Terry explained that any sort of central heating would cause the walls of the house to warp and buckle. After all, I could always take a hot bath!

The months we spent in the teahouse marked the beginning of what was to be for me the never-ending challenge of the Japanese house. Terry desired the comforts of Western furniture, especially the beds, and it took more than a little thought to make our small menage efficient and comfortable by American standards. While I was busy Westernizing the house, it was slowly exerting its influence on me, and as time passed I found myself becoming more and more entranced with the fragile and delicate charm of Japanese living, even while exploding with exasperation or laughter at some part of that life that resisted my most concentrated efforts and remained serenely un-changed. I came to love one of the sounds of Japan, the closing of the heavy doors, the *amado*, shutting out the world for the night. In the morning the conventional Japanese bowed as he opened the doors to the world for another day.

Like most Japanese homes, ours had electricity for lighting, but it was not used for cooking or for refrigeration. The cooking was done with charcoal and there was an icebox to keep our vegetables in. Our hosts had installed a flush toilet, otherwise we would have been confronted with the weekly visits of the receptacle cleaners, who, Terry told me, oftentimes arrived in the midst of company with their "honey buckets." Indispensable as it seemed to me, the toilet was more of a concession than one would think because the fertilizer made from sewage in Japan is vital to the agriculture of the country. As has so often been said, the people would starve if everyone used a flush toilet.

With the approach of spring, I began to find that the house was delightful in warm weather. With the penetrating chill no longer a problem, the spacious, uncluttered interior of the house became very pleasing; the windows on the garden side seemed

15

to draw the garden into the room and to make the house a part of its natural surroundings. It occurred to me that it had not been so very chilly during the winter and that the lack of appliances was more than made up for by the numerous servants. I believe I would always choose servants over any number of labor-saving gadgets.

We furnished one room completely in Western style, with rugs and drapes and overstuffed chairs and sofa. A room like this is commonly found in Japanese homes; it is called a *seiyōkan* or foreign room. As time passed, I began to feel more at home, and the Japanese social customs became less and less involved as I came to understand them. On the arrival of guests, the maid would call, "*Okusama* (Honorable interior of the house, me)" and I would go to the *genkan* or vestibule to meet them. The *genkan* was small and unheated, and I would greet my guests there only briefly, helping them to remove their coats and proffering them slippers to be worn in place of their shoes. This accomplished, I would step to the entrance of the *seiyōkan* and say, "*Dōzo* (Please come in)." When all were inside, my guests and I would exchange formal bows from the waist—I could never do it so gracefully as they—and with each bow I would be asked about members of the family: "How is your mother?" "She is very well, thank you." "How is your father?" "My father is also well, thank you." The bowing and salutations tended to become very prolonged and if Terry was present he would shorten the procedure after the first bow by saying simply, "*Dōzo* (Please be seated)." Then he would promptly fall into his favorite chair and everyone would be seated. In a Japanese-style room the greetings would be exchanged from a kneeling position on the *tatami* (mats) but in the *seiyōkan* with rugs on the floor the kneeling was dispensed with.

We greeted our American guests as one would in this country but they, too, followed the custom of removing their shoes in the *genkan*. This practice is very pleasing and I found myself keeping a pair of soft slippers for inside wear and reserving my other shoes for outside wear only.

16

Gay and happy, I had paid little heed when first told that a Japanese alighting on the docks at San Francisco becomes a different person, and only becomes himself again when he steps down the gangplank at Yokohama. A foreign wife had told me this, and it was very true. Not so much that Terry was different when we were alone, but rather that he became a natural part of what was about him in Japan, whereas I could never fit in quite as completely. Although he preferred the easy American ways in society, the stiffness and formality of the Japanese ways were not the burden for him that they were for me. Of course, he was not confined to the society of women as I was, and that made a great difference.

The other wives, whom we were constantly with at the social functions, seemed to have only one interest and that was to talk about their children and to spin endless gossip about the affairs of women they knew. How I hated to see the men leave us after dinner—I wanted so much to hear them talk! But I was, suddenly, a Japanese wife and unfit to converse intelligently and seriously with the menfolk, and I must repair to the parlor with the shy, unbearably formal group of wives.

When we got home after the first ordeal of a diplomatic party, Terry sat down and called me to him, "Hey, come on!" And I sat on his lap, happy to be at ease again.

"What," remarked my husband, "do you think the Ambassador would say if he could see us now?"

"I don't know, but it wouldn't be as bad as what the Ambassadress would say."

"I know what she would say. She'd say, that's for the Yoshiwara!"

"What's the Yoshiwara?"

A slight note of embarrassment crept into my husband's voice as he said, "Oh, I thought you knew that word. It's the section where the brothels are."

I discovered many of the ladies would have thought exactly that. There are many good things in their upbringing and the standards of *onna daigaku*, or woman's way, which announces the three-fold obligation as a Japanese woman: obedience to her father first, then obedience to her husband, and thirdly, obedience to her eldest son when he is grown. But as a part of this discipline she must accept the fact that her husband will be chosen for her—she might not even see him until the wedding day—and she would do well to avoid any personal choice. The possibility of falling in love with a man not destined to be one's husband portended the loss of all security in the established order of things. It was safer and more proper to feel, as one bride-to-be told me, "I have not met him yet, but I know I will love him. Of course I will love him. He will be my husband!" Under such circumstances where romantic love is forbidden and somewhat ominous, it is not unnatural that there would be a tendency to look down upon it and identify it exclusively with lovemaking.

I felt sorry for the Japanese women; the unreal relationship they had to bear with their husbands and all persons of the male sex was frightful. They continued to find, as they had as small girls, that there was a place for them, not a very comfortable or spacious one, but a place they must get along with. It was hard, but not without its compensations.

Although the wife is kept in a subordinate position, she is respected in her sphere, the home, whereas unmarried women are shown pity but are little respected in any regard. One of the worst short-comings seemed to me the custom of the men to partake of leisure and entertainment almost entirely in the company of other men, most of the time at one of the ever-present *geisha* parties. Being so often left at home with the children, and having little opportunity to know what her husband's thoughts on politics and business and the outer world were, the wives had little recourse but to talk of the subjects they did. And the father's absence often made it difficult to discipline the children. Mothers become overly kind, especially to their sons, and the boys fall into the habit of approaching their fathers for favors through the mother. The habit often persists even when the boys are grown and an officer told me that many soldiers killed in battle died saying, "Help me, *Okāsama* (Mother), help me!"

The divorce laws, written by the men, of course, permit the wife to divorce her husband on only one ground: adultery with a married woman, an offense against another husband. But the husband may divorce the wife without cause. Since he is regarded as legally her superior, his wish for a divorce is sufficient cause in itself. He may have a divorce without a trial, merely by filing papers with the proper authorities signifying his decision for a divorce. By such a simple deed he has the power to renounce her and all further responsibility for her well-being and, needless to say, the custody of the children remains with the father. Upon being divorced, the rejected wife becomes a social outcast, often even to her own family. I knew one such divorcee, and her misery was overwhelming. She had to seek work as a shopgirl and she would stand at the curb to watch her children being taken to school by the woman who replaced her. However, although the power exists in the husband to divorce his wife in this summary manner, that power is very rarely used. The men have a code among themselves against divorce and, as a result, divorce is reserved for the most unusual circumstances. The divorce rate is very low by Western standards. It also happens, more often than one would think, that a couple falls in love after marriage and, because the arranged marriage takes full advantage of similar family background, education, and position, these marriages are extremely happy. Other marriages, whether happy or not, are stable and lasting.

With its sentiment of unity interwoven with the nation's traditions, the family organization is the backbone of Japan. The child owes allegiance to his parents, the wife to the husband, the husband to the elder brother of the family, and the whole attorns to the Imperial Family as brothers of one house. As I came to understand this, it seemed fit and proper to be known as the wife of the house of Terasaki, and I felt proud when Terry introduced me as *uchi no kanai desu*, the wife of my house.

For all his ideas and ebullience of sentiment when we were

alone, Terry was not only a true Japanese outwardly but a formal Japanese at that. If he met me on the street, he would remove his hat and say, "How do you do, my beloved wife." It disturbed him not at all that he might have referred to me in something very like baby talk but a few hours before. His strict demeanor was such that all his friends had thought he would be the last to marry a foreigner. I wondered how many more of the rigidly orthodox in appearance were like Terry underneath.

Our marriage was something of a challenge to their customs and many of the young men in the Foreign Office, fretting under the yoke of convention, used to come to ask my advice about their romances. I always told them the burdens were very great and they must not try to swim against the current. It seemed to me that any who felt any strong attachment would see from what Terry and I had done what my opinion must be. But they should not risk the venture unless they were as sure of their love as we of ours, and I thought many of my inquisitors were simply infatuated by the notion of breaking with precedent.

Terry told me, "You know, the Japanese think I am the most un-Japanese in the world. When they compliment you I can't help but say, 'Oh, thank you very much. I think so too. You are very kind to say so!' You know what they think I should say? They think I should say, 'No, she is really the inner lining of a very green lemon!' "

So I became accustomed to my life in Japan, knowing that when we should return to San Francisco I would again be permitted to go first when the party moved to the dining room for dinner. I knew that I was already known at the *gaimusho* (Foreign Office) as "Terasaki's folly" and felt that I must fit in as best I could so as not to embarrass my husband.

3

CHINA SERVICE

WE went to Japan expecting to visit there but briefly with Terry's family before being reassigned to Shanghai, but I became ill and we remained for nearly eight months. I was pregnant and suffering minor complications that were very distressing and made it unwise for the time being for me to travel. My pregnancy was too precipitate, a fact we understood thoroughly as soon as it was too late. As the Minister to China, Mr. Shigemitsu, a friend of Terry's family, told us soon after our arrival in Tokyo, "You two children must learn to love people from all the world. There is great work for you to do. Don't have a family too soon—take time to get fully adjusted."

Then, comprehending Terry's sheepish look, "Oh, so that's the way it is? In that case my heartiest congratulations!"

The Foreign Office had a position for Terry in Shanghai and held it open for him as long as it could. In late July it appeared Terry must proceed without further delay. Faced with remaining in Japan to have the baby alone, I determined to go with him. We sailed on the day the baby was due—thank heaven it was three weeks late! The ship had the Lytton Commission aboard, en route to Manchuria to investigate the fighting there for the League of Nations. When Terry discovered Lord Lytton on the passenger list and learned he was ill in his room, he sent a message offering his assistance. Lytton sent for him to come to talk over the situation.

Terry had never seemed much interested, except in an academic way, in the baby; he spoke of it as a "bridge" between our two countries. Not until his child was born did he show the intense personal interest new fathers are supposed to exhibit. Immediately upon arriving in Shanghai I looked for a doctor. I did not want one of the Japanese doctors because they follow the German method and refuse to give an anaesthetic for the mother's pain. I found the name of a Dr. Barry in the telephone directory and called him. He was reluctant to take me, knowing nothing of my case, but when I explained my situation to him, he was very sympathetic and arranged for my lying in at the British hospital on one of the extra-settlement roads. This was in a sort of no-man's land, being neither under the Municipal Council nor under the jurisdiction of China. I visited Dr. Barry several times and felt confident of his kindness and ability when my time came.

Terry was off in the outer part of the city when I felt the beginnings of labor one afternoon as I sat alone in the big house with only my Oriental servants. I called the taxicab company and told them to send a careful driver who knew the way. He arrived and took me out Bubbling Well Road en route to the hospital. I had the taxi stop so I could go into McTavish and Twiggs pharmacy to purchase baby powder. McTavish waited on me and inquired if I was ill. I told him no, I was not ill, I was in labor.

"Oh, dear!" said McTavish and hurriedly escorted me back to the taxi. The Chinese driver kept saying, "Oh, missy, wait, wait, missy, wait a little."

We arrived in time at the hospital and I placed another call to the Japanese Consulate for my husband, who came at once; but the baby did not arrive for several days. Terry spent as much time at the hospital as possible, coming out before he went to work and as soon as the day was over. A typhoon was raging off the coast at the time when it finally appeared that the baby's birth was imminent, and Terry could not get across the city to me at once because of the storm. His anxiety to join me was needless, however, because it took another four hours before the baby was delivered. Terry kept sending messages to the doctor, a kindly old Canadian. The doctor repeated their contents to me with much amusement, saying, "I have another love letter from your husband. He wants me to spare his wife—he doesn't care what happens to the child. I must remember that you are the most important. He says to forget the child and take care of you."

A Chinese *amah*, with a great scar across her face and a humped back, sat there with me to call the nurse if needed. She kept repeating until I could have screamed, "Poor little missy, no catchie baby, poor little missy, no catchie baby." Finally I did "catchie" baby, and our little girl was born.

We had asked Mr. Shigemitsu, who had been so close to Terry's father and regarded us as his children, to be the child's godfather. He had chosen the name "Mariko" for our daughter, and in time her nickname became "Mako."

I was anxious that she not be mislaid among the other children and kept asking the nurse to put an identification tag on her. The nurse thought this unnecessary and refused to do it until Dr. Barry said, "That's her baby—do as she says!" An arm band was quickly found and placed around the baby's arm.

Then I was wheeled out of the delivery room and down the hall past where my husband had smoked a pack of cigarettes and drunk many cups of coffee during his four-hour vigil. As I came by, Terry looked at me and then sat down hard in a chair—he had fainted! What pleasure we had repeating that story! Each time it was mentioned it took all his diplomatic training to retain his composure. As a rule, Japanese fathers do not appear at the hospital at all until notified that the baby has arrived.

Terry's duties in Shanghai were to investigate and pay the claims of foreign nationals resulting from Japanese action during the First Shanghai Incident. As he explained the solatium mission to me, it was rather like insurance adjusting on an international scale; only the victims had suffered a bombing instead of an automobile accident and their claims were exaggerated accordingly. A Frenchwoman was one with whom he had to deal. Her magnificent Wedgewood, en route to her from Hong Kong, had been destroyed when the docks were bombed. She did not want the money for the china but wanted Terry to find a like set of Wedgewood to replace the original. Another file he had concerned an English lady whose expensive new furs had been destroyed in a dry cleaner's shop far removed from her neighborhood when the shop was burned to the ground. Several days of investigation went into settlement of that particular claim; I think they finally agreed that the furs were not exactly new and payment was made for their depreciated value. Terry told amusing stories about his troubles and detective work. In all, he handled several hundred claims and he enjoyed the work, at least for the first few months. Partly as a result of his command of English and his knowledge of Western customs, he completed the mission successfully and was afterwards promoted to vice-consul.

Terry enjoyed argument and he also enjoyed negotiation, which as he told me is "quite another thing." He preferred, in dealing with Americans, to deal with Southerners. Part of the reason for this was his loyalty to me, I think, although I told him the mountainous part of Tennessee, my part of the state, had fought for the Union. He saw through this quibble, it seemed. Yet, his liking for Southerners was not wholly inspired by me; he had it long before we met. He said he found in them a quicker and broader understanding, more interest in people and personal quality. He tended to generalize this opinion into the view that

24

there was an exclusively "Southern" brand of thinking. This led him to congratulate an American official, Dick Buttrick, whom he had recently met and found most agreeable, with the remark,

"Mr. Buttrick, I can tell from your manner that you must be from the South."

"You are exactly right, Mr. Terasaki, I come from about as far south in New York State as one can get!"

Ordinarily in the Japanese Foreign Service a man is moved each two years, but Terry was kept in Shanghai for five. We enjoyed those years when the tension and strain among the powers had not become as severe as they were later to be. But more important, the China service is essential to the Japanese career diplomat. Without a knowledge of the 500 million people on the continent, composing Japan's nearest and most natural market, he is never fully qualified.

Much of my own knowledge of the Chinese came from our Chinese *amah*, Ah Mei, whom we engaged soon after arriving in Shanghai. She was a young woman of eighteen, a person of squarish build, short, and with fine white teeth. Her past had been starkly tragic but she seemed unmarked by it. She had been sold into slavery by her father when she was a little girl. The family lived on a small farm near Soochow, China, and the father could not support his numerous children. The little girl's mother was blind, but she went to the man who had purchased Ah Mei and agreed to pay an exorbitant sum to get her back. She washed clothes the rest of her life to pay out the debt. The father suffered from dropsy and Ah Mei helped her mother nurse him. He was bloated and swollen with the disease, and one day while the mother was out searching for a doctor, he died. The little girl stayed in the house alone with the body for five days, watching in horror as the swelling subsided and the body shrank. She had been told to stay with her father and knew nothing else to do when he died.

Ah Mei was kind and gentle with Mako and taught her the Chinese equivalent of the Uncle Remus stories I had heard in my

25

childhood. Although we were at war with the Chinese, I had absolute trust in Ah Mei and she remained with us for years. She was the chief retainer of· a diplomat's family, and a diplomat herself. When we would move to a new neighborhood, she would go about and meet all the house boys, the store people, the *amahs*, and the gardeners, saying, "What fine man my master is all same Chinese man. He good man. Lookie Chinese, too. Got Chinese face. Chinese heart." As a result all the working-class Chinese loved us.

Ah Mei was in charge of our staff at the house. I had some difficulty getting a number one boy who would be number two to Ah Mei, but I insisted that she was to be the boss, and by perseverance I found men who would work under her. We had two guards and a half dozen other servants under her charge. There was the number one boy, who was in general charge of arrangements for parties and guests, a number two boy who helped him, one cook and a "helpie" cook, a wash *amah*, the gardener, the gatekeeper, and an *amah* to watch Mako. The number one boy usually hires and pays the other servants and does the serving at a dinner party, but I had Ah Mei do these things because she was more capable. She got a percentage of the grocery bill, but she was careful not to be wasteful on that account, as the number one boy would have been. She could provide when Terry called at four in the afternoon to say he was bringing a group of eight or ten home for cocktails and dinner that evening. So reliable was she that I thought of her as "Can do, Missy." She carried all the keys and kept tight control over the other servants.

Ah Mei was not without a sense of humor. We had a fat Japanese gentleman to dinner one night who slurped his soup, making a considerable sucking noise as he did so. Everyone but Ah Mei intently engaged himself in ignoring the noise. She was so amused she almost fainted in an effort to keep back her laughter and finally she left the room rather than disgrace us.

She loved Terry and took special care of him. When she was serving something special she would inch the plate around to show him which piece to take, and he would happen to seize on it. They did it deftly and without the slightest sign. She knew he loved food just as he loved comfort, and he was pleased to help himself to the best piece just as he would stand in front of his favorite chair so he could sit down in it when greetings were concluded. She used to tell me to put his newly washed shirts on the bottom in the drawer. "Master always go top side down. Top side all wear out, wash too often, put new wash shirt on bottom then all wear same." And she would turn the frayed edges on Terry's collars for him.

We lived in a British apartment house on Yu Yuen Road near Jessfield Park. It was a lovely place. The previous tenants had left owing the Chinese comprador and he sent a collector. In spite of Ah Mei's instructions, the collector kept returning. I heard her tell him,

"You go away and don't come back. New master doesn't know anything about bill. Go away. Next time you come, I throw you down stairs!"

He returned and found it was not an idle threat. Although he was a tall person, she hefted him up and sent him bumping down the winding back steps.

"He no come back, Missy!"

When we took her on a visit to Japan with us, Taro wanted to hire her away from us. I told Ah Mei to see how she would react to such a proposal. "Big master, master's big brother, wants you stay over at his house, work his house, he thinks you very good."

Ah Mei's reply was, "Missy, I more better die!"

What a delight it was to relate this to Taro.

Taro took it in good grace. Once while we were visiting him in Tokyo he took the children and Ah Mei to the park at Ueno to see the statue of Saigo, the rebel *samurai* who had fought the newly-formed national government in the seventies and lost. Ah Mei was greatly impressed.

"Big man, all same master. Lookie master, same got big ears like master."

When Terry had his appendix removed and went to Japan to the hospital, I left Ah Mei in the apartment and told her to stay there until we got back. We were gone two months and Ah Mei was very pale when we returned. She had understood she was not to leave the apartment at all until our return, and she had obediently stayed inside all the while.

Her fine teeth she attributed to the salty cabbage and rice which were her steady diet until she had come to work for us. She could not read or write and her ignorance was amazing. When she saw Japanese soldiers boarding a ship to go to China, she asked me if they were Japanese or Chinese. She had never been anywhere in China except from Soochow to Shanghai and had the idea when we took her to Japan with us that it was many times larger than China. "Japan belong much bigger China," she said. She thought the Japanese Emperor was Chiang Kai-shek. And yet with all this lack of knowledge, she was an intelligent person with a very good mind. When it came to managing the house and the staff, and to planning meals for the staff plus thirty or forty guests, she was unbeatable. She did not know figures but could add with facility in her head.

We had a nurse for Mako who was called "Little Feetie Amah" because her feet had been bound in the ancient Chinese manner and this made her a virtual cripple. When Mako got large enough to run and play she would elude Feetie Amah and jeer at her. We had to get another person in her place. Feetie Amah came to me on her knees and begged me to keep her. We found her another position and she left in tears but was well satisfied with the other house. She always took her money on pay day and splurged by buying herself a slice of ham. Then she would wait with the rest of the money for her husband's number two wife to come for it. Number two wife was a younger, more attractive Chinese woman. Feetie Amah was very proud of her. She would bring number two in to see me.

"Missy come see my husband's little wife, so pretty—not many old men can get such a pretty sweet little wife. Look what pretty arms she has! I bought a pin for her hair."

This was the regular pay-day performance for Feetie Amah as long as she was with us. After she left, she always came the day after pay day with a vile looking piece of Chinese cake for Mako, whom she called "little Mako missy."

Number one boy was Lui Dai Yeh. I made it a practice to use the names of my houseboys rather than refer to them by title, as so many of the British and Americans did. Some never knew the name of their number one boy although he had been with them for ten or twenty years. Unsuspectingly, I once gave Lui a box of Whitman's candy for his wife. He told me, what was altogether news, that he had two wives.

"Just one box candy give to number one piece wife, number two piece wife make big walla walla my family. Two boxes, o.k., but one box, no, I not take big walla walla my family."

I got him another box.

Terry used to enjoy chatting with Ah Mei. She had lived on the farm at Soochow in territory that had been fought over by the contending forces and had changed hands with the seasons. He asked her what was the difference between Japanese and Chinese soldiers. Ah Mei considered a moment before replying:

"Chinese soldier, he wantie first chicken, second pig, third woman, fourth rice. Japanese soldier first he wantie woman, then he wantie chicken, then he wantie rice!"

Very handsome Chinese men used to hang around the gate waiting for Ah Mei. I never understood her attraction, but unquestionably there was a strong one. Her face was flat and square, she wore her hair straight, and she was very neat and clean. But she had no figure except for a big stomach partially hidden by her coolie uniform of white jacket and black trousers. She had been engaged since she was eight years old to a boy from Soochow, a Mr. Ba. She told me when it neared time for the marriage ceremony,

"Missy, I don't wantie marry him. I no love him. I love Shanghai man. You know, Missy, I already catchie baby."

But she married the man from Soochow and as far as I ever knew he had no knowledge the baby was not his.

It was customary to fire the *amahs* when they got pregnant, but I wanted to keep Ah Mei. I hired a little *amah* to help until she was strong again. She went to a Chinese hospital when the time came but until then she sat around with Mako, telling her fairy stories and looking after her. When the baby came, I called the Consulate to tell Terry that Ah Mei had a baby boy; he was in conference but I had the call put through to him as urgent. He was delighted at the news and turned to the joint meeting of the Municipal Council of Shanghai to exclaim, "My *amah* has a boy!"

"Well, Terasaki, is it yours?" was the obvious rejoinder.

It was a beautiful child. Ah Mei used to bring him to the house often. It was there that he came down with pneumonia, and Ah Mei got a Chinese medicine man to bring a dragon stamp to paste on the baby's stomach.

"Missy, Chinese man can make baby well. You thinkie foreign man can do. I no think, but Missy, make you happy, you gettie Melican doctor, all right."

I got the doctor to treat the baby and at length he recovered.

"Missy, Chinese man make baby well, Chinese dragon make true well. But make Missy happy think Melican doctor do it."

There were things about Ah Mei I could not understand. At first I felt a moral superiority to her, but the more I saw of the Orient the more doubt I had. It was in her attitude toward human suffering.

For example, Ah Mei said it was "bad joss" (bad luck) to help a person injured in an automobile accident. She would stand by and watch a stranger bleed to death in the streets of Shanghai, rather than incur "bad joss." Many Chinese would. The evil spirits were attacking the injured and would attack anyone who helped. Her superstitions were incredible. The Chinese karma, or religious spirit, sanctioned mistreatment of animals because they were bad men returned to life in animal form and deserved punishment. Likewise, the human suffering all about us in Shanghai was not to be relieved, for by present suffering people secure happiness after death. Such being the dominant attitude, there were of course few Chinese charities and those who gave alms openly declared it was not given to help the beggar—he did not deserve help—but to add to the giver's heavenly status.

When I was first in Shanghai, I was totally unable to prevent myself from trying to help. It was at first unimaginable to me that there should be dead and dying babies lying in the gutters of the city and that civilized men and women would step aside without concern as they passed, the man guiding the woman to one side with a casual pressure on her arm as if to avoid a puddle of water. But, when one witnesses the unimaginable each day there is a disregard, a callousness, that comes upon one of necessity. Life would be unbearable if it were otherwise; yet, one feels that if one's shock at such things ceases entirely, his life will no longer be worth living. Thinking like this, I got so I could almost ignore the crowds of starving wretches on the streets appealing to me for food when I went out.

One day at the market place I saw a crowd of people stoning a girl. Frightened by the sight I asked a British lady, shopping there, what is was all about. With an almost imperceptible lift of her shoulders she let me know that she was not interested in what was happening, nor did she care to speak to strange Americans. I dashed into the crowd to see, impelled irresistibly by the screaming of the victim. The child was a little older than Mako. She was on her hands and one knee dragging the other leg. She was crying hysterically to the mob to help her, but several in the crowd were throwing stones the size of hen's eggs, bruising her on the body and legs. As the girl thrashed around trying to get away, I saw the leg she was dragging. It was a rotten stump, off below the knee, dead from leprosy and alive with maggots.

I could not think clearly about the incident until the next day, nor have I ever since been able to think calmly of it, but after some time I realized that I had seized a British policeman and told him to take the girl to the hospital. He had refused politely, saying it would not do to become involved. Then I pounced upon a Japanese officer, shouting at him that I was the wife of

31

a high-ranking Japanese official and that I was *ordering* him to get an ambulance for the girl. He had done as he was told and the girl was taken to the doctor.

Terry was not surprised at what I had done, but he was much amused by my threatening the officer as the wife of such an important man. The day after the incident when he came home from the office, we sat on the huge sofa in the living room of our apartment and Terry said to me gently,

"Gwen, I understand how horrible it is for you to see these things and not be able to help everyone and change it all. But you must realize it can't be done. Therefore, you must not look at Shanghai with American eyes too much. If you try to do charity here for all the miserable people who deserve it, as you would in the States, you will lose your mind.

"In Shanghai we have three classes of people. A few who eat all the rice they want and have *sake* on occasion, that's one class. A few who eat caviar at the Cathay Hotel and drink all the champagne they please, that's another class. The third class is an army of people who never have enough to eat and never have enough to drink. They have no houses, they have little food, they have no clothes. They are the superfluous people the Englishman wrote about—what was his name? Malthus, the man who wrote about population and war."

"Is it really that bad?" I ventured. "It looks to me like they would try to get something by force before they would starve."

"Ah, that is what they would do in America and succeed. But not here. A child is born in the streets along with many other children who are born in the streets. Most of them die but he lives. He sleeps in the alley and eats garbage and wears clothes he steals from the dump. He knows how to do nothing but beg. He doesn't know his parents but he knows they were beggars. Always he is weak because he has never had a full meal in his life. If there are public works jobs, it is no help to him because he can't do manual labor. There are hunger riots from time to time but he achieves only additional misery from the riots when they are finished. And if he does get enough to eat that he lives, then he has children and the circle begins again. There are thousands upon thousands of these people here already. They can't be fed. If all the food in Shanghai were divided equally among everyone, all of us would starve."

He told me of the American relief work and of the soup kitchens the Quakers ran. He hoped the eventual industrialization of the surrounding country would create a subsistence standard of living if the increase in population could be controlled.

He said, "You must do something, however, otherwise your conscience will die. But you must be sensible or you will have a nervous breakdown."

"What can I do, Terry?"

"Do this, Gwen. You pick out one beggar in the crowd and do something for him. But do not let the other beggars know. They would mob you every time you go out. Do you have a sufficient allowance to take care of that?"

"Yes, I have more than enough."

"And I'm going to give Mako an alms-giving fund, too. So, you understand now. Let's have some tea and think of happier things."

With her allowance, Mako began to support a little beggar child. She was so happy to see the child respond that she began using money she had hoarded to spend on herself. Her father was very satisfied to see this in her.

Outside the theater one night, I saw a beautiful little Chinese girl about two years younger than Mako. Her cheeks were rosy, and her bright eyes told me she was intelligent and from good stock. At once she caught my eye and stretched out her grimy little hand for money. Beggar children develop a keen instinct about people; she knew I was sympathetic. She became my special pet, receiving from me clothes and food and money and silly little gifts. I could not have another child and wished to adopt this little girl, but Terry said it would be unwise. He was generous and did more to help the poor than he ever permitted me to learn, but he suggested I visit Taro and his family in Japan to forget the tragic side of Shanghai. He told me we could not do enough to help, that we must get used to our helplessness and realize that the situation was beyond us; we must keep healthy and plan to do what we could on a long-term basis. As time went by I understood more about the indifference of the Chinese to human agony, but I have never thought, and can never think of the girl they were stoning, without sensing pity and contempt for them and something akin to guilt for myself.

I became somewhat conditioned to expecting the unexpected. I knew of the great prevalence of opium smoking in the Orient, as well as how it was fostered by the British, and I had heard that when one has taken opium for many years it becomes impossible for him to keep any food on his stomach except mother's milk. So when on a trip into China by train I chanced to see a bearded old man nursing a young Chinese woman in a Pullman berth, I tried very hard to act like an "old China hand" and to take it in my stride.

Life in Shanghai was comfortable, happy, and always interesting, but there was one significant drawback. Our social obligations were so demanding that we could save no money but used up much of Terry's salary in entertaining. How extravagantly people lived! The white man was shouldering his burden for the last time and doing it in great luxury. But the white man was not alone in his wealth; many were the Chinese, Japanese and Indian officials and businessmen whose scale of living was almost regal. Their homes were as sumptuous as any in the world and were furnished in all styles known to Occidental and Oriental lands. Through these homes were was a continual round of parties attended by the international set and their exotic ladies vying in the splendor of their native costumes.

Terry had worlds of friends. Among the Chinese, he had warm personal relations impartially with those who were anti-Japanese as well as those who were pro-Japanese. Both sides used to come to dinner with us in large numbers for Terry was a generous host. His guests enjoyed as good a table as Ah Mei and I could manage and there was never a lack of good bourbon and scotch. Terry spent hours debating the issues between the

34

warring countries with his enemies, and I soon learned not to be alarmed at this. No one ever showed the least personal animosity. No college bull session on the merits of socialism or other subjects dear to the undergraduate heart was ever carried on with more fervor or better will. I was vastly amused when the Chinese would remark as they so often did, "Why, Terasaki, you don't look Japanese at all—you look Chinese!" in the same patronizing way as my English friends sometimes told me, "You aren't like an American at all!"

Sometimes Terry found himself in difficulty with his superiors because of his unlimited friendships, notably when they found him at a restaurant one night seated cozily with the violently anti-Japanese O. K. Yui, the two of them happily devouring a large roast duck. Always his defense was that he needed to understand the point of view of the enemy. That was only part of the reason, however; he also enjoyed a good argument.

In discussion of the China situation my husband took the position that it did not matter whether the Chinese had actually blown up the railroad at Harbin in 1931. He stated that the invasion of Manchuria and the taking of Shanghai were justified because Japan, for her own survival, had to occupy Manchuria to keep the Russians out and that the creation of a buffer against Russia would be to the advantage of the Chinese and Japanese alike. Terry asked the Chinese why Chiang had not helped the Chinese 19th Route Army defend Shanghai from the Japanese if it was not because Chiang knew the Russians controlled that army. He always insisted Russia was the real enemy of both China and Japan.

When the Lytton Commission reported to the League upholding Japanese rights in Manchuria stemming from the Treaty of Portsmouth but finding that Japan had violated the Covenant of the League in attacking China, Terry was dismayed. Yet he seemed to feel that if the League would guard Japan against Russian expansion and insure free trade for Japan with China, his government could withdraw from Manchuria as, obedient to the League's request, it had withdrawn its troops from

Shanghai. But the government was coming more and more under the influence of a new brand of militarists, the younger men who had assassinated the moderate Premier Inukai and whose attitude was becoming more truculent each day. They withdrew Japan from the League rather than comply with its mandate that the troops be withdrawn from Manchuria. When nothing was done to enforce the League's decision, Terry said it showed that the League would not have tried to control Russia and was nothing but a debating society.

During the latter part of our stay in Shanghai, toward the middle 1930's, Terry became greatly concerned at the reports being received from Tokyo about the excesses of the younger militarists. The elder generals and admirals were more reasonable and some of their group supported the principles of Saionji, but whether they were for democracy or not, he felt they would not have used such violent means to advance their views. But the new group of officers, whose memories did not antedate the Japanese triumph over the Russians and who were convinced their German-modeled army and British-modeled navy were all powerful, were radical imperialists who would stop at nothing to gain their ends. The navy and army officers who assassinated the Premier in 1932 were of their group and had been largely successful in explaining their deed as necessary to rid the Emperor of an "evil adviser." An atmosphere of fear had come over the business people, and their great industries were being controlled by the military to provide war material and munitions. Jingoistic slogans about a "national spirit" were being fostered to replace the deliberation and discussion directed by the Charter Oath of the Meiji; the newspapers were censored and dance halls and Western languages and dress were being denounced as opposed to Japanese patriotism. Terry was aghast at the code of conformity gradually being foisted upon his people, but he thought the militarists would soon hang themselves because a powerful group of moderate statesmen still held the ear of the Emperor, Saionji, Admiral Saito, Takahashi, and the others. When the proper time came they would reveal the militarists to the

36

people and to the Emperor for what they were, put a stop to imperialism in China, and bring the country back to a democratic course.

Sometimes Terry's deep-rooted distrust of the military caused him to do wrong, such as the episode that occurred shortly before Mako was born. An officer boarded an elevator we were on; he was the last one on and the little place was crowded. He elbowed people aside and swung around so that his *samurai* sword, a long unwieldly object that nearly touched the ground when he walked, struck me in the side. In a fit of anger, my husband took him by the shoulders and kicked him violently with his knee. I was terrified and the crowd stood agape, fearing Terry would be killed. The Major turned around fiercely, "*Dō shitan da?* (What's the big idea?)"

"Didn't you see the lady here? You come on pushing and shoving like the world belonged to you and hit your sword against this lady who is expecting a baby—a fine thing, that sword, when you use it that way!"

The officer removed his cap and bowed low to me, "*Gomen nasai,* I am sorry, I am not in the habit of bumping people."

I assured him it was all right, that I knew it had been accidental, and that I was unharmed. He got off the elevator at the first stop.

I pounced on Terry for this outburst when I had him alone, but all he said was that the military needed disciplining from civilians. I think the root of his trouble lay in his father's admonition in his youth that he should not carry the "tin sword." It rankled with him that the sword used by the officers as a mark of distinction bore the name of the *samurai,* from which his family, along with most of the leading families of the country, had sprung.

One night my husband came in late. He was rumpled, his shirt was torn, and he seemed agitated. I asked him what was wrong, and he said,

"I don't know, don't I look all right?"

"You look very informal, to say the least. What have you been doing?"

37

Terry looked a bit like a small boy caught misbehaving.

"Well," he began, "I guess I had better tell you to keep you from thinking something worse. I had a fight. It didn't amount to much. A fellow made a remark. Let's forget it."

Later he told me that he had been to dinner at a downtown restaurant with members of the staff. One of them suggested to him, while imbibing deeply of *sake*, that he should be tired of always living with an American woman and should find him a Japanese woman in addition. Terry had jumped up and struck the man on the jaw. The poor fellow was only half Terry's size and he found himself in a pile on the floor. He turned to the others and appealed to them,

"Are you going to let Terasaki-san beat me up like this?"

No one stirred and he begged them again. Then someone from the crowd yelled to him.

"You've got just what was coming to you."

I was glad Terry had explained it to me, for the next morning, after Terry had gone to his office, the little man appeared at the door to beg my pardon. He said he had been too drunk to know what he had said, but when he had sobered up and had been informed of it he was horrified. It took me some time to quiet him.

But Terry's temper did not affect his ability at the office, and I soon saw what it was that Ambassador Debuchi and Taro had meant when they talked of my husband's future. The young men in Terry's office seemed to anticipate his slightest wish. He could not open a door or a window—someone was there to do it for him quickly, gracefully, without being told. He spoke to his secretary and the young men about him in a low tone, sprinkling his opinions with many of his beloved "therefores"; and he listened with attention to their views. I must say this power of decision was reserved for the office—he could hardly dress himself without me to choose the tie and tell him what suit to wear—and when questions arose at the Consulate he was confident and decisive. And when the decision had been reached, his subordinates obeyed him cheerfully and implicitly. He lent them money when they needed it and they came to him with their personal problems. I knew they were probably working as much for Terasaki-san as for their own futures. As Terry was promoted he found higher places for "my young men," as he called them.

To my dismay I would find that Terry wanted me to have dinner for ten or twelve people on a few hours' notice. He thought nothing of it; of course I could do it and everything would be perfect. Then he would brag on me and tell me how he liked a woman with spirit who walked side by side with her husband and not to the rear. Without being aware of it, I was doing things, entertaining literally throngs of people, remembering names and prejudices and idosyncrasies of our guests, and feeling myself the hostess *par excellence*. I wondered if the secretaries, the attachés, and "young men" who had become my husband's disciples did not feel much as I did, an unquestioning desire to please their leader.

Our first months were troubled by my failure to understand Terry's moods. Sometimes he simply wished to be alone. I could not get it through my bride's head that there could be a time when he could be so worried, or concerned with the world and his career, that I could not console him; but there were periods when he would retire to the library and firmly close the door. When I saw that this meant a need for solitude and not a lack of confidence in me, I ceased to thrust myself upon him and our course became smoother.

When I would get home from a party which he had not attended, he would inquire eagerly, "Who was there? Did you have a good time? What did they have to say?" But when he was the one returning he would say nothing. He would proceed about his affairs and only gradually and by fits and starts would I learn what had occurred. I turned the tables on him once and refused to tell about a dinner I had been to, to show him how he was treating me, but it made no difference. He could not talk unless he felt it at the time. I had to learn to let him take his time, and when I did I never lacked for information, although I was on pins and needles to hear the gossip once in a while.

Notwithstanding his rare displays of temper, Terry was a formal person. Although he was a liberal, thoroughly Western in many of his views, and not the conventional Japanese as to the family system, he was at heart and personally a formal man. During all our married life he never once entered my bedroom without knocking. It took me years to get over my surprise that it was he—I always thought it must be the bell boy or the porter. I told him he was a silly ass to knock, but he would no more have entered without knocking than he would have called his grandfather by his first name. Some of his formality was reassuring at times. I never had the least hesitation to bend over to tie my shoe or stir the fire or for any other purpose in Terry's presence. He might be standing there with a ping pong paddle or a rolled up newspaper or even a fly swatter, and I was perfectly safe. He never took advantage of a pose irresistible to American men, and I am sure the mere thought of it caused him pain.

Terry was furious at the sight of "maidenly" tears. It was more than unwise to make use of weeping to gain a point with him; it moved him to extreme fury to see them employed as weapons. If one wept in front of Terry, it had to be for a calamitous reason. When we had arguments, as we did frequently at first and very infrequently later, he would be consumed with rage. I found I must sit quietly and let him storm. He would go out and slam the door till the foundations of the house trembled. I would wait a few minutes. Then he would return, calm and regretful, eager to be reasonable. I think slamming that door did something for him; he would shove it back against the door jamb with such loud violence that it could be heard for a block, I am sure, and that gesture seemed to dispel his frustration and anger at once, as a pop-off valve dispels steam when the boiler gets overheated.

And Terry had another safety valve—his indiscreet, sudden fits of laughter. He loved to laugh, and his laughter was uncontrollable. When he was confronted with too much of the "stuffiness," as he termed it, connected with the social events we had to attend, he was likely to explode. But how good it was, the

40

few times it happened at affairs of state, to hear that wonderful laugh cutting through the oppressive atmosphere of diplomatic solemnity like a refreshing breeze.

His humor asserted itself in other ways—for instance, the time we went to a meeting of the Oxford group for moral rearmament in Japan shortly before leaving for our new post in Havana. It had much in common with an evangelistic meeting, members of the audience being called upon as witness to the powers and happiness of their own moral rearmament. As time went on, the cloying mixture of sentimentality and academic wishfulness became unbearable, or so it must have been for Terry. I had not noticed it until he was called upon. The leader pointed him out in the audience and called upon him to declare what his purposes and hopes were in his new service in the foreign field of Cuba, where he had been called to work for amity among the nations. Terry arose with his usual marble composure to announce quietly,

"I am going to drink Bacardi rum and learn to smoke black cigars."

That was all he said. I could have crawled under the rug. I wanted to announce as vigorously as I might that Terry was only having his little joke, that he was really going to do his best to work for good relations with the Cuban people by learning their language and living with them as a friend. But the dismal silence that had greeted my husband's outburst intimidated me. I could only sit and wait until the meeting concluded and I could speak my mind in the taxi on the way home. Terry gave me no satisfaction; he said my remarks were what they had expected him to say.

He was tender in the important things, and he was terribly proud of the house and the way I managed it. He never asked me what I had done with money, and he was extremely generous. I never lost the feeling that I could depend on his loyalty, that he was always there.

A year or so after our marriage he formally released us from the Japanese family discipline under which it was our duty to obey the elder brother, Taro. Thereafter, although Terry never addressed him as Taro but always as *niisan* (elder brother), it was purely a conventional courtesy and no indication of legal subordination. He gave me a copy of the papers which he had filed in Tokyo. They were in Japanese and were very official looking with a big seal and red ribbons. He explained that they would make me free to do as I wished and to return to my country with Mako if he should die.

He told me when we first went out in Japan that it was an atrocious breach of manners to kiss in public, that if one greeted another in that manner at the railroad station or at the dock the Japanese would be embarrassed. I took due note of this very unreasonable restriction on natural impulses and behaved myself as best I could. But when Terry returned to Shanghai, a year or so later, from a short business trip to Tokyo and I went to the boat to meet him, he took me in his arms right in the middle of the companionway jammed with crowds of people. The Consul General, who had gone with me, was so humiliated at the sight that he stepped into an open cabin to avoid being seen with us. When I commented on this later in Terry's presence, he said, "Oh, never mind!" It may have been, if we had had long enough, that he would have come into my bedroom one celebrated morning without knocking.

Terry's hopes for internal reform in Japan looked bright just before the general elections in 1936. He thought the people would vote strongly for advocates of the parliamentary government so bitterly opposed by the militarists. His predictions were accurate, but his hopes were crushed by the barbarous outrages of February 26.

In Shanghai on February 26, 1936, our telephone rang and I answered it. A newspaperman, greatly excited, was calling from Tokyo. He asked to speak to my husband. I explained that Terry was in the bathtub and he said,

"Is this Gwen-san? I have only a moment."

"Yes, it is."

"Tell your husband that there has been an insurrection. Many leaders have been killed. That is all we know right now."

I hung up the phone and told Terry. He ran out into the living room with a towel wrapped around him, spilling water all over place.

"You must be mistaken. The man didn't speak good English and you have gotten it wrong. I will call the Embassy!"

When he had telephoned his office I knew at once from his face that I had not gotten it wrong.

Only gradually did the full revelation of the tragedy become known. A group of junior officers of a Tokyo regiment had murdered the liberal statesmen Admiral Saito, Watanabe, Takahashi, and Suzuki. The assassins had been armed with machine guns and at the Watanabe house they had killed the entire family and the servants. Prime Minister Okada, Count Makino, and Prince Saionji had been marked down for execution but had escaped. The conspirators had intended to kill all the prominent liberal statesmen and their plans had been carefully laid. It was through chance that some escaped. Count Makino was saved by his little granddaughter Kazuko, who was a playmate of Ambassador Grew's daughter. Makino was not in Tokyo but was at a hot springs resort in the country. The assassins sent an officer with a detail of soldiers to kill him. This band attacked the hotel in the middle of the night. The Count's bodyguard shot the officer but was cut down by the soldiers who then set fire to the hotel. The old gentleman and his granddaughter sought to escape out the rear of the burning building by climbing a cliff that rose sharply from the rear of the inn. They climbed part way up and onto a ledge, but from there they could not climb higher. The flames from the inn soon lit the cliffside as though with daylight. The soldiers saw them and raised their guns. Before they could shoot, the child jumped in front of her grandfather, holding her arms outstretched as if to hide him. For an instant the firelight shone on the beautiful silk of her kimono. The soldiers dropped their guns and permitted the Count and his grandchild to escape.

Immediately the government took effective steps. Other troops were called out to maintain order. The Emperor called on the conspirators to return to their barracks and they obediently complied with the Emperor's wish. The ringleaders were given two hours to commit *harakiri* and those who did not comply were court-martialed.

The thought that those distinguished men had been killed for believing as I knew my husband believed terrified me. Terry tried to assure me that since Prince Saionji and the Premier had escaped and the assassins had been punished, things might yet improve. But from that day on, I knew what it was to fear for one's husband and realized how wide an abyss separated his country from democratic rule.

4

INTERLUDE AND
GATHERING CLOUDS

LATER that year we were transferred to
Cuba, where Terry was to be Chargé d'Affaires and acting Minister. When we sailed more than four hundred people were at the
dock to see us off, a great many of them Chinese who felt great
animosity toward Terry's country.

Cuba was like a vacation for us. We lived in the suburbs of
Havana in a huge house with high ceilings and entertained easily
because of the excellent staff we had. Terry invited many Cubans
and Americans to dinner, but there was not such a whirl of
parties and entertaining as there had been in Shanghai. For the
first time we were able to save money. With the promotion in
rank, Terry now had an expense account and we did not have
to use his salary to entertain.

After we had been there only a few months, I found that I
was the only one in the family who could not speak Spanish.
Mako was delighted to find herself in the role of interpreter
for her mother. She tried a few times to tease me by saying
something to her father in my presence that I could not under-

stand, but Terry was Japanese in his attitude toward that sort of teasing. It was distasteful to him, and when Mako would say something about me in Spanish he would admonish her,

"Mari-chan, it is very rude to use Spanish in your mother's presence. She cannot understand."

The Chancellery was connected to the legation residence, a greatly convenient arrangement. Terry's mission was to open Cuba to direct trade from Japan and he worked hard at it but without success. Japanese goods continued to be imported into Cuba by way of the United States. It was not long before it clearly appeared that the mission would be a failure and after that there was little for Terry to do.

Fortunately, he enjoyed Cubans and the tempo and zest of life in Havana. I found it a little odd that a person so much in the Japanese tradition of restraint should fit in so well with the gaiety and exuberance of the Latin spirit. Terry said Cuba was like a carnival, and he delighted in it. I saw he had meant it when he told the moral rearmament people that he was going to relax with the Bacardi rum and black cigars in this new post. Every morning he arose at dawn and left for the golf course—his standard was eighteen holes during the week before the Chancellery opened at ten o'clock, and on Sundays he was not content until he had gone thirty-six holes. It helped him work off his frustration in his job but the golfing was not a success as a weight-reducing exercise. He came in ravenous for *arroz con pollo* and the other well-seasoned dishes that came from our Cuban cuisine. His weight went gradually up instead of down. He took advantage of his leisure to enjoy Mako; they went to the beach and he taught her to swim, they played Ping-pong and became good friends.

Only once did he punish her with any severity. She was misbehaving at the table and when he scolded her, she flew into a tantrum and struck him in the face with a large serving spoon. He seized her, put her across his lap, and gave her a paddling which drowned out her cries until she began to scream in earnest. She would not stop and Terry became afraid he had hurt her; we took her up to her room but she still would not stop wailing,

46

and Terry was beside himself with remorse. Finally I went out of the house to let both of them calm down. The servants were standing at the foot of the stairs pale-faced, listening to the awful commotion.

I stayed away for an hour or more, and when I went back I found them in bed together, sound asleep. I suspect that our little girl first gained the upper hand on her father during that episode.

Mako acquired pets everywhere we went and in Cuba it was a baby turkey. One night we heard its strange cry coming from the private park across from the legation. Mako insisted that the maid, Belen, go to rescue the "poor little something." She went out with a lantern and soon returned with the awkward little bird. Mako was never at a loss to name her pets and immediately dubbed the queer creature "Pockie." At once Pockie became her favorite playmate.

Terry would call the bird, "Come, Pockie, Pockie," and he would sit in Terry's lap. Business visitors were startled to find the young turkey perched in Terry's lap at the office, listening attentively to all that transpired, but my husband saw nothing unusual in it at all. He gave Pockie free run of the legation and one of the porters was assigned to follow after him to clean up the marble floors. "*Diablito!*" the porter called the bird.

While Terry was adjusting himself to the ease and near idleness of our Cuban tour of duty, I took advantage of our nearness to the United States to visit my family in Tennessee, taking Mako to meet her relatives. But Terry and I both remained restless. We thought of asking to be transferred to London next. Mr. Shigemitsu was Ambassador to the Court of St. James, and Terry might get a position on his staff. We thought of the trips we could make to the continent. Eventually, we decided not to request anything until later—a time might come when we would need a transfer more—and we did nothing. When, at the expiration of our two years, orders came, they were for us to return to Shanghai.

We sailed on the *Florida* from Havana in 1938. The Cubans surprised us with a room full of roses and a *bon voyage* party during which they presented Terry with the Order of Carlos

47

Manuel de Céspedes. This was a great surprise, but Terry was delighted and made an acceptance speech in flowery Spanish.

We went by ship to New York, then to Washington and across the continent by train to San Francisco, where we embarked again. The languor of the long trip across the Pacific was broken only by the Ping-pong matches between Mako and her father and the horse-racing games we all took part in. At Shanghai, Gretchen Buttrick, the wife of the American Consul, was at the dock to meet us as we came again through the Yangtze and into the muddy swirls of the Whangpoo River. It seemed as though she had not moved in the two years since she had been there to see us off.

We secured a roomy apartment and began to get settled once more. Through the Consulate, Terry was able to locate Ah Mei. What a joy it was when she returned to us!

Things had changed in Shanghai. The second "incident" had occurred. It had been set off by the pretended loss of a Japanese soldier at the Marco Polo Bridge at Peking and, like the railroad incident in Manchuria six years before, seemed to be a fabrication of the overeager militarists calculated to force the civil government to yield to their martial ambitions. Japanese troops had occupied Shanghai in a drive up the Yangtze toward Nanking and Hankow, while the civil government meekly supported the war it had never desired. The Japanese were in almost complete control of Shanghai, but there still existed a municipal council composed of the great powers with interests to protect in the city. Dick Buttrick, Gretchen's husband, was the American representative on the council along with Terry and men from other countries. Mr. Miura was there as Consul General, with Terry and another consul serving under him.

Terry was placed on the committee for the relief of the Jews who had refugeed to Shanghai from Hitler's Germany. These thousands of people were walking the hot summer streets in winter clothing. They had no work and no place for shelter. Barracks were built for them at Yangtze-poo, a section near the city, and arrangements were made to see that they were fed. Many of them came to Terry for help, knowing that he was one of the authorities in charge. They had to sell those personal possessions that they had been able to smuggle out of Europe with them. I bought a scarf from a distinguished-looking old lady who approached me piteously on the street one day.

The military dominated the city and this grated on Terry's nerves. When the troops moved into Manchuria, and later into Shanghai, it was a part of my husband's job to present this altered state of affairs in such form as to be acceptable to the other nations whether he thought well of it or not. The growing might of the militarists alarmed him and he was bitter at their interference in the orderly administration of Japan's foreign policy which had been built upon the trust and good will of the countries with which it must trade. He became tense and preoccupied.

An American newspaperman, a Mr. Burgner, was arrested by the Japanese naval landing party on the claim that he was taking pictures in a restricted area. I never knew exactly what happened when this report reached the Consulate, but it was a serious matter and boded no good for relations with the Americans. When Terry heard of it, he immediately ordered his chauffeur to bring his car around. He found out where Burgner was being held and had himself driven there, the Rising Sun waving jauntily from the fenders of the official limousine. When he arrived at the jail, he brushed past the guards and had the cell opened. He told the surprised American curtly, "O.K., Burgner, let's go." The two of them marched past the puzzled guards and sped away.

The wires buzzed between the headquarters of the naval forces in Shanghai and Tokyo when the release was discovered. The naval authorities considered it a high-handed invasion of their jurisdiction for a member of the civil government, a mere consul certainly, to have shown such brash disregard of their prerogatives. There was for a while some question as to how the Consul General and his superiors in the Foreign Office would view the matter. At length the Embassy stood behind Terasaki and, in time, the navy expressed reluctant agreement that he had done the right thing.

The city was not the enjoyable, exhilarating metropolis of contrasts it had been in 1936 when we had left it for Cuba. Now Japanese were being assaulted and stabbed almost every night in the crowded Shanghai streets. When we went out, Dick Buttrick and Gretchen would walk on each side of Terry, and I would walk behind him with someone else in our group leading the way so that no one could get near him. The Chinese had reason to hate the Japanese. The army of occupation was behaving with Prussian arrogance and taking a bully's pleasure in humiliating the Chinese. Army orders required that the Chinese, of whatever rank or age, should bow to the ground when passing a Japanese soldier, even a private. There was a need for a curfew and strict policing of the streets, but the kowtowing was outrageous and barbaric. Terry was aghast at this and became more anxious and depressed each day.

One afternoon the door bell rang, and Ah Mei and I went to the door. It was early for Terry to return from work and we did not know who it might be. We opened the door and there stood my husband. He looked at us with an agonized face, tears streaming down his cheeks. We were terrified. Somehow we got him inside and into the living room. He was sobbing and muttering something unintelligible. Ah Mei made him a cup of green tea and we tried to calm his hysteria. For several minutes he could not speak. Then he began to tell us, still weeping,

"I can't stand it! Gwen, I can't stand it. I can't bear it, I am going crazy—I'll break down and what will happen to you and our child?"

He had come across the Garden Bridge and witnessed the Chinese lined up and forced to kneel and bump their heads on the pavement for the Japanese sentry. His chauffeur had been required to get out of the car and kowtow. The sight of this spectacle was more than his overwrought nerves could stand. He kept repeating that it did not hurt the Chinese, that they had not lost any dignity, but it was destroying the Japanese people. All that he was proud of in his people was being betrayed. He started crying again,

"My father, my father, I want the Japan of my father. Where are you, father? Where is *my* Japan? Where is the *bushidō* spirit, the code of the warrior?"

When I could calm him, I said, "Terry, we'll go. You will be needed sometime for bigger things. We will get out of this piddling place. We'll leave. We'll ask tomorrow to be transferred."

He insisted it would be hard on the Consul General for him to ask for a transfer then, but I was determined that we should get away. Terry was going to pieces, and I knew he was intended for more important things in the future.

The next day he asked Miura to relieve him and send him to another post, and he was transferred to Peking as second secretary of the Embassy. It was the spring of 1939.

I had feared that Ah Mei would not make such a long journey with us to Peking, but she sent her baby to her mother, saying she was afraid we would be unable to take care of ourselves in Peking without her. She made one request of us.

"Missy, only one thing I ask, give me enough money buy my mother's coffin."

"Your mother's coffin! What on earth for?"

"Yes, my mother no die, but maybe she die before I get back. No got coffin that disgrace in China. Chinese must have coffin."

I spoke to Terry and we provided Ah Mei with four or five hundred Chinese dollars and a Japanese military pass to get through the lines in Soochow. She took the money sewed in the bottom of her shoe. When she returned, she was triumphantly carrying a chicken. It was tied in a basket with its head sticking out from the *furoshiki,* the cloth wrapper used in Japan for all types of packages. Because of the black market it was strictly forbidden for people to carry any kind of food or produce into Shanghai from the country. We were astonished that she had brought a live chicken through. We asked her about it.

"Missy, I had big military pass from master. Everybody afraid of me."

Terry went on ahead of us while we packed for the move.

The packing was soon done and I was leaving Shanghai the second time.

As soon as we got on the boat, Ah Mei became violently and noisily seasick. She wanted to move to my room, and I had the amazed steward move her. She slept on the floor on a blanket. We were both very sick, and Ah Mei kept up a perpetual whimper, "Ah ya, ah ya, one day all same one year. Why for I go Peking side? I am going to die, going to die, not going to see my mommie again."

"Never mind, she has got a coffin."

Mako, who was never seasick in her life and had only contempt for weaklings who were, shouted, "Ah Mei, if you don't keep quiet I'm going to throw you in the sea!"

She got quiet then and pouted the rest of the way, but the minute she saw Terry at the wharf in Tientsin, she was all right again.

Our ship was carrying troops and some of the soldiers had adopted Mako. Two non-coms asked me if they could help us disembark. We had to get off the ship and onto a tender for inspection of our papers before a small boat would land us on the wharf. The sea was rough and I was glad to have some help. I let the soldiers carry some of my bags and two silver fox furs. After we were on the tender we had to wait on the slow processes of the bureaucrats to unfold four hours' worth of red tape before we could be taken ashore. The soldiers entertained Mako, who was unbearable because of her prickly heat; they gave her candy and calmed her down. At length we were put aboard a boat and towed to Tientsin. Terry forgot how long he had waited for us in his amusement at seeing the two soldiers, their arms full in carrying Mako, the bags, and the silver foxes, yet still trying to salute their superior officers as they disembarked from the boat to the wharf.

My husband was dejected and unhappy, and as we sat in the train from Tientsin to Peking I tried vainly to think of something that might dispel the gloom that had settled over him.

An elderly Chinese, dressed as a scholar in old clothes of very good cut and good quality, was sitting across the aisle from us. When the Japanese soldiers came through inspecting visas and travel permits required to travel in that troubled country, they ordered the Chinese to stand and hold his hands above his head. Roughly, they ran their peasant hands over his body searching for hidden weapons. They made him stand with his hands raised while the sergeant tried to read the papers the old gentleman presented to show he was entitled to be on the train. It was tiring to hold his hands so high and slowly the old man let them down until his palms rested on the back of his neck; the sergeant glanced up and fairly shouted at him, "Put your hands back up!" Totally undisturbed, the old gentleman gave a faint shrug of his shoulders and shook his head slowly back and forth as if to say, "I cannot— go ahead and do your worst!" Standing close and looking up into his face, the sergeant cursed him; then he threw the papers down on the seat and abruptly the soldiers were gone.

With a peaceful sigh, the old man reached down for the documents and carefully placed them back in his pocket. Then he sat and resumed his thoughtful attitude with just the faintest gesture of long graceful hands brushing himself off.

Terry arose, went over to the Chinese, and stood there introducing himself. He was politely asked to sit down and he said to the older man,

"You know I don't like this."

In beautiful Japanese a gentle voice replied, "I will survive without difficulty. It is your people who are being damaged."

All that long afternoon they sat together talking of Chinese art and history; they discussed the question of whether Japan owed more to China for what it had learned during the T'ang period or more from the Western world for what it had learned since Admiral Perry's time. When Terry returned to Mako and me and we went to the diner for supper, I thought some of the serenity and peace of the ancient scholar had come into my husband's face and I was greatly relieved.

We were happy and able to do important work in Peking. We breathed the poetic air of that ancient place until we felt that all the fear and frustration of our frenzied lives had taken but a brief and unimportant moment compared to the life of the astonishing, blue-roofed Temple of Heaven. We loved the old buildings and the pastel shadings, the smokiness that seemed to hold every view in a distant haze. It never seemed quite a part of reality. We sat under the trees and cracked watermelon seeds and drank green tea before walking to the Forbidden City to gaze at ancient scrolls and curios thousands of years old. Terry was adding to his collection, finding pieces to go with his revered Chung Yao, a small and perfect porcelain piece from the T'ang dynasty. He would hold the Chung Yao for me to touch, exclaiming,

"Think, Gwen, how many hands have held this fragile beauty. Who were they, how did they live, what did they feel and think?"

We shopped up and down Old Brass Street and Old Jade Street, heard the Marine Band at the American Embassy, and listened to talk of the Boxer Rebellion. We went to see the chair in the Forbidden City on which the Chinese rebel leader had sat on a cushion made of the skin of the German Ambassador who had bravely sought to parley with the besieging forces before the city was relieved by a Japanese naval landing party. We were amazed at the many clocks of the Forbidden City, presented to the Empress Dowager by knowing diplomats who sought favor by catering to her hobby.

Ambassador Debuchi visited us, and we had a delightful time talking of our early days in Washington. The kindly old gentleman drew me aside to apologize for having opposed our marriage. He said if he had known how well it was to work out he would never have hindered us, remarking, as many Japanese did and with the same wistfulness,

"It is rare that a Japanese has opportunity to have such a romance."

That feeling toward Terry and me was often shown, manifesting itself in little protective acts done to help us by many people we scarcely knew.

Peking was not a continuously idyllic life. The war went on

about us and General Homma blockaded Tientsin, the seaport for Peking. He was in command of the city and had the British closely confined there without water in the summer's heat. The British women were stripped and searched for weapons, and another dangerous incident was in the making.

Terry had formed the habit of fraternizing with the younger officers of Homma's staff. Several of these officers, majors and colonels on the General's staff, came each Monday to dine with us. Terry thought it would do their provincial minds good to see a Western woman running a house and caring for her husband quite as well as an Oriental woman could. One of the officers, growing friendly with me, showed me a picture of his little boy whom he had never seen and of his attractive wife. He told me his boy was strong and could already walk with *geta*. I could not forbear asking him then how he would like to see his wife and child treated like the British in Tientsin, thirsting in the heat and searched for weapons, caged like common criminals. He did not answer but hung his head until I was embarrassed for him.

Later the blockade was lifted and conditions were bettered in Tientsin. Terry and I thought our circle of officers had had some softening effect.

We looked about Peking to find a dog for Mako and could not decide among several puppies we found at the pet shops. We needed a small dog that we could keep in the house and take on trips with us. Then we were given Pechy.

A funny little man with a Manchurian cap like a coonskin came to our house one day and asked for Terry. His appearance was so outlandish I did not quite know what to say to him. He told me he had been at the Imperial University with my husband and had been living in Mongolia. At that reassurance I bade him a puzzled welcome. Mako asked him where he lived. He said he lived in a "yurt." Then she wanted to know what he ate in Mongolia. "Yogurt." And what on earth did he do for company. Oh, he had his "yak" with him. I began to feel all the more uneasy, but when Terry came in from the office soon after, he greeted our queer

55

guest most warmly. He was Mr. Suzuki, and he had been in school with Terry and then had gone to Mongolia to study the people. I suppose he had also lived in the yurt with a yak and shared his yogurt with him. Suzuki had found Pechy in Tibet and offered him to Mako, who accepted the little fellow with delight.

Pechy was a small poodle, about the size of a large housecat. He resembled an animated mop, his long hair falling over his face. The first day he was frightened and would not eat, but the next morning he responded to Mako's blandishments, had his breakfast, and became a member of the family.

Mako taught him to "sit up" and to "chin-chin," holding his paws just under his chin and wriggling them in a gesture of supplication. When he became adept at this, he would come to the dinner table and beg from each person in turn, very quietly when he was noticed and fed, but clamoring for attention when he was not. He came to think he could have anything he wanted by "chin-chinning" for it. One day we saw him in the backyard where he had scattered a bunch of blackbirds; the birds had flown into a tree from which they peered down disdainfully at the furry mop of a little dog vainly "chin-chinning" for them to come down and play.

Pechy's hair was snow white—when it was clean, which was never for long. Soon after a bath, his heavy coat would take on a slight grayish tinge, and then proceed through various stages of darker shadings until family conferences on the subject of his appearance would finally end in the decision that he must be washed again. Lying there, listening to us talk, he could somehow tell as soon as such a decision was reached and he would quickly depart to hide under the bed in the guest room. Once he had been forced to take a bath, he knew he was a person of privilege and disported himself in his shining new plumage by bouncing from one chair to another, a ball of white fur racing about the living room. It was a time of cheer for all of us to see his infectious delight and his pride in his freshly-laundered state. Occasionally when Terry came home tired and discouraged, with little time for his family, he would ignore Pechy, whose spirits would immediately sink.

When we said, "Pechy has had a bath," Terry would remark, "Oh, in that case—" and greet the little fellow with due respect. Pechy would begin cavorting again.

Each time we were in a different hotel with the dog, Pechy would be on his guard until Terry arrived. He would sit alertly at the door, showing no interest in investigating his new surroundings—things simply were not right to him until the master of the house was there. As soon as Terry stepped into the room, Pechy would jump up and greet him; only then would he feel free to wander around the room to sniff at things and the situation would be normal once more.

I could not prevent Mako or Terry from taking Pechy to bed at night. Mako claimed that he served her as a hot water bottle; she pushed him toward the foot of the bed and slept with her feet against his warm furry side. Pechy knew perfectly well that as far as I was concerned, at least, he was not supposed to get on the beds. He would slip into Terry's room secretly and when I found them in the morning the same look of guilt would show in both pairs of eyes that peered at me from the bed.

We took Pechy everywhere with us, and when we travelled by train we carried him in a special traveling case. Regulations prevented boarding a train in Japan with a dog, but it was considered permissible if the dog was put aboard without the knowledge of the conductor. So, we simply kept Pechy in his traveling case until the train had started. He would walk with me, too, when I went in the afternoons to meet Mako returning from school. He could tell her from a distance by the tall cap she wore and would run breathlessly to meet her.

We considered him one of the family and there is no doubt but that he did, too. If any one of us so much as patted another dog, Pechy would immediately be overcome with jealousy; he would pretend to be crippled and in acute agony, only regaining his well-being when the other dog was dismissed and attention was focused on him once more. He felt responsible for his misconduct as a member of the family, also. At times when he came crawling into the living room on his stomach, in an attitude of abject apology, we knew to go in search of the broken vase or flower pot or whatever else he had upset.

We watched Ah Mei and Mako cavorting with Pechy and enjoyed the tranquillity of Peking as best we could, but in the back of our minds was always the awareness that world events were continuing an ominous course. With the outbreak of war in Europe, the cross-currents of intrigue on the diplomatic front became as intense and complicated as the actual fighting. The combatants were striving to draw in the two great powers still at peace, my country and Terry's, against their enemy. America was slowly, but it seemed certainly, going to the assistance of Britain, while Germany was reaching an accord with Japan which would pose a threat to the United States in the Pacific and divert her from the European hostilities. Japan wanted the Burma Road closed and the flow of British, French, and American supplies to China stopped; China wanted active participation of these countries in her war with Japan. The East was involved in the European War and the West in the Sino-Japanese War—the inner complexities of the tangled situation were beyond my grasp. I did understand, however, that in diplomatic warfare the weapons are moral force and economic sanctions and that, unless these were effective and concessions made on each side, no settlement could be made short of war.

Added to the political tension, we faced a personal crisis.

Unknown to me, there were rumors that Matsuoka, the Foreign Minister who was strongly pro-German and anti-American, was about to issue an edict that all Foreign Office men with foreign wives must either resign or take inferior positions. Terry heard the rumors and, without telling me anything, was suddenly off to Tokyo. After he had gone, I began to feel myself the object of undue solicitude and affection from the Embassy wives; in a most friendly way, and with unusual frequency, they called on the telephone and "dropped in" at my home to see me. They had always been good to me, but as I had already begun to wonder about the Tokyo visit, something in their protective manner aroused my suspicion.

When Terry returned, obviously anxious to tell me a secret, I was careful not to let him know I had guessed the reason for his trip.

Terry had gone to Matsuoka's office, where the little man—he was half Terry's size—arose to greet him. Terry put a letter firmly on the great desk. Matsuoka picked it up, read it, and asked urgently, "What does this mean, Terasaki?"

"I have been told on very good authority that there is a directive going out to the effect that certain Foreign Office men will either have to resign or take unimportant posts. That implies that my wife is embarrassing to the Foreign Office—therefore, I am resigning." Abruptly he started for the door.

In much confusion his superior called out, "Oh, wait, Terasaki, wait! I beg you—this in no way applies to Mrs. Terasaki!"

So the personal crisis had been surmounted and we talked gleefully of Matsuoka's discomfiture. I also had a story, a less happy one, to relate of happenings in Terry's absence. While he was in Japan the Tripartite Pact became known. Events which we had watched with such anxiety, now hopefully, now fearfully, had taken a drastic turn for the worse. After the agreement was reached, the German special envoy, Stahmer, his mission accomplished passed through Peking en route to Germany. This called for a celebration in honor of Stahmer, now an ally of the Japanese, and the ranking Japanese official, the Counsellor, whose wife was away, needed a hostess for the party. As the wife of the second ranking official, it fell my lot to serve in this capacity. The task was extremely unpleasant, but I did my best and found that Madame Stahmer and her husband were most delightful and pleasant to know. As we sat at the great table the inevitable cry went up for a toast to the Tripartite Pact. Each guest raised his glass and they all looked at me. An officer said loudly, "We are waiting for you, Mrs. Terasaki!"

"Please don't wait. I am not drinking tonight."

As they drank I received a warm and understanding look from their host, the Counsellor—how grateful I felt toward him! The

Stahmers remained cordial and charming; I talked at length with them, thinking what good friends we could be at another time.

The alliance with Germany and Italy portended the end of peaceful attempts at settlement. Terry was plunged into deepest consternation. The Japanese propaganda declared the agreement was for the purpose of guarding against Russia—but had not Germany entered into a pact with Russia the year before, looking to the joint conquest of Poland? It seemed to us that the Tripartite Pact could be nothing less than a design for war. The military party must have been dazzled out of their senses by the German blitzkrieg in France. With mounting anxiety we watched the dreadful march of events.

5

A MISSION FOREDOOMED

THE months passed slowly and it was the spring of 1941. Nomura, who had known Roosevelt years before, had been sent to the United States as ambassador. This was hopeful as Admiral Nomura was a sincere liberal and a great friend of America. We knew he would seek some agreement that would thwart the recklessness of the war party. Relations between our countries had become so tense that domestic public opinion in each country made concessions by either government difficult. President Roosevelt had brought the moral force of America to bear on Japan in 1937 with his famous "quarantine" speech in which he branded Japan as an aggressor. Now, economic opposition was being employed more and more stringently against Japan as the United States, Britain, and the Netherlands tightened an embargo around the islands. Rubber, oil, and minerals were shut off from the Dutch East Indies and the Malayan Archipelago, and the flow of scrap iron from America had ceased. With each such restriction the rich, undefended countries of southeast Asia—abounding in the raw materials Japan must have—became more and more tantalizing before the calculating eyes of the Japanese militarists. We knew Nomura opposed their rash designs and that he was a good choice for ambassador if a peaceful solution was to be sought.

After four costly years in China the Japanese army was bogged down, and a decisive victory over the Chinese seemed as elusive as catching a handful of smoke. Japan held the coast and all the large cities. After losing Nanking and Hankow on the Yangtze River, the Chinese retreated to Chungking and now interposed the formidable Yangtze gorges between themselves and the advancing Japanese. Although it appeared that Japan should have won, the war had become a stalemate because of the regrouping and resilience of the Chinese. Japan was trying to wait out the Chinese but resistance mounted.

Taro had been appointed chief of the American Bureau of the Foreign Office. He wanted Terry to go to Washington to help Nomura with the negotiations and to report to him if anyone tried to sabotage the efforts at a peaceful settlement. It was known that China and Germany were doing their best to hamper negotiations and that the military was committed to a collision course directly into the war on the side of the Axis powers. It was important that Nomura have all the help he could obtain and that no one in the Japanese Embassy cooperate with those who wanted war. Terry told me before we left Peking that if there should be war between my country and his, Japan was certain to lose and that Russia would be the only victor. I told him Russia was a third-rate power and he must be mistaken. He said he hoped I would never be proved wrong but he knew I would be. I could never understand his profound fear of the Russians.

That summer, after we arrived in Washington, Terry spoke to Taro often over the trans-Pacific telephone, using Mariko's nickname as a code word. If things were going well he would tell Taro that Mako was in good health, and if not, then Mako was ill. Mako's illness was critical. Kurusu had been sent to join Nomura but had not been armed with authority to concede to the American demand that Japan retire from China and Indo-China where they had recently landed. Kurusu and Nomura were doing their best but they simply had nothing to bargain with. Konoye repeatedly asked President Roosevelt to meet him in the Pacific, on American soil, to work out a settlement, but on October 18, 1941, as the negotiations dragged along, Prince Konoye's cabinet fell. Taro immediately resigned as chief of the American Bureau rather than take orders from Tojo's government. Tojo, a dangerous man who stood in awe of Germany's might and had little understanding of the United States, was poised in a position of great power over Japanese policy as premier.

As Taro had suspected, there were Japanese in the delegation who were bent upon sabotaging the mission. I had personal knowledge of one of these men. He looked for opportunities to show his disdain for the Americans and made trouble at the discussions by his truculence and self-importance. Once, just after they had returned from a conference to their offices at the Embassy, Terry upbraided him for his rudeness. The man was very casual about it, and Terry lost his temper and struck him violently in the face.

"Terasaki-san, this is insupportable! You have insulted my ancestors! You must let me hit you back to appease them," he said.

"Turn your other side and I'll hit the other jaw and get all your damned ancestors!"

I was secretly pleased when I heard of this, for I had had an encounter with this boorish fellow myself at a state dinner a few days before. When asked politely by an American diplomat how he liked Washington, he had said,

"O.K. You have great natural beauty. It is lucky you do for the buildings are frightful—but nature makes up for the lack of culture in the people."

I kicked him twice under the table. The first time he looked about in astonishment, not imagining it could be me. The second time I kicked him while he was looking at me. He asked me the meaning of it later and I was delighted to tell him. The American, a former consul at Harbin, realized what had happened and was greatly amused.

63

On November 26 the Americans delivered a note to the Japanese envoys demanding that they get out of China and Indo-China forthwith and retain no trading advantages with the Chinese mainland. Japan was in a box. The military could not agree to such a move, especially without some concessions elsewhere, without encountering disgrace for having initiated the Chinese war. Something had to be done and done quickly.

The wires from Tokyo directed the Japanese Ambassador to make all efforts at settlement but stated that a conclusion must be reached by November 29. The deadline was ominous.

Dismayed at the emergence of Tojo and his group to power, Admiral Nomura had previously wired Tokyo that he wished to resign. Tojo told him he could not resign for the present. Again Nomura had cabled the Foreign Office that if his country was planning to take "free action" his resignation must be accepted. Then after the cable carrying the deadline of November 29 was received, Nomura sent the following wire: "I am an honorable man. I will take no part in any deceit or duplicity of action nor do I wish to be the bones of a dead horse . . ." and demanded his resignation be accepted. No response came from Tokyo.

Terry remarked that the discussions with Secretary Hull, my fellow Tennessean, had been in vague, "around-the-bush" terms and got nowhere. He sensed the approach of disaster and wanted desperately to do some last-minute bargaining which might avert it. He kept telling me, on the rare instances when we could talk, that they must be plain-spoken and bold at the conferences, dissolve the diplomatic niceties, and get to the heart of the matter. As first secretary, he was a right-hand man to Nomura. Daily he became more affected by the tension and pressure of the mounting crisis. Working night and day, he was largely sustained by quantities of black coffee and the cigarettes he constantly smoked.

Then he did something that reminded me of the Burgner incident years before. He said to Kurusu, "Ambassador, why don't you become a national traitor? Why don't you go ahead and say to the Americans, we will get out of China? We can't remain in China for long anyway. The war party knows that. They will have to leave China but they would prefer war with the United States as an excuse for leaving to admitting they have made such a mistake. You may be executed but they may honor the treaty. It will give them a way out and we may get some concessions in exchange."

Kurusu said he would consider it.

There had been many proposals in the air. One was that Japan be granted New Guinea for colonization by its excess population in return for stopping the Chinese war and giving up claims to China and Indo-China. New Guinea was far less desirable but the Japanese leaders under such an agreement would have done something toward handling the problem of surplus population, in addition to obtaining raw materials and having something to show to save "face."

On the twenty-ninth of November my husband went to Dr. E. Stanley Jones, the well-known Methodist leader who was using his prestige and friendship with the President to help the parties reach an amicable settlement of the crisis. He asked Dr. Jones if he could get in touch with the President and explain to him the Japanese situation psychologically so that he might be more receptive to their proposals. The Japanese were to see Mr. Roosevelt at 2:30 that afternoon and it was 12:30 when Terry reached Dr. Jones. A call was placed to the White House and the President's secretary, Mr. McIntyre, read off the engagements already made for the intervening time before the Japanese delegation was scheduled to see the President. It was not possible for Dr. Jones to talk with Mr. Roosevelt but a message could be transmitted if Dr. Jones would dictate it to Mr. McIntyre over the telephone. My husband and Dr. Jones then composed a letter, unmistakably in Terry's style of English: "We Japanese have been four years at war. When one is in a war mentality, he cannot think straight. The Allies were in a war mentality at the close of the last war and made a bad peace. You help us from a war mentality to a peace mentality. Don't compel us to do things but make it possible for us to do them. If you treat us this way, we will meet you

65

more than half way. If you stretch out one hand, we will stretch out two. And we cannot only be friends, we can be allies."

The message was delivered to the President and the conversations that followed shortly after centered on the Japanese psychology in the crisis. Kurusu and Terry were delighted.

Soon afterward, Kurusu called Terry into his private office and closed the door.

"Terasaki, you have suggested that I be a national traitor. How about being one yourself? I think we should approach the President through an intermediary, someone who has the President's ear, and suggest that he send a cable directly to the Emperor appealing for peace. I must warn you that I have already asked permission of Tojo to do this and have been ordered not to. The cablegram must be sent over Tojo's head directly to *tennō heika*." Kurusu paused a moment, looking up into the eyes of the taller man and added quietly, "Of course, if your part in it is discovered, it may mean your death and death for your family also—but you thought I should take the same risk, so now it is your turn."

"It is an excellent idea. I will get to work on it at once."

When he came home that night, Terry told me about it. By then he had a little speech about his decision for my benefit, "There are only three members of our family—our sacrifice compared to the death of millions is unimportant." Back and forth across the living room he paced, thinking over people he knew who might serve the purpose. He had golfed with Walker, the Postmaster General, and it occurred to me to suggest his name. Terry thought it would be better to have someone who was not in the Cabinet. We spoke of several men and then Terry decided to approach Dr. Jones again.

The next day Terry telephoned me hurriedly with directions to arrange a luncheon for Dr. Jones and Dr. Robinson, his friend and companion in efforts to placate the nations, at a place where they could talk. I called a restaurant known as the Purple Iris and reserved a private room.

Dr. Jones had just come from Dr. Hu Shih, the Chinese Ambassador, whom he had urged not to block Japanese-American negotiations, reasoning that if Japan and America went to war the winner would be the Communists and that China's difficulties with Japan could be worked out without taking on something much worse in the process. He warned that the American public would react unfavorably if it were known that China was trying to drag us into their war with Japan. When Terry explained to Dr. Jones the plan for having the President cable the Emperor, he immediately agreed to act as intermediary.

The entire message was to be delivered by Jones by word of mouth and nothing was to be in writing. Mr. Roosevelt was at Warm Springs, Georgia, where he had gone for a few days' rest. Dr. Jones called the White House and spoke to Mr. McIntyre again, asking if he might take a plane and speak with the President in Georgia. Mr. McIntyre said he might, but he suggested that if the message could be written it could be brought to his office at the White House and sealed in his presence. It would then be put in a special bag and taken by plane with a courier to the President the following Monday morning. Mr. McIntyre would guarantee that no one would see the contents of the message until the President opened it himself. Terry agreed that most of the message could be delivered by that method, but he insisted that unless one part of it could be handled verbally it could not be sent at all. The message was written, except for this reserved portion and taken to the White House, but by this time the situation had worsened. The President had changed his plans and was returning to Washington by train to arrive on Monday morning.

The letter was given to the President at the railway station and he read it on the way to the White House. The suggestion contained in the message was, of course, that the President send a cable to Hirohito appealing for peace. The Emperor rarely took part, but if he interfered, it was known that the Japanese leaders would comply—all of them, including the war ministry.

On December 3, Dr. Jones requested audience with Mr. Roosevelt to deliver the verbal message. It was arranged for him to talk with the President if he got there within twenty minutes, and he was instructed to go to the east gate where someone would meet him and take him in the back way in order to avoid news-papermen.

Mr. Roosevelt told Dr. Jones, "Two days before I got your letter I thought of sending the cable, but I've hesitated to do it, for I didn't want to hurt the Japanese here at Washington by going over their heads to the Emperor."

Dr. Jones replied, "Mr. President, that is the purpose of my visit. I have come to tell you that this suggestion of sending the cable did not come from me, but from the Japanese Embassy. They have asked me to ask you to send the cable. But obviously they could not let me write that, for there must be no written record, since they are going over the head of their government to the Emperor."

"Oh, then, that wipes my slate clean; I can send the cable."

"But," Jones said, "the Japanese tell me that you must not send the cable as you sent the other cable to the Emperor over the sinking of the *Panay*. They tell me that the reason you got no reply from the Emperor was that it never got to him, but was held up in their Foreign Office. This time, they tell me, you must not send it through the Foreign Office, but direct to the Emperor himself. I don't know the mechanics of it, but that's what they suggest."

Mr. Roosevelt said, "Well, I'm just thinking out loud. I can't go down to the cable office and say I want to send a cable from the President of the United States to the Emperor of Japan, but I could send it to Grew, for Grew as an ambassador has the right of audience to the head of a state and he can give it to the Emperor direct, and if I do not hear within twenty-four hours—I have learned to do some things—I'll give it to the newspapers and force a reply!"

It was hoped that the cable would not be held up by the Japanese telegraphers who would handle it before it reached Ambassador Grew and that Grew could obtain immediate audience with Hirohito; this might have the same effect as the proposed meeting with Premier Konoye.

At the conclusion of the meeting Dr. Jones mentioned that the

68

President must never refer to Mr. Terasaki in connection with the message. Mr. Roosevelt told him, "You tell that young Japanese he is a brave man. No one will ever learn of his part in this from me. His secret is safe."

The cable was long and was not sent until December 5—two days before our world had burst apart.

What could have happened to it, I wondered. Oh, God, what could have happened to it?

6

INTERNMENT

THE next morning the doorbell rang and we opened it to admit a member of the F.B.I. We were to have a close association with that office for six months. The agent was brisk, efficient and stiffly polite. He took down our names and addresses, including the address of my parents in Tennessee. I was instructed to stay in the apartment unless accompanied by one of their men. I could take walks with Mako and Pechy, the agent with us or at a protective distance. These regulations were not so much to restrict us as to provide for our personal safety. Feeling was intense and the government did not want to risk any unnecessary incidents. I welcomed our ever-present escorts and made the best of the cumbersome situation.

My paramount concern during those first few days of the war was for my mother. Since she was visiting us at the time of Pearl Harbor, her position was delicate; she was caught at the outbreak of the war in the home of an enemy alien, even though the alien was her son-in-law. She was greatly astonished when told by the agent that she could not leave my apartment to return to her home. She was not released until arrangements had been made through our congressman.

Our last night before my mother departed, she and Mako and I slept together in a large double bed. Three generations of us, close and secure for a few hours wondering what was to come. I lay wide-eyed again for most of the night and doubted whether we would meet again.

When at last I fell into a troubled sleep, I awakened with a start and saw a light from the kitchen. Springing up half-drugged with sleep, I looked through the crack between the wall and the door. There sat mother fully dressed, peacefully having her breakfast. I stood watching her intently, saying an inaudible goodbye. When the actual parting came, the firm set of her shoulders and the erect way she walked down the hall to the elevator braced me for things to come with the memory of her graceful strength. Her black cape moved from side to side and she never looked back. When the elevator closed after her it occurred to me that she had never asked me to stay in America.

There would be time enough to grieve later; now there was too much to do. I had to pack, pay the household bills, do some shopping, and make whatever arrangements I could for the impending move. I was competent to do the packing by virtue of our previous frequent journeys but was under considerable strain as to the rest of the planning. We had been told that we would be allowed to take all our personal effects, with the exception of furniture. Happily our apartment was furnished so there was no worry about storage.

The government men settled down outside the entrance to our flat and everyone coming or going had to check with them. Several friends, a cousin, and an aunt came to see us. The Negro porter who helped me box my things was very kind and the Jewish grocer in the basement came twice a day to keep me supplied with groceries.

My colored maid, a husky six-footer named Clementine, had fled in terror when war was declared, and I had to cook all our meals and do the cleaning. This unaccustomed labor helped me keep my senses.

The weather was clear and crisp, and we took a walk every day with the F.B.I. agent. He was a kind person and sorry for us. Mako, with Pechy on a leash, would scamper through the leaves and play along the way. We went shopping several times, and often our escort was bewildered at my purchases. Tacks, nails, shoe strings, rubber bands, soap and vitamin tablets. The nails were such a treasure in war-time Japan that often I was to use a couple of them, suitably wrapped and be-ribboned, as a very well-received gift.

Many of the wives of the Embassy personnel spoke no English. They were interned in their apartments, as I was, and were not allowed to communicate with their husbands. Several were completely at a loss when it came to arranging to move. To help them manage, I kept in touch with them by phone and relayed their problems to George Atcheson, Jr., of the State Department, who was temporarily in charge of their welfare. In that way I was able to help both sides through a most difficult time. As a group and with only two well-remembered exceptions, those Japanese women were magnificent; and they were treated well by all the Americans with whom they came in contact. Mr. Atcheson would telephone and I would tell him how each wife was getting along, whether she needed medical attention or some other special service. He would always end our conversation with a kindly, "And how are you?" Primarily because of his friendship and helpfulness, I could truthfully say, "I am all right."

The Consul at New York called me. His name was Morishima and we had known him in Shanghai. The consulates had not been closed and the staffs were not under surveillance, as the Embassy people were. This puzzled and alarmed the poor man. He wanted me to ask George Atcheson what they should do. This disturbed me greatly, but I refused to interfere. Terry told me later I was right in this; I should help with the Japanese wives at the Embassy and do what Mr. Atcheson wished but not volunteer in other directions.

One day I received a telephone call informing me that Terry would be brought to the apartment at nine o'clock that evening and would have to return to the Embassy by nine the next morning. The hours passed slowly as I waited.

My husband's face held grim lines of fatigue, sorrow, and frustration. His eyes that had been so brilliantly alive spoke an ineffable sadness. His career seemed to have gone for nothing, and the future held only the inevitable, violent doom of his beloved country for him to witness, an impotent and wretched spectator. He seemed to have lost all hope.

We had much to say to each other that night. I was indignant when he asked me what I intended to do. He was fond of repeating the phrase he had used with Ambassador Debuchi, "I have shot the ball down the fairway," to emphasize the permanence of our marriage and now I told him that I, too, had "shot the ball down the fairway"; that what I intended to do had been decided ten years before on our wedding day. I suppose his question was only his way of saying I could remain if I chose. He reminded me of the cablegram and that if his part in it was known in Japan, as it might be, it would probably be the end for all of us. I told him that I realized the danger and was prepared to face it. He was much moved and solemnly announced, as if to the world at large, "Japan will lose—utterly." He played handball with Mako before we put her to bed.

Far into the night we whispered to each other, and daybreak and the F.B.I. came with brutal suddenness.

I was the last wife to enter the Embassy. I packed everything, paid all the bills, and closed the book, so to speak, but I held off as long as I could. I wanted to breathe the clean, sweet air of my native land, to walk its streets; and, as the leaves were being raked, smell the odor of burning leaves, a nostalgic reminder of my childhood. The aroma of burning leaves is not half so pleasant in other lands as it is in America.

At last I told the man from the F.B.I. that I was ready to go into the Embassy to join my husband. I telephoned Mother in Tennessee to hear her voice once again. She charged me, "Keep a stout heart, my darling, you're going to need it!" I said goodbye to my friends and at last to my aunt, who came to see me. I walked to the elevator to see her off, and her weeping face was too much for the agent, who turned his back so as not to embarrass us. I called Mr. Atcheson to thank him for his care of all the Embassy women and his courtesy to me. He said in parting, "I hope we'll meet in happier times and that this war will soon be over."

Mako with Pechy, and I with the luggage, climbed into the agent's car and we drove to the Embassy. I told the agent that I hoped to avoid newspapermen and photographers, so he circled the Embassy several times to see if there was danger of being detected. There was one photographer asleep in his car and the agent told me, "Hurry, Mrs. Terasaki, run for it!" He wished me the best of luck and I thanked him with much feeling for his thoughtfulness.

Mako raced into the Embassy and I followed with Pechy's leash in my hand; but Pechy had seen a tree and made for it. I yanked him, dripping, into the Embassy and, to the butler's horror, across the hall. I had planned to enter my internment with more dignity.

The entire staff was lunching in the big dining room. I had to go into that crowd with the bombing of Pearl Harbor fresh in my mind. My husband rose to meet me and so did Admiral Nomura. He took both my hands and said,

"Now all my children are here. I am very sorry for you, Mrs. Terasaki. You are a brave woman and I hope you will always feel that I am your friend."

He, like Terry, had done his best to avert the tragedy that had befallen us.

The Embassy was greatly overcrowded and the allotting of sleeping space was difficult. We were given a small room on the second floor. I got a bed with springs but no mattress. The mattress went to someone without a bed, no doubt. Every morning I found the pattern of the springs imprinted on my body. Mako had two large chairs put together for a bed and Terry slept on the floor. It was a race to the bathroom; even at an early hour a long line had already formed.

INTERNMENT

I spent most of my time reading and listening to the radio. Christmas was near and the Christmas music so constantly on the air could not become tiresome for me. I prepared our presents and we had our family celebration in our little room.

There was a tall Christmas tree in the lower hall. I took Mariko down to show her the lights and we talked about Christmas. She announced happily, "I'm glad there's Christmas, mama, even with the war." I assured her there would always be Christmas.

A tall, slim major was watching us. He introduced himself and asked me to tell him about the Christmas story; he knew the Japanese version and wanted to learn the American story. We talked it over and found that the two accounts were remarkably alike.

A few days later we were told to pack up and prepare to go to the Homestead Hotel at Hot Springs, Virginia, where we would be interned until our exchange for American diplomats would be effected.

Terry was to ride in the Ambassador's car with the other ranking officials; Mako, Pechy, and I were to go in one of the large buses provided by the government for wives, children, and men of lesser rank. We knew that there was a crowd outside the Embassy gates and that all along the route there would be photographers and newspapermen. Many of these people were Secret Service agents for our protection.

Mako was excited—a trip, and such a confused, noisy one— made her black eyes shine. She carried Pechy in his "traveling bag." We all congregated in the large reception hall of the Embassy and each person was told the number of his bus. There was no way of avoiding having our pictures taken, but I tried not to hear those in the crowd who yelled at me, "Hey, you're no Jap— you're in the wrong place." One woman thumbed her nose at me. Perhaps she had a son at Pearl Harbor. Before the Japanese got into their cars the men doffed their hats and all bowed low to the Embassy in farewell.

At Union Station all was confusion, flash bulbs popping and people staring and shouting. I raised my eyes to look away from all those faces and caught sight of the flag fluttering atop the station building. The crowd could not know that it was my flag as well as theirs and they could not know with what sorrow I was being separated from it and them. Somehow we were jammed aboard and the train started.

Immersed deeply in thought and calmed by the sedative clickety-clack of the wheels sounding the joints in the rails, I realized we were in Virginia and I had just read one of that commonwealth's historical markers. We were near Manassas Junction. I fell to thinking of the great battles fought over these rolling hills as we journeyed on. There came into my mind the consolation that some eighty years ago there must have been many desperate soldiers battling over these fields who would have understood my position. I had a sense of communion with the mothers of the sons who had fought each other. People had made the hard choice between conflicting loyalties before. I realized I was fortunate in that I would not have to take any active part against my country, that Terry and I could maintain a neutrality. Perhaps when it was over I could again reinforce my husband in his efforts to find a means for the two nations to live together in peace. I knew that Terry shared with me a sense of outrage that we, who held a common love for the good things of both countries, should have to endure a war between them.

I was shaken from my reverie by a porter serving sandwiches and coffee for lunch. A few children became travel sick, and I dispatched Mako to carry wet towels and water to the rescue. She went off happily to her nursing with a glow of unmistakable superiority in her eye. Soon she was able to be of service again. When the immigration men and F.B.I. agents went through the coaches to check all the personnel, they had great difficulty with a number of the Japanese who could not speak English. Mako, who was tagging along with them, began translating as though the big fat immigration inspector with the service ribbons from World War I had appointed her official interpreter. Things went more smoothly for the men, and they offered her a reward of chewing gum and candy if she would accompany them through the other cars. I told her to go along and make herself useful, and she went proudly off, jabbering first in Japanese and then in English, a happy nine-year-old go-between for the enemy adults.

The countryside was beautiful. I tried desperately to memorize the tall bare trees, the hills, and farm houses in the gathering twilight, to hold this picture as though it were a tangible thing, fearing I might never see it again.

We arrived that evening at Hot Springs and I was taken aback to discover a huge crowd of mountaineers assembled to watch us come in. These were the lean descendants of the Scotch-Irish who had settled these mountains and my east Tennessee homeland late in the eighteenth century. I was curious and somewhat fearful to see how they would react. There was not a sound, only silent, unfriendly faces. It was a relief when Mr. Muir, of the State Department, informed me that there was a car waiting to take Mako and me to the hotel. The men were to walk to the hotel and I know that it must have been an anxious time for the F.B.I. men who were responsible for getting them safely there. The safety of the Japanese was in their hands, and they well knew that if one Japanese official should be killed or injured some American interned in Tokyo would suffer for it.

The Homestead Hotel is surrounded by some of the most breath-taking country in the United States. The inn has much dignity and charm and also it provided the seclusion desirable for an internment camp. I am sure it was chosen for us because of the ease with which it could be guarded.

We were assembled in the vast lobby to be assigned rooms and to try to fish out our luggage from the mountain of trunks, valises, suitcases, hand bags, hat boxes, and impedimenta of all sorts piled there. Terry arranged for things to be brought up to the room and I escaped to a hot, relaxing bath. The forced move through the staring crowds of my countrymen had unnerved me. I was tired and tense. Mako was greatly excited in her new home. I heard her telling Pechy that he must never bark inside the hotel, because he might wake up all the babies and they would start yowling and that would be terrible.

When we went down to our assigned table for dinner that first

77

evening, I noticed the official table was placed just inside the main door. Here sat the F.B.I. agents, immigration officials, State Department people, and a Spanish and a Swiss representative to serve as liaison between the two governments. They were eating and occasionally glanced up as the Japanese filed in. When Terry and Mako and I came in, I caught the alert look that passed among them all.

We became friends with all our official keepers. Being thrown together there for nearly six months, it was fortunate that almost everyone showed a spirit of cooperation and willingness to get along. Many of the Japanese had never lived so luxuriously or amid such beauty, and they enjoyed the novelty of it almost as much as they looked forward to returning to Japan. For me it was frustrating to know that I could not go out and walk that highway just visible through the trees. I could imagine it going south to Tennessee and my people.

Terry was appointed a committee of one to represent the Japanese group. This kept him busy the first few days seeing what privileges we were to have and what medical attention would be available. There were five pregnant women among us, and, with my smattering of Japanese, I offered to help them. Some of these women were extraordinarily shy and timid with an American doctor, and I was able to make things a bit easier for them. Dr. Jarman, the hotel's doctor, was in charge of the Medical Center and the medicinal baths. He was a kindly Southerner and cared for his enemy patients with skill and solicitude.

I assisted at one of the childbirths because the mother knew no English. It was my first such experience and I was more than a little frightened. The doctor was almost as much concerned about me as the mother and child. Several times he inquired anxiously, "Don't you want to sit down for a while, Mrs. Terasaki?"

One thing rather puzzled him. There was no sound from the mother. Once only she said to me, "*Itai* (It hurts)," and that was all. She had the prettiest tiny baby I have ever seen. We named her "Izumi (little spring)," and she was written up in *Life* magazine. Not only was *Life* interested, but one of the Negro waiters wanted to see her and remarked when he did, "Why, ma'am, she's as cute as any baby I've ever seen!"

Mako had learned to swim when she was only five, while we were in Havana. There was a beautiful pool at Hot Springs and we had the instructor work with Mako to improve her strokes. Every morning she and the big red-headed lifeguard had a workout and frolic in the warm pool. I went down every morning to watch them play water polo and swim to the tune of Strauss waltzes on the record player.

We were allowed to read *The New York Times* and we could buy magazines and books provided they were not of a political nature. Only fiction was available and much of it was of poor quality. We read Adams' *The Epic of America* and the *Oxford Book of English Verse* which we had brought with us. A number of classes were organized among the internees. They studied Spanish, English, and French in the language group. Some studied painting and poetry, and there was a glee club of sorts. I taught them "On a Bicycle Built for Two," and that became a great favorite.

The officers in our group, immediately feeling the dominance of the military at the outbreak of war, took it upon themselves to give orders to the diplomats. Perhaps they had nurtured a jealousy through the long period of subordination to the civilian officials whose advisers they were. They set up a schedule for calisthenics in the mornings for everyone and posted it in the lobby and the dining room. Terry announced publicly he would have nothing to do with it, nor would his family.

One morning, while taking a stroll, we passed the calisthenics grounds where the motley group of men, women, and children of all ages were responding in awkward fashion to the curt directions of a lieutenant. One of the officers ordered us into line, to do knee bends with the rest. Terry told him the idea was absurd. The officer came up to Terry to lecture him and to my shocked surprise my husband slapped him in the face. The astonished man turned to the group and asked if they were going to let Terasaki-san do that to him. He got no reply, and we continued our stroll.

Thereafter the number of people showing up for calisthenics dropped off sharply.

An officer by the name of Yano became friendly with Terry. He remarked at the dinner table one evening, "Terasaki-san, you would make a wonderful army officer, a general. How in the world did you ever happen to be a diplomat?"

Terry told him his father had warned him against carrying the "tin sword."

Yano's face paled with anger. I was embarrassed for him and argued with Terry about it later but to no avail. Terry resented Yano's suggestion that the military was superior in any way to the diplomatic corps. Mako and I made it a point to be especially friendly to Yano so that eventually he got over it and became devoted to Terry, who was careful never to allude to the subject again.

Concerts were held in the lobby every afternoon and we had music for dining. We thought our prison was about as comfortable and luxurious as it could be. There is no truth in the reports that the State Department stopped the music and reduced the menus to very scant fare. Some of the nationalistic Japanese among us thought the internees would get soft and asked that the menu be table d'hôte instead of the varied à la carte menu we had been choosing from. They also thought that listening to music while their countrymen were fighting a war was unpatriotic. At their request, the music at dinner was discontinued and the à la carte menu was withdrawn. I was glad no protest was made about the nightly movies; whether it was in the proper spirit of patriotism or not, our family enjoyed them very much.

Among the Embassy personnel there was a young man named Yoshida. Before going to Washington he had served in a consulate on the west coast. There he had fallen in love with one of the *nisei* secretaries in the Consul's office. They became engaged just before he was sent to Washington. She had been born in the United States but educated in Japan. Somehow she was not listed for one of the relocation camps into which most of the west coast Japanese, citizens and aliens alike, were herded, and she had not been interned when the Consulate was seized. Mr. Yoshida was in a desperate frame of mind and threatened suicide if we had to leave for Japan without her. We were sorry for him and even more disturbed that if he should kill himself some innocent person might be held responsible. My husband talked it over with one of the F.B.I. agents and the agent promised to see what he could do. After several weeks which were very trying to Mr. Yoshida and equally trying for his friends, the young woman in question arrived. The internees had little enough to talk about and this development got full attention. The girl had traveled alone across the United States but no one had bothered her; no one had even spoken to her. I do not know who was happiest at her arrival, Mr. Yoshida, the kindly agent, or Mr. Yoshida's patient friends.

We planned a wedding. It was my responsibility to buy the ring and flowers and to help dress the bride. She looked lovely in a spring-like dress with a corsage of gardenias. The wedding was simple and impressive. The minister was the Episcopal rector who held regular services in the hotel each Sunday. He was a thoughtful, considerate person, and his little talk after the ceremony touched us all. The agent who had intervened on their behalf and other Americans attended, and all took the groom's nervousness very much to heart. It is not unusual for the self-contained, reserved Japanese man to cry at his wedding, and Mr. Yoshida furnished the astonished American witnesses with copious proof of his happiness.

About this time an old friend, Hélène Feier, a French girl married to a Foreign Office man, arrived at the hotel. I had not seen her for several years and was overjoyed when she joined us with her husband and two children. She had been a secretary at the League of Nations, a brilliant person, who spoke many languages and had great political sense and acumen. She was a vivacious, clever person. She contributed a certain *ambiance* to any group which shared her conversation. She had a full measure of the *esprit* of her courageous people, and her common sense and courage cheered and bolstered me on many occasions.

With us there was a beautiful *nisei* girl from Seattle who had married the Consul at Houston. Her name was Jeanie and she was as American as corn flakes and apple pie. More than anyone else, she reminded me of home. Whenever I think of her, I remember a letter she once wrote to me which to my mind epitomizes the tragedy of the *nisei:* "Gwen, if you took my skin and made a dress, it no doubt would turn out a kimono. But if you opened my heart, you'd get a squirt of Yankee blood in your eye."

Hélène, Jeanie, and I shared a unique loneliness. We made the return to Japan with our husbands and witnessed, impotently, the destruction of that country, which was and was not our own, by the forces of our homelands. We three, the Tennessean, the Parisian, and the *nisei,* were to share the destinies of our diplomatic husbands.

Daily new rumors were begun. We were all to sail within a week from San Francisco, we were to sail within two weeks from New Orleans. Eventually we were told by the authorities that we were to be moved to the Greenbrier Hotel at White Sulphur Springs to join the German internees. Many of the Japanese had misgivings about being with the Germans but did not talk much about it. Again we packed and again the mountainous luggage was collected for transportation, but the move broke the monotonous life of the Homestead and we wondered what our new surroundings would be like.

We got settled at the Greenbrier with somewhat more ease than at the Homestead, and we found the Germans hospitable and glad to see us. There was much wining and dining and a number of gay cocktail parties among the higher ranking people of both embassies. Altogether, there were five American wives of German diplomats there. Some were frankly apprehensive about going to Germany, especially those who had never been there before. Others were well satisfied; I remember one such wife who was more Nazi than Hitler. She was vigorously instilling National Socialist doctrine in her German children and also in her American children by a previous marriage. I became friends with Frau Thomsen, the Hungarian wife of Hans Thomsen, the German Chargé d'Affaires. She was a very pretty woman, so fond of animals that she is reported to have gone down to the zoo at Rock Creek Park to say goodbye at the beginning of the war. She seemed desperately unhappy and permitted herself to make a number of remarks against Hitler and the Nazis. We spent much of our time together, trying to forget our situation which we could not remedy.

The Axis powers were incompatible at several points. For some reason he did not disclose to us, Pechy felt an ingrained aversion to Germans which extended to dogs belonging to the super race. An international incident occurred one afternoon while Terry was taking Pechy out for his customary run in the garden. A stout German lady was airing her large, shiny black, and thoroughly disdainful French poodle at the same time. Pechy, without the least provocation from the haughty poodle, suddenly made a furious, undeclared assault. He sprang unexpectedly toward the large dog, jerked the leash out of Terry's hand, and bit savagely into the poodle's aristocratic jowl. Terry raced up just in time to witness the woman belabor Pechy with her walking stick, whereupon Pechy turned to her and sank his sharp white teeth into her sizable ankle. Words were had at a great pace and in three languages before Pechy was again collared and dragged, still growling defiance, away from the Germans. For days thereafter we received cold, nasty looks from the woman and her husband, which caused Terry to break into peals of uncontrollable laughter.

Babies were born with surprising regularity. One or two of the mothers had to go to a hospital forty-five miles away to be confined. They had to go alone except for the ever-present agents and in the cases where the mothers knew no English, it must have been very difficult. I knew one girl who took a tiny Japanese doll along to make her feel more at home. I never heard one of these mothers mention other than kind and considerate treatment from the doctors and the hospital staff.

It was a snowy winter and the children were busy sledding down the slopes near the hotel. Mako did not have a sled and she was smaller than the other children. I watched her pulling their sled, a big red one, up the long hill time after time on the promise

83

she could ride down with the larger boys and girls who owned it. Then they would not let her go down, but each time she was eager to try again and kept trudging back up the hill with the rope thrown over her thin shoulder. Terry watched with me, saddened that he could do nothing for the little girl. He wished she could have a sled of her own and not have to endure the bullying of the other children. I told him it would teach her patience, but her father said that Mariko would see enough hardship in the future; it seemed a pity for her to be unhappy now. What impotence he must have felt, after years of comfort, to be unable to do anything for his only child, to see her so used irritated his sensitive pride. But we were helpless and knew we were.

Unknown to us, the same thoughtful agent who had helped in the wedding, had witnessed the spectacle from his office across the way. He too felt sympathy for the child. The next day he came to our room carrying a large red sled to present to "little Meriko."

I noted, however, that Mako did not let the others ride her sled very often, and that a tiny little boy did most of the job of lugging it up the hill for her.

As time went on, we began to wonder again when and how we would be exchanged for American diplomats. Many people had no extra money and none of us knew how long our funds would hold out. Our bank accounts were frozen, of course, and we had to be very thrifty to make our money last.

I bought an ironing board and an electric iron and ordered a wooden drying rack from Sears, Roebuck and Co. Thus equipped, I proceeded to tackle the family wash. I am sure the elegant Greenbrier Hotel has never before or since had washing and ironing going on in so many of its luxurious rooms. I learned to turn out a very well-laundered white shirt. Sometimes, when I thought of the numerous servants we had enjoyed in our homes in various countries, I thought with amusement how some of them would have been amazed at the chores I did.

There was no extra food for Pechy, so we all shared our food with him and every night I carried a covered dish of left-overs to my room. At first, an army officer who dined at our table did not

84

seem to approve of such a fuss over a little dog. But as time went on we eventually won him over to the cause, and before we left the hotel he, too, was cutting his contribution for Pechy into tiny pieces. The night we were told by the F.B.I. that no dogs would be allowed to return to Japan, this officer could not eat his dinner.

The Germans were to be repatriated first, and one evening they left amidst much saluting and "Heil Hitler-ing." The hotel staff remained in their offices and only those Japanese who were pro-Axis gave them a rousing send-off. I sent a corsage to Frau Thomsen because, somehow, she seemed to me like a small bird lost from its nest. I have heard nothing of her since.

After the departure of the Germans we felt our leave-taking would come soon. I felt a poignant sorrow as I thought of Mother; she could not be informed and would learn by radio when we had gone. It grieved me deeply to think of the anxiety and worry I had brought to her.

I was anxious over my husband's mounting depression and lethargy. Terry had believed in peace as the pious believe in religion. Peace was a tangible and obtainable thing. It was a personal thing, it was Terry's career and his game. He was like the sprinter who believes he can run a four-minute mile or the schoolboy who believes he can win a scholarship. He had felt that Japan should withdraw her troops from China where, in his view, their situation had become hopeless, and thereby remove the major immediate threat of a clash with United States. It was an old argument of more than ten years' standing, and I had heard it often, but Terry kept repeating it to me as though in a trance. The war party, having thrown the steel dice in 1931 and won in Manchuria, had erred on the second throw in 1937, gambling to conquer China and make Manchuria secure. The Chinese, with the new vigor of nationalism, had rallied after successive defeats and held Chungking, which lay in central China far up the Yangtze behind great natural barriers. Meanwhile the would-be conquerors found themselves far from their base of supplies and scattered over a tremendous, densely-populated area among people who had been made increasingly stubborn by maltreatment from Japanese soldiers. Faced with these difficulties, Japan had tried to blockade the Chinese into submission, thinking that without access to the sea and their principal cities they would come to terms. When this plan was unsuccessful, and the British and Americans had imposed costly economic sanctions, Japan was in the position of having worsened the evils she had sought to cure: her population was still far beyond her ability to feed, and the abortive attempt to annex colonies with which to trade had caused the shutting down of trade with most of the rest of the world. The militarists, who had imposed the policy of conquest upon the nation over the hard-fought opposition of the moderates, were unwilling to admit they were wrong. They preferred to reason that Germany would overwhelm Russia and England and that, by the calculated risk of attacking the American fleet, they might occupy southeast Asia readily. With the raw materials and food gathered there, Japan could entrench herself to withstand what the war party guessed would be a half-hearted American effort to dislodge her. The militarists calculated it would take years for the Americans to rebuild their Pacific fleet. Thus, by further boldness, the China defeat would be turned into victory and the betrayers of Japan would become its heroes. This ill-considered course was viewed by the moderates and liberals as presaging certain doom, a total eclipse of the Land of the Rising Sun. Pearl Harbor was their defeat, and it had brought a peculiar spiritual destruction to Terry, in the long run as fatal to him as to the American naval vessels at Oahu.

Over and over, day by day, he reviewed the past as if mesmerized. Sometimes he seemed like a child that keeps saying to itself, "It has not happened—it is only a dream." With worried eyes I followed after him until I realized that a man's work is the heart of his hope and happiness, that when the work is smashed, nothing—not love nor family nor wife—can replace it; all the wife can do is to keep his likeness alive, tend the wounds she cannot cure, and wait until he can work again. Then, when

86

he ceases to live automatically, the incubus may depart and hope return.

We were told that we must pack up and be ready to leave. Something had to be done with the dog. Pechy was to be the first casualty in our family. Again the kindly agent helped us and made it possible that Pechy be sent to my mother in Tennessee. However, when we studied the train schedules we found that the connections were so bad that the trip might take days. The agent informed Mother it would be best if someone came for Pechy at the hotel.

I knew nothing of this and was greatly surprised one day when I was told to prepare the dog for travel, that my mother and brother were downstairs to get him. As we put Pechy in his little travel-scarred case, Mako began to sob. Terry and I wished there were something we could do but we could not help her. We saw Pechy off with his little tail beating a swift tattoo on the sides of his case. The prospect of another trip excited him and, as a true diplomat's dog, he looked forward to new vistas. With those excited thump-thumps he went out of our lives. He died in July, 1945, a month before the conflict between the two countries to which he belonged was finished.

I asked the agent if I could see Mother to say goodbye. I begged him to accompany me—I only wanted to look into her face once more and shake her hand in farewell. The regulations forbade this strictly and the agent had no choice but to refuse. Then I asked him if I could go to the roof of the hotel and wave to her. The regulations were silent on this possibility and the agent assented willingly. We went to the roof.

There I waved sadly to Mother and my brother, Bill, where they stood about fifty yards away down the road by the car. The road ran along beside the hotel and on the other side was a tiny church with a cross topping its steeple. Their car was surrounded by immigration and F.B.I. cars, and I saw Mother and Bill get out. I lost all control and fell to weeping. Mako was in Jeanie's comforting arms. I remember the flutter of Mother's pink handkerchief and the forced calm of her voice calling up to me, "Goodbye, darling, keep a stout heart!" I knew why Bill said nothing. I turned to Terry and beheld an expression of controlled suffering. Shocked at his face, I stopped my crying and stared at him. He seemed a different person, so intense was his agony. Sorrowfully, we watched the car pull out, gain speed, and disappear into the Virginia twilight. Without a word, we trooped downstairs, washed our faces, and went into the dining room for a dinner we could not eat.

Mother and Bill drove a few miles and then stopped the car to give way to their grief. They took Pechy home and cared for him lovingly as long as he lived. Throughout his life he looked down the street for the little girl who never came. When she did come at last, she was tall and grave and he was dust.

7

THE *GRIPSHOLM*

On June 10, 1942, we left the Greenbrier and White Sulphur Springs. I went up to the roof one last time to gaze wistfully at the green countryside of my native land. We were being sent to Lourenço Marques in Portuguese East Africa, there to be exchanged for Americans. The American diplomats were to come from Japan and other posts scattered throughout the East on Japanese ships, and at Lourenço Marques we would exchange ships with them and return to Japan while they sailed back to the United States. The countries had made safe-conduct agreements with regard to the exchange of diplomats, but many of the Japanese feared that the agreement would not be kept.

I had taken pains with the packing, putting in woolen things as well as summer wear, because on the long voyage we would change climates. I had packed our emergency bag for the life-boat, putting in vitamin tablets, bouillon cubes, and a first-aid kit. I had been working too hard to think much about whether we would be safe on the ship, and only now, when I looked at the

Blue Ridge Mountains from the hotel roof, I wondered what would happen when we got to Japan.

There were many tears when we said goodbye to the hotel staff and the official personnel who had been responsible for our safety and welfare. The agent who had befriended us had done as much for others and was especially popular and well liked. Of course, he held a tender place in Mako's heart because of the sled he had given her the past winter.

After an overnight train ride to Jersey City on a hot muggy day and an endless tedium of "processing," we were herded aboard the Swedish liner *Gripsholm*. The ship was clean and brightly painted in blue and yellow, and she carried a huge sign on her side, "Diplomatic." There were three times as many passengers aboard as the ship was intended to carry.

Our cabins were assigned according to rank, and we received a good cabin with three bunks and a shower bath which we were told not to use because there would be a shortage of water on such a long voyage. The heat was terrific and we were dismayed to learn that we could not sail until some Japanese who had not yet arrived came aboard. We found out later that the Japanese government had withheld the sailing of the *Asama Maru* at Yokohama and the *Conte Verde* at Shanghai until all the Japanese nationals were on the *Gripsholm*. That took eight days of boiling hot sun in New York harbor with the boat filled to capacity. There was nowhere to go for a cooling breeze, and we were not told why we were held up.

At night we all went on deck after dinner and sat in groups, gloomily discussing why we had not sailed. I was especially moved by the dim-out of New York and the fantastic view of the skyscrapers outlined in black against the summer sky.

We were closely guarded by Coast Guard sentries and small tugs that seemed to do nothing but blow their shrill whistles. It was impossible to sleep for the heat and the incessant din.

Finally on June 18, 1942, the familiar throb of the ship's engines was felt, the pilot flag went up, and we moved slowly out of New York harbor. Many of us were greatly afraid. We had been ordered to wear or carry our life belts and to have them with us at all times. The Swedish crew laughed and asked, "What are you afraid of?" They explained that the ship was kept ablaze with lights at night so that the submarine captains would know not to attack it.

As soon as we got to sea the Japanese naval officers in our group seemed to think they had complete authority over us all. The Swedish officers patiently endured the flag signalling, order-giving, and general nuisance made by these navy men on the top deck at the time of sailing. I shuddered to think what would happen if we had trouble at sea.

Jeanie and I stood together on deck as New York faded away in the distance. We did not speak. We both were thinking of our parents—Jeanie's parents, naturalized citizens, who had been sent inland from the west coast to be interned for the duration of the war, and my parents, living among their patriotic neighbors in our Volunteer State. We knew that it would be years until we could contact them again or they would have news of us.

There was another American woman on board. She had joined our group at New York and I did not know her. She was in a bad state emotionally. Over and over she cried and sobbed, "Fare-well, New York!" She continued in a state of hysteria during the entire trip. Mother read newspaper reports that an American woman on the *Gripsholm* had tried to commit suicide. It may have been this woman, but I heard nothing of it.

Once at sea, we settled down to a routine shipboard existence, trying to make it as similar as possible to what we had known on our previous voyages. Mako, who always enjoyed the ocean tremendously, was in glowing health and spirits. She and her father won the Ping-pong doubles and she was runner-up to him in the singles. Her highest ambition was to best him some-time, but that time had not yet come. At nine years old she had great fun humbling the adult players, especially the naval officers who played her. The crowd would jeer when a grownup was soundly defeated by the long-legged little girl with the serious expression, and few aboard except her father could defeat her.

Almost all of her time, when she was not having classes, was spent at the game. She was being tutored every day in Japanese, both the spoken and written word, by a young friend, Mr. Honjo, and as a result she was able to enter the third grade instead of the first when she began school in Japan.

We had many boat drills, and each time I was in constant difficulty. I could not remember my lifebelt but would leave it in my cabin or on my deck chair. For this I would be roundly scolded by some young navy man. We had instructions to pack a small emergency bag in case we were torpedoed. It was to be ready so that we could carry it to the lifeboat. Terry wanted to include the Chung Yao, his most cherished treasure. I thought this was somewhat impractical and said to him, "Darling, if we have to die together, am I not enough? There is no room in the bag for other than dire essentials." Perhaps I was not quite fair in this, for all during the war, in each of the emergency and make-shift houses we used for homes, we found a special niche to display the Chung Yao. His scholarly reverence for this master-piece of delicate porcelain was such that Terry made it a habit to arise early in the mornings, take it down, and sit gazing upon it until Mako and I arose. The steady view of the rare curio served him in about the way that attending church inspires some, and he did not feel whole without it. He took solace, as the Oriental spirit can, in the perfect form and color of the cup; and he could sit and look at it for hours, knowing tranquillity in its exquisite appearance and in his wonderment at the centuries of strife and alarm that it had quietly overcome. Perhaps for my husband it could never have been impractical, even in a lifeboat.

There was a little white-haired man on board who always came on deck for the lifeboat drills heavily laden. Many of the other passengers laughed at him because each time there was a frying pan and a huge box of matches, plus rope and a hatchet, hanging from his small shoulders. I frequently thought that if we were stranded on an island he would be a good man to know, although with his impedimenta he would doubtless be much in the way in an open boat.

I am one of the world's worst sailors but, oddly enough, I was seasick only once on that entire voyage. I believe that even though we were not consciously afraid, we were subconsciously in a state of tension. If the ship rolled unusually or if there was a different creaking noise, all of us were instantly awake and alert; and one often found oneself standing in the middle of the dark cabin trembling.

I found myself losing weight rapidly. Even my Swedish steward noticed it and was sympathetic. He was a big blonde man and kindly, and his morning greeting was something that sounded like "Hup, Madame." All the stewards and stewardesses were grossly overworked and faced with almost insurmountable difficulties, but they carried on in good spirit.

Our greatest difficulty was keeping clean. The ship was greatly crowded and we were two weeks at sea before docking at Rio. It was necessary that our water supply be strictly rationed. I became very adept at taking a sponge bath and then washing out my underwear and stockings in the bath water. This procedure seemed revolting at first, but there was nothing else to do under the circumstances. With the daily wash swaying to and fro in the sea breeze our cabin resembled a Chinese laundry. "Hup, Madame" was especially helpful. At midnight he would bring a ewer of hot water to me as a special favor, and then I would give Mako her scrubbing.

The days struggled by. Terry spent them at the Ping-pong table with Mako and in long hours at the bridge table. He enjoyed cards and he was delighted at Mako's Ping-pong prowess, or so it seemed, but I knew he was forcing himself into these diversions. His work had kept him so busy in the past that he had to be active in something now, however trivial. He tried to stay at the card table most of the night, mechanically dealing and betting at bridge or poker, going to bed just before dawn and sleeping restlessly until noon. He played roulette in the game room, placing bets on number 23, the date of Mako's birth. The first afternoon out of New York he had helped arrange a lottery on the ship's daily run. He was lucky and he won at roulette, at cards, and on the distance the ship had traveled. But when he won, it was not like the times when he had won betting on the horses in Cuba. Those two years we had spent in Cuba seemed to have been a part of another world. Terry never mentioned his fear for us once we should dock in Japan, but his old confidence was gone and I had not seen happiness on his face since the war began. His life was now a void. He must watch Japan be destroyed and could do nothing to help. Once while we stood on deck to see the Southern Cross rise before us, he took my arm and told me quietly,

"Gwen, Japan died with Saionji. Therefore, we must not be sad at the war; it is only the funeral. You know, Gwen, I think it may be that it was ordained. Japan could not become great until she was once conquered by enemy soldiers as she hoped to conquer Asia. You and I must live this time out and when it is over we can help bridge our countries again. We can do nothing now but suffer. We must not allow it to overcome us; we are young and the war will be over shortly."

In this way we steeled ourselves with fatalism to await the end of the war.

Mr. Muir, the State Department official who made the trip to facilitate the exchange, was a very likable and fair person. It was a great source of satisfaction to me that, almost without exception, those Americans who were officially connected with the internment and repatriation of Japanese diplomats displayed such human understanding and ability that they were not only respected by the Japanese but often held in deep affection.

On July 2, after two weeks at sea which took us from summer to winter, we arrived in Rio and steamed slowly into that most spectacular harbor in the world. I stood on the top deck with tears in my eyes, discovering for the first time the beauty of the floodlighted Christ of Corcovado.

Everyone wished we might be allowed to go ashore, but we could only look toward the bright, vibrant city from where our ship rode at anchor in the stream. We could see the streets crowded with throngs of people going about their everyday affairs. We had lived in such constraint and anxiety that it seemed most remarkable that outside our isolated world aboard ship normal lives were being lived.

At Rio 380 additional Japanese from the capitals of the South American countries were jammed aboard the crowded ship. Among the new passengers was Mr. Itaro Ishii, Ambassador to Brazil, our first chief when we had gone out to Shanghai. Mr. and Mrs. Ishii had taken a protective interest in me then and had helped me to accustom myself to Japanese society. It was good to see them again and to talk of the old days.

Another passenger taken aboard at Rio was a prospective bridegroom who was separated by the war from the Brazilian girl he had planned to marry. They said farewell at the wharf and the girl with her parents kept a sorrowful vigil all night before the boat sailed. The silent young man stood on deck, gazing hopelessly throughout the long hours of darkness. As our boat crept away from the dock, the girl got into the car and, with one last desperate look toward the ship, drove away.

The first day out of Rio, Terry and I became seasick. There was no room service, of course, so Mako served our meals. It seemed incredible how that little nine-year-old sea dog could balance two trays, one for her mother and one for her shame-faced father, down the corridors of that heaving ship. She reported proudly that few people were in the dining room.

There was a very pretty blonde beauty operator managing the beauty parlor on board. All the young men were getting manicures just to hold her hand. She received many amorous notes and each time showed them to me, asking me to point out the writer to her. I often thought how embarrassed the young men would be if they knew I had read their notes. One note I remember in particular ran, "Blonde Nordic daughter of Neptune, give me your smile."

One night off the Cape of Good Hope, as I was walking on deck, a young Japanese joined me. We walked around and around the boat deck while the wind-blown spray whipped at us. It was midwinter in this latitude, and we wore our heaviest clothing. We spoke of the Portuguese sailors who had passed there in their tiny sailing craft centuries before. In the inexplicable way of conversation, the talk digressed to Greek mythology. After some discussion on this subject, my young companion chanced to remark, "I want to find the daughter of Neptune and marry her!" I did my best to hide my sense of delighted discovery.

On July 20, 1942, we arrived at the port of exchange, Lourenço Marques, on the east coast of Africa. The weather was milder than it had been and we were bursting with eagerness to go ashore; all of us were on deck to see Africa as the ship slipped into the harbor. I had the impression of one color, a melancholy, brooding purple and its shades of lavender in land, water, and sky. I remembered that my grandfather, paralyzed and helpless for nine years, had dreamed of going to Africa. He used to tell me about Africa and its purple skies when I was a little girl. Grandmother used to ask him, "Why Africa of all places?" His response always was, "Yes, God damn it, Africa!"

At this obscure African port our paths crossed for the final time with that of the gay and handsome Sotomatsu Kato, who had befriended us and our plans to marry over a decade before in Washington, the man whose picture had appeared by mistake opposite mine in the newspaper announcement of the engagement. He had been serving as Ambassador to France at the time of Pearl Harbor, and soon after the outbreak of the war had become known, his crumpled body was found in the street below the high windows of his living quarters in Paris. We had previously heard many rumors as to the cause of his death. Now his body lay in its casket on the docks at Lourenço Marques to be loaded aboard the *Gripsholm* to complete its return from France to Japan.

Wanly, Terry said to me, "Come, we must go down on the dock and keep our old friend company until he is brought aboard." I went with him to watch over the body, thinking vaguely how in the old days in my country people had sat up with the bodies of their loved ones.

96

The next day the Japanese exchange ships, *Asama Maru* from Japan and *Conte Verde* (chartered by Japan from Italy), glided into port, bringing Ambassador Grew and American Embassy and consular officials. Many on our ships were wildly exultant when they first saw the rising sun flag at the mastheads. Not so with me. As the two ships eased in next to our *Gripsholm* I realized my last contact with America was about to be ended. I was sorry to leave the impersonal, hulking *Gripsholm* and forgave her for being so stuffy, crowded, and short on water, and I even wished her *bon voyage* back to New York. It would be many years, if ever, before I would see New York or my home again.

Americans and Japanese mingled on the wharf and I saw many old friends. They wished me luck, adding ruefully, "You'll need it."

We shopped delightedly. I bought remarkably cheap toilet soap, British woolen underwear, and a case of Portuguese wine. These purchases were carried to the ship, balanced expertly on the head of a tall, speechless African. Male and female natives looked alike. The only difference, as Mako observed, was "bosoms."

The ranking members of our diplomatic group were invited to attend an "Axis Party" given in our honor by the German and Italian consular officials in Lourenço Marques. Buses and cars were sent for us in the evening, and we went forth in our hastily unpacked and unpressed finery. The party should have been most pleasant; surely we had been pent up long enough to be gay if given the chance. But Terry was withdrawn and remote. I was fearful that he might say something bitter to the Germans which would make trouble, but he hardly spoke during the whole evening. I had the distinct feeling that our hosts did not really like us, that their hospitality was insincere and somewhat forced. The party was not a success. This was the beginning of my conviction that the Tripartite Pact appealed to none of the people represented by the signatories. All during the war I was to see how unnatural and even hostile the Germans and Japanese were to each other in all their relationships. There was none of that respect and hearty admiration for the Germans that I had always seen shown to the British and Americans. The hostility I was to experience toward myself throughout the war occurred almost without exception because I was mistaken for a German. As for the Italians, Terry remarked that they could only be described as "among those present."

There were many speeches. If I were casting a play and wanted an actor to portray a perfectly typical German diplomat, I would have chosen His Excellency the German Consul General at Lourenço Marques. He played his part with a crisp perfection. Admiral Nomura's response in German to the Consul's speech was incomprehensible to Germans and Japanese alike. He seemed like a small boy forced to "say a piece" before company, displaying a grim determination to get through with it as quickly as possible.

We danced until a late hour but there was little gaiety or spontaneity. Many dancers, especially the Japanese, seemed grimly intent on enjoyment, like wooden dolls making the motions of happiness.

We learned later that the German and Italian colonies in Lourenço Marques had exerted every effort to entertain us. Food was not so abundant as it had seemed and they had given from their own larders to serve the sumptuous buffet.

At last we changed ships and on July 26 were ready to sail. Some of our people left the ship because they had been ordered to various posts in Europe and were to go on other vessels sailing from Lourenço Marques. Again the unhappy goodbyes were said. "Goodbye," it occurred to me, is the most overworked word in the vocabulary of war. We steamed out of the bay on the final stage of the journey, a small group of people waving to us from the pier.

Since there were two ships after leaving Lourenço Marques to carry the passengers from the *Gripsholm*, we had room and could exercise freely on deck. There were baths and the evening meal was Japanese. But I began to feel the war-time tensions at once, for daily those things we were compelled to do began to supplant those things we did because we wished to.

The voyage from Lourenço Marques to Singapore was a succession of days, following monotonously one after the other, alternate light and dark. Each day the weather was warmer as we sailed northward into summer again. There was nothing to do but endure the growing heat and the constant screaming and commotion of the small children everywhere about. Everyone was growing a little fat on the varied foods served so sumptuously at mealtime and the delicious cakes of all sorts served with tea. The stewards told us delightedly of the scant fare they had offered the Americans on the way to the port of exchange, and Mako told them how she had made bets with her father about the number of weevils she would find in the rice we had aboard the *Gripsholm*. It appeared each nation had reserved the ship's stores for its own people, for we later learned from diplomat friends that the *Gripsholm* table was remarkably improved after the Japanese were replaced by Americans. Mako gorged her small self on the cakes at tea time and the steward encouraged her, saying, "You'd better eat plenty of those cakes, Mari-chan, there won't be any when you get back to Japan!" Mariko did not understand what he meant but it did not worry her, and she ate until I was forced to stop her for fear she would make herself sick.

On August 9, 1942, several months after its capture by the Japanese, we reached Singapore amid great noise-making and color-waving. Every small craft in the harbor came out to welcome us and circled the *Asama Maru* again and again, with whistles blowing and flags flying. I was struck by the sight of Mako's dazzled eyes. In an ecstasy of excitement, she ran over the decks from side to side for fear that she would miss something. But as we steamed into the bay my own spirits were not so high. I had seen an American plane half submerged in the mud. It may have been British. Either way it sobered me to see it there. Involuntarily, I breathed a silent prayer for the Allied airman who had flown the stricken craft.

After we docked Mako and I were besieged by Japanese newspapermen, and I decided to spend the time we were in Singapore in my cabin. As a result, I saw nothing of the city; I remember only the heat, intensely oppressive in our cabin because I had closed the porthole and locked the doors against the reporters and photographers.

As our boat left Singapore for Tokyo, I noticed British prisoners of war working on the wharf. They raised their hands in farewell, making the sign "V for Victory" with two fingers. No Japanese on board seemed to know what the sign meant.

At Singapore the exchange ships had been boarded by several military police and a navy officer who gave lectures every day to the passengers. The lectures were intended to imbue the Japanese with a patriotic spirit and to assure them of Japan's inevitable victory. Attending these classes was compulsory. I had to be there, too, and sit among the returning Japanese and their children to hear the instructor go about his task of purging us of the Western ideas which officialdom suspected we had acquired through long sojourns abroad. I hardly understood a word that was said. Most of the military and naval officers had had their hair clipped, ready for action, I suppose, and I found it hard to recognize them when we met on deck or in the dining room. The ladies were told not to wear hats with veils when we arrived in Yokohama—we must not look fashionable or frivolous during war-time. We arrived there after only about ten days at sea from Singapore and two months after we had departed from New York harbor. The night before our arrival, when our ship was off Tateyama, we had to close the curtains and stay indoors to "protect" that fortified zone from our inquisitive eyes. I wondered how we could have seen anything at all so late at night, and I questioned if anyone among that diplomatic group would have had any interest in the military installations.

8

TOKYO, THE HOMEFRONT,
1942-1943

I WAS happy no newspapermen or photographers came near me at Yokohama. I had been dreading them all of the way, especially after being mobbed at Singapore. My brother-in-law, Taro Terasaki, and his wife Sugako came aboard and bustled us off to the Imperial Hotel in Tokyo. I said goodbye to all those people with whom I had been associated for more than eight months and watched them go off to meet the war, each in his own way. At once Terry told Taro about Roosevelt's cable. Taro did not think the militarists knew of it and said for us to keep still—maybe nothing would happen.

Upon arriving at the Imperial Hotel I became very seasick, or land sick, I should say. I had to lie down for several hours until I regained my equilibrium after so many days on shipboard. I suddenly felt very tired and alone. Gone was the gay international atmosphere of the prewar Imperial Hotel I had known so well in earlier years. War was evident on every hand and one could see the beginnings of the shortages that were to become more and more severe as time went on. There was no soap in the bathrooms, and there were fewer maids and boys in the dining room and lobby. The only foreign people one saw were Italians and Germans.

I noticed that people looked at my clothes, especially my shoes and hats, and I decided to pack away my smartest clothes for the duration. I spent the war years in slacks, sweaters and skirts, and one gray flannel suit for more "dressed up" wear. We wore no hats and when cold winds blew we tied scarves over our heads. Later on, as fuel became a thing of the past, I put on the regulation *monpe*, a Japanese-type pantaloon which made up for its ugliness by being very warm and practical. I would put woolen underwear, a woolen skirt, and woolen socks on and then pull the *monpe* over it all. The baggier one looked, the smarter one was supposed to be. Like the Chinese and his numerous coats, as the day got warmer one began to pull things off and then in the evening add garment upon garment until we could cope with the bitter cold without freezing. Mako wore leggings and overalls and did not seem to mind the cold.

My brother-in-law had rented an apartment for us in the Bunka Apartments in beautiful Ochanomizu (tea water), a section of Tokyo not far from the Imperial University. There was one large room with twin couches and one small room with another couch. A kitchenette and tiny bathroom made up the rest of our menage. Hot water for baths was available every night between 5:30 and 7:30 but at no other time during the day. Gas and electricity were rationed. I was taken aback by all these regulations and the austerity of our life, but I came to view those days at the Bunka as most luxurious before the war was through with us.

Everyone tried to help me understand the ration books. My sister-in-law and friends helped me to get accustomed to the routine and gave me tips on buying our daily necessities. I had all my household furnishings stored in a warehouse in Yokohama, but, as our apartment was furnished, there was no need to have any furniture brought over. With our own bedding and linens, I was able to make our apartment livable.

Sometimes I had to stand in line for two or three hours for a few pieces of fish or a bunch of carrots. The repeated air-raid drills also took up a large part of the day when they were called. I took active part in only one of these drills and I think my neighbors were glad when I did not reappear. People looked at me instead of listening to the warden and that created too much confusion. Running uphill with pails of water, without spilling any water from the buckets, seemed to me a silly and tedious way to fight a war. We had to fill small bags with sand and stack them outside each dwelling, supposedly for use in putting out fires the air raids would start. We never knew and were never told whether that was the purpose of the sandbags or not, and I could only guess what the authorities had in mind. Additional fire protection was supplied by a large container of water outside each house and what looked like a huge fly swatter (to beat out the flames).

Sometimes a smudge pot would be placed in the lower branches of a tree and the women would have to line up with pails of water to throw in an attempt to extinguish the smudge fire. Usually these exercises were at night when the women were exhausted from their household chores. The warden would shout "next," and I would hear the clap-clap of the wooden clogs and then the splash of the water.

We placed Mako in the Roman Catholic school, Futaba, soon after we got settled, and she went every day by railway, carrying her little lunch box. She had to wear the uniform with long black stockings, a navy blue middy blouse with pleated skirt, and dark blue felt hat trimmed with navy blue grosgrain ribbon and the Futaba insignia. For the hot days, the middy blouse was white cotton and the hat was of straw. I knew she was struggling daily through a maze of unfamiliar words and customs. Her Japanese was not good enough to follow all that was being said in class; and when one is nine it is fearfully oppressive to be stared at, marked down for the strange and foreign one, every place one goes. Mako was taller than the rest, she could not speak their language, and to them she was an American. She lost her gaiety and spontaneity and became habitually silent. However, she was able to enter the third grade and managed to hold on. The head mistress was a Japanese nun of unlimited compassion and understanding. She spoke fluent French and English and was a source of much comfort to me. The school had been founded by the French Catholics but during the war years it came under the direct jurisdiction of the Education Ministry. The head mistress told me sadly how they had been forced to carry on under great stress and difficulty owing to the enforced regimentation. I used to fetch my child in the late afternoons and sometimes watched the military drills the little girls had to take part in. Mako, tall and straight, towered over her classmates, her hair bound in two hard little pigtails.

Terry and I were fearful for Mako's safety should there be an air raid. It was several miles to Futaba and we would be unable to reach her. We expressed our fears to Yano, a friend whom we had known at Greenbrier and who was stationed at Imperial Headquarters very near the school. Yano promised to look after her if bombers should come.

One afternoon at a school function she sang the solo part in a chorus for the entertainment of the mothers. I went to hear her and sat alone in that auditorium of more than three hundred Japanese mothers. No one spoke to me. Mako's clear, bell-like tones drifted out over the hall. I listened to her, weeping. I had to powder my nose quickly for I knew Mako would be ashamed of me before her schoolmates.

There was no sun in our apartment except for about an hour every morning and then only in the corner of one window. I bought a little narcissus bulb and put it in that corner. There it sat week after week with no sign of life. I felt that my soul was like that narcissus, closed up with war and loneliness. The winter grew cold and there was no heat except the charcoal brazier.

I bought a small red lacquer brazier to put my feet on. I called it my "Dutch husband." The "Dutch wife" keeps one cool in the Indies, so why not a "Dutch husband" to keep one warm in Japan? All my friends brought me extra charcoal and I remember one young man carried on his back a sack of the lovely type of charcoal made from cherry wood that glows for hours with a haunting fragrance. Always a little tea kettle was kept bubbling on the brazier and it whispered to me "like wind in the pines," the Japanese say.

The war news came in with intensity and volume during that winter of 1942. The only news we had in English was the government-controlled *Nippon Times;* like the Japanese-language papers, it carried only stories of victory. One day I read of the "punishment" of the Doolittle flyers. By the wording of the article, I knew those men had been executed. That day was one of the blackest of my life. For three days I did not leave my apartment.

The Foreign Office put Terry on the waiting list. He had hoped for a position where he could be kept informed and at least be prepared for service when peace came. When no work was found for him, I felt that he was being discriminated against because of me and my heart ached.

He was not well and I urged him to see a doctor. When he did so, it was found that his blood pressure was dangerously high. The doctor's advice was to "take life easy and not to worry." Doctors have the most complacent way about them all over the world; they love to inform you in bland tones that all you need do is to perform something impossible and everything will be perfectly all right.

Terry was not the only sick one in the family. Mako was ill off and on until she became so tired and weak that we were greatly concerned about her. Even during that first year, our diet was not balanced, and her school work was so trying I do not see how she kept on so long.

Terry kept close to the house, trying to get as much rest as possible, so I met Mako at the school frequently and we would ride back to our apartment by street car. One day as we were hanging onto our straps, I noticed two university students were discussing me. Americans always expect all foreigners in America to speak English, but the Japanese take it for granted that no foreigner in Japan knows their language. It is interesting, if somewhat risky, to hear one's self being discussed by onlookers, frankly and casually appraising one as though they were looking at a snapshot. Once, on a train, one woman said to another, looking me over, "Don't you think this foreigner is beautiful?" With tingles of pleasure I waited to hear the verdict. Finally the other woman announced, "No, she's much too dark under the eyes!" Another time a harassed mother told the crying child on her back to hush or she would give him to the foreigner, me. The child immediately choked off his cries and became fearfully silent. And so I listened cautiously to the students. They were in doubt as to my nationality. They agreed that I certainly was not German but could not decide whether or not I was Italian. Then one of them noticed the school identification on Mako's blouse. He asked her in Japanese if I were her mother. She replied, "Yes," and then they asked me, again in Japanese and somewhat sheepishly, about my nationality.

"I am an American," I told them. They acted as though that were the most usual thing in the world but fell to inquiring how Mako and I came to be in Japan. I told them about the exchange voyage and internment in the United States. Suddenly, one of the boys turned to the crowded street car, and, to my intense embarrassment, yelled in a loud voice:

"Behold this courageous American woman and her daughter! She has braved all danger to stay with her husband. Let us be kind to her and show her that war is between governments, not individuals!"

Everyone in that mob of people began to repeat, *"Erai wa ne* (How brave)," and when we hastily got off the street car, they waved their handkerchiefs out the windows until the tram had disappeared over the hill out of our sight. All this was most bewildering to the policeman gaping at us from his box on the corner. He must have imagined all sorts of things.

We had our first Christmas and New Year celebration after reaching Japan in our apartment in the Bunka. I decided to bake a cake. I had brought some spices from the United States and had conserved our sugar ration by not using sugar in either tea or coffee. The cake was gorgeous, well done, and was equally approved by its cook and the rest of the family. But it was unexpectedly expensive. I had used the gas oven to make it, in forgetful violation of regulations. As a result the gas was cut off. I had to hie myself to a *konro* (charcoal cooker) shop and thereafter cook our meals on smoking charcoal. With practice I soon learned to make my fire outside and bring it into the kitchen after the coals were glowing red. I even learned to bake beautiful cakes, first in frying pans over the coals and later in a tiny oven which I acquired, especially made to fit over my charcoal cooker. I found that there is more satisfaction in turning out a splendid meal by primitive methods than there is in doing the same thing with the wonderful assistance of modern appliances. I also got a lot of satisfaction out of showing my Japanese friends that a Yankee could carry on her homemaking under the same severities they endured. I managed to arrange my kitchen work so that I could spend the minimum amount of time there because the kitchen is always the coldest, darkest room in the Japanese house. Many of my Japanese women friends came to see how I had worked out my ideas.

The apartment house furnished maid service so I had no cleaning to do, but the thing that took up most of my time was shopping. One had to line up and wait long, dreary hours for everything. Many women carried books and magazines to read until their turn came. It was the only time, I imagine, that they could snatch for themselves from their busy day.

Pregnant women were given priority in the rationing procedure, and one day a pitiful but amusing incident occurred in the ration line. A "pregnant" woman went to the head of the line and, after receiving her rations, started to walk off when out slipped a cushion from under her *obi* (sash). The other ladies sent up a howl and the poor woman broke into tears, explaining that besides seven small children to care for she had her mother-in-law, who was ninety, on her hands. We all had a good laugh, but in the future pregnant women were expertly scrutinized.

The rationing was carried on through the *tonarigumi*, neighborhood group. There was a chairman or head of each association, called *"kumichō-san."* These chairmen rotated so that a member of each household had to serve in that official capacity. The *kumichō* received all the information from the ration center, which she in turn passed on to the members of her association. Usually a *tonarigumi* consisted of ten to fifteen houses.

When the rationing authorities had food for distribution, runners were sent about the neighborhood to notify the people to go at once and join the long queue. Everything was hit or miss and the women were at the mercy of the back-door yell, *"Haikyū ga mairimashita* (Rations are here)." The air-raid drills, too, were usually carried out without advance notice, thus throwing most households into confusion. Many of the women had to work late at night, every night, to catch up with their housework. In addition to that, most single women above a certain age were mobilized for war work and industry, leaving a heavy burden on the housewives at home. The women of Japan carried on magnificently. They did not receive enough credit and recognition for their tireless cooperation in a war that had overtaken them without their playing any part in its making. They carried out orders humbly and obediently, without protesting that they had no choice in the matter.

After spending seven months in the apartment at Ochanomizu I became very restless. The rationing of electricity, gas, and everything else had become so stringent that we had no comfort at all. There was only a rare gleam of sunshine in our apartment all day and we could not use our bathroom because there was no hot water. I knew that a Japanese house built to the sun would be more comfortable and that the Japanese bath heated from wood or coal would prove much more practical for us. Besides that, I had a longing to have my own things about me. I wanted to create my own sense of security and have one spot in which I would really feel intimately at home, something I could never do in a furnished apartment or a hotel suite. Finding a house was virtually impossible but we began to make inquiries.

TOKYO, THE HOMEFRONT

I had not seen my household things, which were stored in Yokohama, for three years. Terry and I took the train there to see what their condition was. On the way Terry suddenly told me to look down at something on the floor of the train, but something in his tone startled me; he could never carry off deceit with success, and I glanced quickly out the window. The blonde heads of tall American prisoners of war came to my view. They were marching on a road parallel to the tracks. Our train rushed on and I tried to control my tears.

One of my friends who had no inkling that I was searching frantically for a home called one day and casually inquired if I would be interested in a Japanese house. This was exactly what I most wanted. Terry and I boarded a train and went to Meguro, a lovely suburban district of Tokyo, and there was our house. It had a large sun porch and was perfect for us. All the rooms had southern exposure and the sun poured in all day long on clear days. We were to live there for several months.

We hired a man to help me arrange the house, a professional gardener, who agreed to stoop to ordinary work only after much persuasion. In Japan all working people have a special title and a gardener is called *uekiya-san*, Mr. Gardener. A carpenter is *daiku-san*, Mr. Carpenter. I became most fond of my little *uekiya-san*, a man about five feet tall with a cast in one eye. The only way he could understand my broken Japanese was to look me in the eye. To do that he would stand on one foot, cock his head to one side for better vision, and look somewhere over my left shoulder. All this so intrigued me that I would forget all my carefully thought out phrases and flounder along with a slow-witted and awkward tongue.

Notwithstanding this we somehow got along and soon we had the house whipped into shape. I called him the "Eighth Dwarf." He was always sure things would turn out right and I found him very consoling.

The biggest problem for the European in a Japanese house is the lack of closets. I find from old prints that with the exception of the additions of electricity, gas, and sometimes a telephone, the

Japanese house remains much the same as it has been for hundreds of years. The kimono being the traditional garment, the *tansu* (chest of drawers) is built to accommodate them. Also the large *todana* (built-in cupboard) is designed to hold the bedding that is laid out each night to be rolled up and stowed away each morning. There are no closet arrangements for Western style clothes that require hangers. I consulted the Eighth Dwarf and his sole contribution to my dilemma was a long drawn out, "Sa-a-a-a." That meant he was perplexed.

I decided to take the drastic step and tear out the heavy shelves in the *todana* in each of the three bedrooms. Then I would put pipe the length of each closet and have room for our clothes. When I explained my wants to the Eighth Dwarf he cocked his eye over my left shoulder and howled. First he said it could not be done. I showed him how easy it would be. Then he said that I had no right to tear up another's house. That I settled by calling my friend, the owner, and having her give him authoritative consent. Then he said that all metal was used in the war effort and there was no pipe available. That put me back on my heels for awhile. I sat down on my sun porch and gazed unhappily into my garden. The wind whispered through the bamboo trees and Fujisan (Fujiyama) serene in the distance looked down at me. I watched the tall slim trunks of the bamboo trees crack together and it came to me that the bamboo would make a good substitute for the pipe in my closet to be. The Japanese had always used bamboo for clothes lines. I rushed out to tell my man Friday. Knowing he was finally defeated, he trotted off to get the poles and I thought I detected an approving gleam in his one good eye.

I tried to put the war out of my mind as I unpacked my dishes, linens, and other household effects brought from Peking. The Eighth Dwarf seemed to enjoy the unpacking and when I would place a vase or a spray of Peking glass flowers in the *tokonoma* (honor alcove) or on a table he would jump up and down and laugh to show his happiness. One box when opened proved to have eight large cans of Bre'r Rabbit molasses that I had quite forgotten. That was a real windfall. The little gardener was beside himself with joy for me and I loved him from that moment. I promptly went to the kitchen, made some pancakes, and opened a can of molasses. From then on our friendship was firmly established.

We put some vegetables in half of our garden and I enjoyed watching the gardener at work, for Japanese methods of agriculture are greatly different from ours. It seemed to me that every clod was handled with loving care. Large farms do not exist in Japan; most of them are an acre or less, small enough to be thoroughly worked by hand. They must be highly fertilized and are used to produce several rotated crops a year. Of necessity extensive use is made of "night soil."

The Eighth Dwarf put crushed dried fish in my garden. That was available at the beginning of the war. Later on we had to use "night soil" because we had to eat the dried fish ourselves. We had radishes and cucumbers, green beans and lettuce. The cucumbers grew so fast I could not believe my eyes. I tied a red string around one tiny one just to prove to myself that the phenomenal growth was actually taking place. That summer of 1943 was to prove the only one during the war which provided me with American-type vegetables. Later, there were no seeds and, even if there had been, orders were to raise only native vegetables, all others being considered luxuries.

One of my friends had promised to find a suitable maid for me, and one day shortly after our move to Meguro the girl arrived with her father. Father wanted to look me over and make sure that I did not have horns in the place of eyebrows. I could understand that he was anxious about leaving his daughter in the hands of one of the enemy even though the enemy was married to a Japanese. The father, a farmer from Ibaraki Prefecture, and his daughter, Kikuya (Miss Chrysanthemum), had never known any Americans and had only seen other foreigners from a distance. I am sure there had been a family council around the *hibachi* to decide whether the girl should stay with us.

I was encouraged because she carried her luggage, and I invited her and her father in for tea. After many bows and with downcast eyes on the part of Kikuya, the father explained that his daughter, being such an unworthy creature and a mere woman, was not really fit to live with the *okusama*. I assured him I would care for her to the best of my ability but I did want him to realize that since I was an American, Kikuya might have some unpleasant reactions from neighbors and shopkeepers. He said he had taken all that into consideration, that Kikuya understood and wanted to shield me from any such troubles. Besides, Kikuya was bored in the country and wanted to learn city ways, and he added, "She's not afraid of work." It seemed she especially loved to wash. "Ah, Kikuya, heart of my heart," said I, with my mind on the hamper of dirty linen in the bathroom. "Ha," replied Kikuya seriously. I took her to her room, the tiny two-mat (6' x 6') room next to the kitchen which is the traditional maid's quarters in the Japanese house. A great feeling of peace came over me as I heard her humming, of all things, "In the Sweet Bye and Bye," as she stowed away her things in the *todana*.

The peace was short lived, however, for Mako was soon sent home from school with a high fever which turned out to be measles. This was just one of a series of childhood diseases that filled the entire next year for her. That year included whooping cough, which I promptly caught. The Japanese call it the "hundred days cough" and we both certainly put in our hundred days.

During this time, the government was pushing forward the air-raid drills which made life a nightmare. The so-called shelter each household had to prepare in its garden was often only a deep hole, exposed and damp. These holes always depressed me; they looked so like open graves, gaping expectantly at us. Kikuya had to dig ours, and our new dog Kuri did his bit, too. Like a true war dog, he worked side by side with Kikuya, and I longed for a movie camera to record the scene.

Besides the shelter, every household had to have on hand one rucksack filled with supplies, bandages, a few first-aid articles, rice, a cooking pan, and the padded hoods which we were required to wear. Many people were to be badly burned because of those hoods. The padding used was made of thick cotton, and when it caught fire the wearers were unaware of the blaze until it was too late to avoid serious burns. All women were requested to wear either *monpe* (the Japanese "pantaloons" I had learned to appreciate) or slacks, although slacks were frowned on as too Western. Permanents and nail polish were also considered in bad taste. But the Japanese woman, in spite of having been taught obedience from birth, rebelled at the prohibition of permanents. She continued to have her hair done, sometimes under great stress, and often incurring real danger during air raids. These governmental restrictions were short-sighted. The Japanese lady had always been a colorful, well-groomed person. She should not have been robbed of such attractiveness unnecessarily and forced to adopt drab, muddy colors in place of her gay, delightful kimono. A happy woman is a more efficient woman, even in war-time.

The men were requested to wear what was called "the national uniform," a dull khaki affair with puttees wrapped around the trousers. This uniform included a field cap identical to the army cap except it was without insignia. My husband, always clumsy with his hands, was never able to manage the puttees, and with his poor circulation his legs would become numb every time he wore them. One day in anger he threw them across the room shouting, "The only way to victory with these things is to use them to hang one's self!" He never wore them again.

On the eighth of every month, to commemorate the beginning of the war, every man was required to wear the uniform and the women had to wear slacks or *monpe*. Anyone dressed otherwise was stopped at the exits of the stations and roundly scolded. Often some poor woman, harried and overworked, was forced to return home and dress again.

At Meguro we found ourselves living next door to an army barracks. Almost nightly we heard the going-away parties for the men called to distant spots in the Pacific, songs and cheers, "*Banzai! Banzai!*" They made Mari-chan their mascot and would wave from their trucks as they passed our house each morning.

One morning one of them used a small mirror to reflect the sun into her eyes as she waved from her sickroom window. She was furious and the next day while the soldiers were lined up at a review, some hundred yards or more past a vacant lot directly in front of our house, she took the mirror from my compact and put a spot of sun in the eyes of a uniformed man standing in front of the regimental line. He was quite blinded.

The soldiers arrived breathless at her window when the parade was over and they were dismissed for the afternoon.

"Mari-chan," they demanded, "Why did you have to pick such a time? Any other time would have been all right. You almost put the colonel's eyes out!" But they brought her a package of army cakes with the red star on each.

I was delighted that Mako had the soldiers to distract her, for, being confined to her room for weeks, she had begun painting as a hobby to withstand the boredom. When she first expressed a desire for some paints, Terry and I had thought it would be fine. Terry had done some rather good watercolors when he was a boy and we were interested to see if Mako had inherited any of his talent. It was certain she could have inherited none from her mother, who scarcely knew the difference between watercolors and oils. Our child took her painting much too intensely— she would work and sketch for days doing faces—faces only— and then in a furious rush of effort would do a strange sad countenance. I shuddered at her paintings. They were faces of the most unremitting and remorseless despair. Always just faces. She tore up a hundred for each that she kept; and those she kept she sometimes hid from us until her father coaxed her into permitting us to look at them. It seemed to me she had too readily absorbed the manifold tragedies about us; she was not yet in her teens but with the things we had given for play, she painted single-mindedly of hopelessness and pain. I watched for opportunities to divert her attention to happier thoughts but knew she must inevitably witness greater misery before peace would return.

As time passed our diet became more insufficient and the

medicines fewer. Mako and I were unable to shake off our whooping cough. We were weak and thin. July came with its intense heat and Terry urged us to go to the lovely mountains of Hakone for a month's rest and vacation at the Fujiya. We needed no encouragement and set off at once.

The Fujiya Hotel at Miyanoshita, an internationally known resort, was owned and operated at that time by the famed Yamaguchi of the impressive, flowing mustache. He had toured the world to study hotels and their management before returning to his native land to run his own hotel with such ease and charm that it became renowned. Yamaguchi was an internationalist who loved people of all races and nations. He died before the end of the war of a stroke brought on by overwork and worry. He had strained greatly trying to make his guests at home with swarms of Gestapo and military police infesting the hotel.

However, during that month of August, 1943, this surveillance was not so obvious as it later became and we had a most pleasant stay. The food was not abundant but what there was, was well cooked and beautifully served. The waitresses still wore lovely kimonos in the dining room and while dining one could look through the huge picture windows at mountains of unsurpassed glory.

Mako and I began to relax and regain our strength. The mountain air helped our coughs and the restful atmosphere of the hotel made us feel like human beings again. There were many German and Italian civilians at the hotel, and now and then officers of those two countries came for a few days on furlough or rest leave. There were always two or three together and they never conversed with anyone. They walked about the blooming gardens behind the hotel with bored and withdrawn faces.

Mako had a wonderful time feeding the friendly fish in the garden pool. There was a large, dark carp called "Jimmy" that was supposed to be one hundred years old. Whether from respect for his great age or superior size, I noticed that the other fish made way for him and he got the choice tidbits that the guests tossed into the pool.

Carp play a big role in the celebration of *tango no sekku* (Boys'
Festival) which falls on the fifth day of the fifth month, or May
fifth, of each year. Large three-dimensional fish made of paper,
cotton, or silk are attached to tall poles in the garden of each
household where there are boy children. Usually a carp is flown
for each son; one perhaps fifteen feet or longer for the eldest son,
and on down in graduated sizes to a very small one for a baby
boy. The carp, like the salmon, swims upstream, exhibiting great
determination to overcome the swift currents of the Japanese
rivers. The Japanese believe it is a splendid example to young
boys, representing as it does the manly virtues of ambition,
strength, and will power. It is an inspiring sight to see these huge
carp filled by the wind and fluttering with the swimming motion
of the fish fighting its way against a current.

During our stay in the mountains we enjoyed our evening
walks just before dinner. We would walk to the nearby village
of Miyagino where there were many buildings converted into
barracks for the children evacuated from congested Tokyo. The
cruelest ordeal the women had to endure, other than sending their
men to war, was sending their children to these children's centers
in the mountains. But the children, long accustomed to discipline
and obedience, soon learned the rigors of communal living away
from their mothers. We would pass these hostels and see the
lines of *tenugui* (hand towels) hanging on the bamboo poles,
each with the child's name and number written on it. Somehow
those rows of tiny towels drying after the evening bath gave
me a sense of total failure as an adult, more so even than the
rows of little wooden clogs left at the entrance.

One evening we walked along at sunset as the children were
having their evening meal. I heard the three claps of their little
hands before they bowed their heads in prayer. While their heads
were bowed I looked through the window, and there sat at
least one hundred children in the dining room. Before each child
was one bowl of rice and two tiny side dishes, one of pickles
and one with a small piece of dried fish. These side dishes were
called *o kazu*, which means literally "to help get the rice down."

Sometimes when we were having tea on the terrace, we would see the children returning from an excursion, tired and hot from their long hike. The teachers looked tired, too, and I wondered how it would be to care for so many strange children in that mountain refuge. Mothers often journeyed to crouch in the bushes and watch their children unobserved.

The Italians and other foreigners staying at the Fujiya at this time were friendly and unassuming. The Germans alone kept to themselves and did not even say good morning to the other guests in the hotel. I, especially, received cold looks from them, and often they treated me with downright rudeness in the elevators and hotel shops. It was revealing that as the war progressed and the German position in Europe became desperate, the Germans seemed to warm up to my daughter and me and find that we were worth speaking to after all.

Miyanoshita had always done a thriving business in catering to tourists and preferred the many American and British guests to the others. One day I was going through the lovely shops on the main thoroughfare looking at the china, brocades, and handicraft. In one shop the owner, an old gentleman in a cool linen kimono, followed me around. He answered my queries with flat, clipped tones and avoided my eyes. I thought that maybe his manner was occasioned by resentment against me as an American, but he handed me a child's book, the charming Japanese story of *Momotaro* (Little Peachling) in a German translation. I told him that I was sorry but I could not read German. With surprise on his face he stammered out,

"If you're not German, what is your nationality?"

"I am an American."

A great smile broke out, lighting up his wrinkled features, as he exclaimed, "Oh, then, Madame, come with me to the back room and I will show you my really beautiful things."

My husband's secretary came to Miyanoshita to accompany us on our return to Tokyo in early September. He carried the news that Terry was ill and the day before had been taken to a hospital in Roppongi, a district in the center of Tokyo. This

117

was the beginning of an endless seige of serious illness for my husband. From then on, I faced not only the dangers of war but also the fear of being unable to get proper care and food for my sick husband.

I went by train and streetcar every other day to carry food and fresh bed linen to Terry because the civilian hospitals did not provide them. I carried these supplies on my back in a large rucksack. Later on when he was in the big St. Luke's hospital in Tsukiji, I even had to carry charcoal to heat water for his tea and bath. A war-time regulation required that one adult must always be in the house in case of bombing or fire, and for this reason I left Kikuya, the maid, at the house and did the carrying myself.

The Great Heat was still on, although it was now early fall, and the crowded buses and trains were stifling. Armed with dark glasses, a fan, and cologne, I would set forth on my journey and return each day, dirty, limp, and dispirited. During the war it required more than a little courage to wear dark glasses. The accepted idea of a saboteur was anyone who always wore dark glasses and often someone yelled at me, "*Supai* (Spy)."

I was afraid of getting caught in an air-raid drill, not to speak of an air raid. Only once, though, during my trips to and from the hospital was the alert siren sounded. We were told by loud-speaker to squat near the walls of the big Shibuya station. My Japanese is very sketchy at best but I had simply to observe the others to know what to do. By some strange manipulation of their fingers my companions covered eyes, ears, and nose and squatted down on their heels, leaning against the walls of the station. It is a very easy thing for a Japanese to squat because from childhood his daily mode of living has involved squatting and rising—but it is quite another thing for a long-legged American woman to sit on her heels, at least for any length of time. I was very much mistaken in assuming the warden would understand this handicap. I raised up once, only to be shouted down. Finally the pain became so intense I just sat down flat in the dirt, thinking it was all a great mistake anyhow, that the railway terminals would be the objectives of the bombs. Later I was proved right in this when during the intensive bombings there was a tremendous loss of life near the stations where people were gathered for shelter. Just as the all-clear sounded, a warden bumped into me in the confused crowd. Looking up, he asked, "What is your country, *okusama?*"

"I am an American."

He looked skyward with astonishment, as if I had just descended by parachute.

Terry stayed in various hospitals for four months. First, he was in a civilian hospital but at the suggestion of a friend in the navy, we had him moved to the large naval hospital at Yokosuka. It was a hard decision to make; the military hospitals were better supplied with medicines and equipment and better staffed—I would not have to take bedding and food any longer—but, on the other hand, I would not be permitted to visit him at all. He was well cared for at Yokosuka and soon after the first of January, 1944, he was able to come home.

Mr. Shigemitsu, whom we had thought of joining in London years before when he was Ambassador there, had been appointed Foreign Minister. He made my husband Bureau Chief of the American Division of the Foreign Office. At last Terry would have some work to do and perhaps this would do as much for his health as any of the hospitals could.

To thank Mr. Shigemitsu for what he was doing for Terry, I journeyed to the beautiful section of Tokyo where the official residence is located and presented myself at his office. He greeted me with warmth, supporting himself with his cane and bowing gracefully for one with a wooden leg. A terrorist's bomb had taken his leg in Shanghai during the thirties; and I thought he typified the struggles of Japan both in his crippled body and his compassionate understanding of his country's torment.

Mako had written him a letter when he was appointed Foreign Minister. Unknown to us, enclosed with the letter was a picture she had done of the moon shining over a medieval castle, though why this was an appropriate salute to a foreign minister only little Mariko knew. When Terry had been called in to receive appointment as head of divisions 5 and 6 of the American Bureau, Shigemitsu had ostentatiously removed some ponderous documents from the glass cover to his desk so the astonished father could see the moon and castle carefully pressed between the glass top and the desk.

"You see, I have been receiving some mail from a very charming fan of mine."

He and his goddaughter were very good friends. In 1941 on arriving in Washington from England, he had brought her a grand French doll he had purchased in Paris. The doll had a magnet in its hand so that it could hold things. I was delighted with it, but Mako, tomboy that she had become, was not interested in the doll except when the donor was around. She loved the donor so much she had a tantrum when she was not taken to the airport to meet him. So when Shigemitsu left Washington to return to Japan, a few days later, we took Mako with us to the airport to wish him *bon voyage*. He was sitting in the waiting room with a group of friends about, and when he saw little Mako he called her to him. There she sat, pleased as punch, on the Ambassador's lap, and as the Japanese adults came up to pay their respects, bowing formally to Mr. Shigemitsu, they received his bow in return, and in addition a solemn nodding of the head from the little girl.

I said to Terry,

"I am going to go get that child and take her down!"

"No, leave her alone. Mr. Shigemitsu wouldn't keep her there if he didn't want her. Besides, she never had so much fun."

Mr. Shigemitsu kept her until the plane was announced, then he kissed her cheek and, with a fond pat on her head, told her to be a good girl and he would see her again before long.

Since that time he had been Ambassador to Russia, where he was stationed when Pearl Harbor was bombed. His career had sent him all over the world. As a young attaché he had served in Germany; and when Ambassador Kurusu was ordered to Berlin to sign the Tripartite Pact, Mr. Shigemitsu asked him to take a sum of money to deliver by some means to the Jewish family with whom he had roomed so long before. I knew that such a man could not have been happy at the partnership between Nazi Germany and Japan.

It was ironical that this able, humane person should become Foreign Minister in the midst of a war he had not wished for or countenanced. If there is a more frustrating position in wartime than that office, I do not know what it is.

He told me not to let Terry work too hard, that about all he could do until the war was over was to learn what he could and save his strength for the future. We talked of many things, of happier days in Washington, of Mako's paintings, of Terry's illness. He said,

"If Terry should die you will be heartbroken, but you and Mariko come to me. My house will be your home."

My husband began going to the office two or three times a week when he was able to be out. There was little for him to do except read dispatches, but he was glad to see them because they gave him a better idea of what was happening than the newspapers. Then, with Mr. Shigemitsu's blessing, Terry and Mr. Ishii, with whom we had returned on the *Gripsholm*, organized the Committee for Postwar Japan, made up of several Foreign Office people. They had never been under any illusion that Japan could win the war and began studying how best to make the transition when the Americans should occupy the country. Terry's "young men" kept coming to see him every time they had a chance, and they talked of beginning life again after the war.

Many black marketeers came to our back door with their wares. Once I bought a small bunch of bananas for Mako; they were to be the last bananas we were to eat until 1949, four years after the end of the war. I needed to be very prudent and prepare for winter while my husband was ill, even if it meant buying on the black market. In the past the Japanese had used small round briquettes made from coal dust to heat with; they lasted longer than charcoal. One day a man came with a whole wagon full, saying he would sell them to me cheaper as they had just been made up and were still wet. He said that if I would lay them in the sun till they dried I could store them away. Feeling very proud of myself, I promptly took the whole lot, and the maid and I painstakingly arranged them in the sun. When they were dried out they crumbled—they were only blackened mud.

The months passed and winter came, bringing the war ever closer. More and more often the air-raid sirens would sound, and, obedient to orders, people threw their houses open to facilitate escape and fire fighting. All members of the family had to be up and dressed. In cold weather this meant that they had to stand in their frigid homes with the door open to the cutting winds. I had a lambskin-lined Chinese coat which I used to wear on such occasions, and once an officious warden stopped and, blinking at me, asked,

"Are you Chinese?"

When I said, "Do I look Chinese?" he walked on.

Terry was determined for us to get out of Tokyo immediately and began looking for a house farther out in the suburbs. I began to pack my things, hoping to store them in a safe place outside Tokyo. I divided our belongings into five sections and placed in each one enough clothing and necessities to carry on in case everything else was lost. Into each trunk I also packed a fervent question, "Oh, God, how will it be when I unpack this trunk?"

There was a sense of impending disaster among the people, and it was intensified when we learned that all dogs were to be put to death and the rumor spread that the animals in the zoos were being killed. There was not enough food for human beings and none for animals. The Buddhists have a special feeling against taking life and many preferred to abandon their pets, but we loved our dogs and preferred having them destroyed to leaving them to wander half-starved on the streets of Tokyo.

One of our pets, Ken, was a lovely beast. Mako had found him on a street, still with rope around his neck, after he had escaped from the dog catchers. She released him and won his whole-hearted loyalty and devotion. He followed her home and we tried to make him leave. We already had Kuri, another stray, and when each of us sacrificed a portion of food, we were barely able to take care of him. Feeding another animal, and such a large one, was out of the question, but Ken stayed in the yard, growing thinner and more gaunt by the day. Terry, opening his window one cold night, saw him shivering by the wall outside. The dog cocked his head to one side inquiringly, and Terry went to the kitchen and fed him from our meager store.

We told Mako we were sending our dogs away to a safe place, and Terry and Kikuya took them one morning to a veterinarian in our district to be put to death. Ken and Kuri were delighted at the prospect of a walk with their master, who had been ill and away so long, and one of our thoughtful neighbors invited Mako over for a cup of morning tea so that she would not see the dogs taken away.

9

REFUGE IN ODAWARA

Taro Terasaki had a large house in Odawara and early in 1944 he offered to share it with us until we could find one for ourselves. Odawara is a small town near Sagami Bay about three hours by rail from Tokyo. My Eighth Dwarf came to help me pack and promised to ride with our things on the truck while we made the trip on the train.

While we were making preparations to move, one of the young men in Terry's office became ill and Terry took him to Dr. Ikeda of the large Episcopal hospital, St. Luke's. While examining the younger man, the doctor noticed my husband's flushed face and remarked,

"You don't look well yourself. Come let me test your blood pressure."

He found it considerably above two hundred and ordered Terry to the hospital again for treatment. Terry submitted with unusual docility and was put to bed at once, but he asked to go to St. Luke's rather than a military hospital so that I could visit him.

This meant that bedding, food, charcoal, soap, and towels had to be taken again. On my first visit to the hospital I found that the cross at the top had been taken down and the red "East Asia" flag put in its place. I mentioned this to Dr. Ikeda and he replied bitterly,

"That cross was good enough to build this hospital, Mrs. Terasaki, but it is considered inappropriate now. The name has been changed, too, from Sei Roka Byōin (St. Luke's Hospital) to Dai Tōa Byōin (Greater Asia Hospital)."

I told my husband not to worry about anything, that I would pack and when he had improved we would move. Every other day I would make the trip by streetcar to the hospital to carry his food. On one of these trips, the transformer at the front of the car exploded. I was hanging on a strap and fell headlong onto the people sitting in front of me. Someone yelled, "Bomb," and panic broke out. I sat down, away from the frightened crowd fighting in the aisle to get out. One man in attempting to get away got a button of his coat entangled in a woman's hair; he hastily removed the coat and jumped from the car. A baby strapped to his mother's back began to cry and the man behind her popped his finger into the open mouth. The baby sucked away and became silent. The woman turned, bowed formally to him, and said "*Arigatō gozaimasu* (Thank you very much)." I watched this as if in a dream during the moment or two until the car was cleared. Then, clutching Terry's lunch in my arms, I got off the car and boarded a crowded bus to continue my journey to the hospital.

The *sakura no hana* (cherry blossoms) were in full bloom, but the people along the way seemed to pay no attention to them. Because it does not wither on the tree but falls in full flower, the cherry blossom is revered as a symbol of the evanescence of life, of youth and courage, and of life's fleeting moments of happiness. Now no one participated in the traditional cherry festival; no one lingered under the laden boughs. Previously there had been an important celebration each summer called the *jūgoya* (the summer Moon-Viewing Festival) on August 15, and in the fall was the *jūsanya* (the autumn Moon-Viewing Festival) on October 13. Offerings of food, flowers, fruit, and autumn grasses were put on an altar placed on the veranda where the moon's rays would fall. The family would gather around and there would be an evening of story-telling and reading of poems; sometimes members of the family would compose their own verses extemporaneously. But during the war there was no heart in the people for their old festivities.

I noticed that many people cultivated flowers on top of their air-raid shelters. When the evening's work was done, they would sit in front of their shops and homes to admire the few blossoms they had been able to nurture. The Japanese have a saying,

> Heaven and earth are flowers—
> Gods as well as Buddha are flowers.
> The heart of man is also the soul of flowers.

At length Terry's blood pressure came down somewhat and he was released with a severe admonition to avoid heavy exercise and "not to worry." We hired professional packers and made ready to move. We found a young couple to stay in our house who could care for the furniture, china, and glassware we had to leave there. I made a cover for the canary cage so that we could carry our bird with us on the train. We had gone through the endless red tape of having our ration books changed so we could receive supplies in Odawara. Everything was ready. I made my *sayōnara* visits to all the houses of our neighborhood association and everyone wished us well. It was hard for me to say goodbye to my first little Japanese house, to my neighbors, to Meguro, and its cherry blossoms. I knew that there would be many changes before our return, if we should return. Unreasonably, the same fears returned to me that I had felt on coming to Meguro, fears that my neighbors would not accept me. But I was invariably treated with tolerance, at least, and almost always with kindness and friendliness. Only once, when I ran to a bleeding child injured in a bicycle accident, the parents snatched him away from me with hatred in their eyes.

REFUGE IN ODAWARA

Carrying our canary with us, Mako and I went on to Odawara with Terry's secretary. The motion of the train and the sound of the rolling wheels brought on such a burst of song as I have rarely heard from any bird. There was no way to stop that flow of music. The man across the aisle was much interested in us. He began to talk to Mako, asking the usual questions. "Where are you going? What is your name? What is your mother's nationality? What kind of canary do you have?" He talked with her for several minutes most kindly. Then as he got off the train he gave her his card to show me. He was an inspector of trains. One of the regulations he was charged with enforcing was that no birds were ever permitted aboard.

Arriving at Odawara we found our truck of household goods there, faithfully protected by the shivering Eighth Dwarf. He had ridden all the way on top of the truck in the cold spring wind. He was dressed for the occasion in a brand new *happi* (workman's livery coat), and his rubber-soled *tabi* (canvas-type shoes with a special space for the great toe) were new. For the first time, he was shaved. The first thing I did after reaching Taro's home was to make hot tea for that chilled little man.

Our host had gotten some men to help unload, the truck was soon on its way back to Tokyo, and I was left to survey my new domain. The large house that my brother-in-law had rented for his family during the first year of the war had been the residence and private hospital of a well-known doctor. We had the hospital side, consisting of three rooms and a large foyer which we turned into a room for Mako. All the rooms opened on a long, narrow hall which ran the entire length of the house. With our trunks stacked in the hall, the apartment looked like a ship's corridor with four cabins, and we dubbed it the *Terasaki Maru*. The Eighth Dwarf and I soon had the house arranged and livable. He stayed in Odawara with us for three days and did all the heavy work for Kikuya and me.

I was sorry to part with our faithful gardener. In war-time even casual goodbyes take on a tragic aspect. We waved him to the gate, and with hat in hand he gave us a low bow with a flourish and walked out of our lives. At the end of the war I made inquiries and learned from one of his neighbors that he fled one night with his wife and six children during the bombing; his house was burned and all his household goods were lost. Nothing further was ever heard of him.

The food shortage gradually worsened, and since we had no space for a garden of our own we had to send our maid on foraging trips. She would take the train and go into the country, walking many miles and returning late in the evening, tired and often empty-handed. She had a pleasant personality and, having grown up on a farm, she managed to find something when there was anything at all to be had.

There was an eye, ear, and nose specialist practicing in Odawara who loved the songs of Stephen Foster. I was ill on two occasions with inflammation of the middle ear, and for a time I was going to him daily for treatments. Odawara is a small place and I could easily walk the few blocks from our house to the doctor's office which adjoined his living quarters. He spoke excellent English which he had learned during World War I when he had served on a British man-of-war. After treatments, we often chatted a few minutes before he excused me and called in his next patient. He was fond of folk music and he loved Longfellow's "Evangeline." Evangeline typified the heroic qualities the Japanese desired in a woman. The story had been translated by the sister of Ambassador Hiroshi Saito and it was much loved by all students of American literature.

One morning the doctor asked me if I could play the piano. I told him I could play a little. He said, "Come with me," and led me through a long hall to his living room where there was a grand piano. He said his son, who played, had gone to war and that he missed the strains of "Swanee River" and "Old Black Joe." He produced a book of songs and I began to play. The tired doctor, his stethoscope around his neck, leaned back in an easy chair and closed his eyes. "Beautiful Dreamer," "Jeannie with the Light Brown Hair," and "Oh, Susanna" filled me with homesickness; it had been a long time since I had heard them. The doctor's waiting room was full of patients but they were forgotten. When I stopped and closed the piano against the dampness, he said, "Stephen Foster and the aroma of good coffee in the morning make me see America again, Mrs. Terasaki; there is so much we Japanese love about it. What a pity, this war!"

Later I learned that I had been breaking the law; the Home Ministry had prohibited the playing and singing of all British and American music.

I used to get on the tiny *densha* (streetcar) at Odawara and ride up the steep sides of the Hakone Mountains to the Fujiya Hotel at Miyanoshita. The hotel maintained a large lending library for its guests. The management kindly allowed me to continue to use the library although I was no longer staying there. In this way I was able to make a life for myself apart from the activity of war around me. The books were mostly classics and this was a very good thing for Mako; it gave her a distinguished taste in literature and built a foundation for her reading life. I discovered also a tiny volume of verse, an English translation of poems of the Emperor Meiji, grandfather of the present Emperor. He was a talented poet as well as Japan's greatest Emperor. I learned to love the poems of Basho and the modern verse of Mrs. Yosano. I had Alexander Woollcott's *While Rome Burns* and doubt that I could have survived without it, at least with my sense of humor intact.

On one of my trips up the mountain foraging for books I found myself seated facing a German who lived at the Fujiya. We were the only foreigners on the *densha* and it seemed very silly for us to sit facing each other without speaking. He was dressed in snow-white linen shorts, white shirt, golf socks, and shining white sports shoes. Much aware of his cleanliness, he was fearful of being stepped upon or soiled by the pushing, perspiring peasants. In spite of the great disdain he affected he was very self-conscious with my amused American eyes upon him. Both of us were squeezed in by the packed crowd and could scarcely move. Next to him sat a farm woman with her baby on her back. The woman looked at him intently, remarking to her neighbor that it must have taken a lot of soap to make him sparkle so brightly.

As we progressed slowly up the mountain, the restless baby began to play with the German's ear. Feeling my inquisitive stare on him, he tried not to be harsh and ducked his head away from the tiny hands. The child reached out again and the man again moved his head away; the mother scolded the child without effect and the child again grasped for its new-found toy. Growing scarlet with mortification, the poor man had to endure this all the way to the hotel.

When he got off the car, I noticed he was carrying butter and jam to supplement his food at the hotel. All the foreigners carried small baskets of extra food to the table and carried it back to their rooms after each meal. Always there was lively curiosity when the contents of the baskets were put on the tables at mealtime.

After Italy surrendered, the Italian Embassy staff was divided in its loyalties and split into groups. One faction remained loyal to Mussolini and these were sent to stay at the Fujiya. The Ambassador and other members who chose to be associated with the Badoglio government were interned in different places outside Tokyo. I used to see the Mussolini group sitting in the lobby, endlessly arguing and talking of the war and politics. Among them was an Italian painter who had an American wife. One day I was sitting by the swimming pool while Mako and her friends were in the water. I was reading and trying to get some sun. A voice just in front of me said, "Hello." I looked up to see the painter's wife. She said, "Fancy meeting you here; aren't you a bit far away from home?"

It was good to hear an American voice, even when speaking such standard American pleasantries. She told me her husband had studied Japan, its painting, and its architecture for many years and had been sent to Japan as interpreter and adviser to the Italian Embassy. She was an attractive, witty person who spoke Italian and Japanese almost as fluently as she did English.

Once she telephoned me at my home in Odawara and, as all long-distance calls had to be conducted in Japanese so as to be monitored by the operators, I had to try to make sense in that language over the phone. It is more difficult to speak a language you partly know over the telephone than one would suspect. I made many blunders and had such a struggle of it that we spent most of the time laughing. Once my friend forgot and in her confusion said, "Oh, hell,"—quick as a flash the operator said, "Put that into Japanese," but we could only laugh. Finally we gave it up.

The warning sirens blared often and we knew that the reconnoitering planes were preparing the way for bombing missions to follow. Yet, daily life had to go on. I had hired a woman to tutor Mako in written Japanese. She came daily and Mako pored over the difficult characters. The child had long braids that hung almost to her waist. She was growing taller, and it hurt me to see how solemn and wise her little face had become; sometimes in repose her face reflected the sadness of an old woman. She was surprisingly gallant and resourceful for a child that had grown up accustomed to having so many things done for her. This gallantry was true of all the children of Japan. A grammar-school teacher told me that when she took the pupils for picnics or hikes, most of them, without any urging, gathered wood to carry home for cooking. Many times they exchanged their cherished pencils or handkerchiefs for vegetables. Frequently I saw small boys and girls toiling home from their excursions laden with wood and vegetables, tired and dirty but sure of a warm welcome.

I used to walk along the streets of Odawara in the glare of the summer sun and look at the bare shops, the empty streets. Sometimes I was much afraid. I had a growing child and a sick husband to care for, and the knowledge that there was no food to be had filled me with panic.

As a foreigner, I received bread instead of rice as my main ration. This was most fortunate because the bread ration was more regular. All three of us had toast for breakfast and for tea, and I ate rice at the other two meals. The people in the *panya* (bakery) at Odawara were unusually kind to me, and whenever they had white flour they sent me a roll of white bread. If they had sugar they often made sweet rolls instead of the regulation small loaves. The smiling face of the baker's wife was one of the brightest sights of my day. The owner of the large pharmacy and his wife were also good to me. Whenever one of us needed medicine they would bring us all they had on hand. They were always most sympathetic, and when things were at their worst, at the end of the war, they did all in their power to help the occupation forces that came to their small town. The husband was an admirer of Bing Crosby, and when the first American soldiers arrived in Odawara he greeted them with the anxious query, "Is Bingu Kurosubi O.K.?"

That June of 1944 the battle for Saipan was in progress and our Japanese friends were depressed and despondent. Every night people held their breaths while the names of the *kamikaze* boys lost were read over the radio. But the newspapers continued to carry stories of simple and uniform heroics reminiscent of the early silent movies. One went like this:

DOMEI

CENTRAL PACIFIC BASE, March 2—Sergeant A. was a youthful wireless operator who won the heart of his commander as well as his comrades with his amiable ways and his cherished moustache. He was a determined fellow who stuck to his post until his duty was performed despite wounds received during a death-defying bombing raid against enemy vessels off Iwojima. Sergeant A. was, at the time, aboard a bomber craft piloted by Kimura which instantly sank one enemy warcraft in the waters off Iwojima. This is the story related by Sergeant A.'s mates at this base.

"Sergeant A. was a popular fellow. He was a young, stalwart, good-natured fellow of twenty-two years of age. About a month ago he suddenly got a strange inspiration to grow a moustache and by the time he was ready to leave this base, he had successfully grown a smart 'cookie duster.'

"One day the unit commander slapped Sergeant A. on the back and jokingly said, 'You'd better shave that moustache off because someone might mistake you for me or for some other

132

high officer.' The sergeant replied, 'But sir, 'twill serve as a break against any enemy bomb blasts,' as he fingered it fondly amid hilarious laughter from the unit commander and his comrades. That evening Sergeant A., chosen as wireless operator aboard a bomber piloted by Kimura, started off on a mission of blasting enemy vessels off Iwojima.

"Addressing his commander, the sergeant said, 'Sir, this moustache will not shame you because I am going with the spirit and determination of my superior officer after those white-livered Yankee rats cowering in the rat holes of their vessels.' The commander warmly grasped Sergeant A.'s hands and chuckled, 'Go to it, my boy!' The Japanese planes roared off the runway. Constant wireless communication was kept with its base. 'That boy is in top condition,' the commander told his subordinates as he listened to messages relayed from the plane. The craft droned toward its objective.

" 'They should be over their target now,' someone whispered. The commander nodded. 'Stand by; stand by. We are now over our target. Have begun our attack.' A few seconds ticked by and then the messages continued. 'Bombing raid successful. No damage to our plane.' It was later learned that the plane piloted by Kimura had wheeled low, ready to fire at what was believed to be a battleship cruising parallel with Iwojima but dived short of its target. Kimura then made a 40 degree turn and winged into the midst of the enemy convoy, with the nose of the plane pointed at an enemy vessel which was either a battleship or a large-sized transport.

"Pilot Kimura then gave the signal to open the attack. The bomber plunged into a dive. Soon it was over its objective and the bombs whined through the air. As Kimura pulled out, terrific explosions rocked the sea, followed by huge pillars of smoke and fire. The enemy vessel split in two, then folded up, and was seen to be swallowed up by the sea. The moon had disappeared and the surface of the sea was enveloped in black. Suddenly a savage rat-tat-tat was heard from an enemy vessel cruising in the darkness on the portside of our craft. A stray machine-gun lead pierced the wireless operator's, Sergeant A.'s, left thigh.

"Despite his injuries he stuck to his post, tapping the wireless keys. Now Pilot Kimura was wheeling the bomber through a fierce squall. Sergeant A. began to feel the effects of his injury. He clenched his teeth, for the fate of his plane and his comrades depended upon him, as blood dripped from his wound.

"The fuel tank began to run dry as the plane roared westward. Minutes slowly ticked by, then like a godsend, Pilot Kimura spotted a beam from the airfield beacon. The bomber slowly circled to its base and taxied down the runway. The commander approached the plane to congratulate his men and especially extend a welcome home to the sergeant. But he died as soon as Pilot Kimura brought his aircraft safely to ground after successfully completing the bombing mission. There was a faint smile still hovering about his trim moustache. The commander sadly said, 'My lad, I am proud of you. The memory of you and your moustache will be with me always.'"

Only victories were broadcast. This involved such obvious contradictions that even the more simple-minded listeners became doubtful. Everyone who could think at all realized that the country was in a more and more desperate state, its back to the wall. When it became impossible to hide the truth longer, the broadcasters would announce a battle or an island lost, and each time they did so the program was ended with music. It was always the same—the sad, sweet strains of *Umi Yukaba*, a well-loved old song. All over the nation people would bow their heads while someone quietly turned off the radio. The conviction of ultimate defeat had become widespread but everyone was careful not to speak his opinion; each carried on silently lest his doubts prevent another from doing his best.

By many little signs I knew how desperate things had become for the Japanese. I saw little boys of ten and twelve unloading the freight from the trains. Children were employed in all kinds of factory work from clothes-making to riveting airplane parts together; they were mobilized through their schools and taken from there to their jobs each day by the teachers. Mako would have certainly been conscripted along with the others but for the fact that she had been studying under a private tutor at home and her name was not on the school list. A friend of ours who had a paint factory that had been converted to do camouflaging put Mako down as an employee of his, to protect her from forced labor should inquiries be made. Always, though, there was the chance that some one of the many people who knew us would complain to the authorities that my tall, thin child was a slacker. Sometimes I thought about it at night and would awake with a start to sit up wondering if I had heard a knock at the door.

Having reported Mako as being on the sick list, we could not afford to have her seen playing about during the day. Still, she needed exercise, so we decided she should arise early with her father and go for a long walk each morning for about an hour. It became their custom to be up and out of the house before I awoke and return just in time for breakfast. One morning during the summer they left the house at about 6 A.M. to take their daily walk along the deserted streets of our village toward the beach. Terry had to depend on his cane to get about more than he liked to admit, and they went slowly down the sidewalk under the trees, two silent figures, watching the approach of day and listening to the boom of the sea. Mako always wanted to walk near the ocean and this pleased her father. Fog had come in from the ocean but it was beginning to lift. As the two of them came down the beach on their return and neared the sea wall where there were steps leading back to the street, Terry's hand tightened on Mako's and he motioned her to stop. A man had come out of the mist in front of them and was moving toward a huge trash can, placed at the corner of the sea wall near the steps, which was filled with garbage and refuse. Before the war there had been no beggars in Japan. The little girl and her father watched. The man grabbed into the barrel like an animal, spilling litter out onto the clean beach. He found some food clinging to a paper wrapper and he pressed the paper tightly against his face to gnaw the food away. A dog slunk down the steps from the street toward the beach and the man at the trash can. The dog was hungry but afraid of the man and cowered at the man's heels, whining low. Hearing the cries of the starving dog, the man turned and patted him on the head. Then, taking courage, the dog dived into the reeking pile of refuse, scavenging side by side with the man. Terry muttered to his silent daughter standing by his side,

"You have witnessed human greatness, Mariko."

Then the two of them walked slowly past the scavengers, who did not look up, mounted the steps of the sea wall, and came home to breakfast with me.

Many wounded, en route to nearby hospitals from distant places in the Pacific, were brought to Odawara station. In my walks I would see them there, rows upon rows of litters. The Japanese would go up to them, and, bowing low, say, "*Gokurō sama* (Thank you)."

Mr. Ishii called one day to tell us he was going to Holland as Ambassador. He hinted at taking Terry with him but I would not have it. For us to be left in Japan, without Terry, was beyond imagination. Mr. Ishii told us he would come through Odawara en route to Kobe to take a ship for Holland, and he added, "If *okusama* wants to do anything for me, please make me a little bowl of potato salad."

I was extremely fond of Mr. Ishii, who had been so kind to me when I was first learning the ways of Japanese society in Shanghai years before, and I got together all the ingredients I could find for his salad. Terry and Taro and I went to the station to greet him as he passed through. We had only a few moments together, and it seemed very sad that such a good friend should be going away and we could not know whether we would meet again. I hardly knew what to say in goodbye. Just before the train was to leave, a nurse came by carrying an object; and we had to step back to let her pass. The object glanced at us, his suffering eyes lingering on our arms and legs. It was a young soldier in his teens. His arms were off at the shoulders and his legs were off at the hips. Watching the nurse take him into the next car, we stood there. No one said anything, no *sayōnara*, no sound. Mr. Ishii boarded the train, nodded to us, and we waved faintly back. The train rolled away.

Realizing the fighting might soon reach Odawara, Terry was

searching for a house away from any concentrated area. A sense of disaster impended. People were restless and afraid. Rations were becoming more scarce by the day and sometimes stopped altogether. Kikuya had to make her trips into the country more often and returned fewer times with anything for us to eat. We were eating so little that a lethargy symptomatic of slow starvation crept over us. Our stomachs had shrunk so that a handful of food, when we could get it, seemed like a feast and filled us very full.

We heard of a tiny house four stations away on the railroad, near Manazuru, the big fishing center on Sagami Bay. Immediately Terry set out to see the owner and negotiated for us to have the house in early November. When he returned he told us about the spot with much animation. The house was situated in a tangerine grove near the lovely village of Yoshihama and looking toward the Seven Islands of Izu and the unforgettable Izu Peninsula. It was high on the steep mountainside, perched on a small ledge like an eagle's aerie. Looking toward the sea, one saw the Seven Islands far below as if viewed from one of the Pan American Clippers that flew over in times past. Clouds sometimes passed below and one could look down on the gulls sweeping over the surface of the bay. The great crest of Nangoyama watched haughtily over the scene from the landward side. There was much irregularity to the shoreline and little surf; the sea lay shining in myriad small coves against hooks and fingers of land where the green vegetation rose lush in the sunshine.

But it was a few weeks yet until we could have the house, so Mako and I went back to the Fujiya we loved so well one more time before leaving.

My old and close friend Hélène, whom I had not seen since we left Tokyo, was visiting there with her husband and their small children, and we had a week together. We sat in the well-kept gardens and talked of how we should best manage our odd circumstances. She had been unable to find a house in the country and, having known bombing in Europe, she was desperate to leave Tokyo. Later things worked out for her; her husband got an appointment which took them to Karuizawa, in the mountains of Nagano, to look after the foreigners who had been evacuated to that famous resort town.

When we went to the station to say goodbye, an Italian woman came up and chattered away at us at such a rate that we had no time to tell each other farewell. Perhaps it was just as well. The Italian woman spoke no English and, of course, I could not converse with her except in Japanese. We walked back through the village in the fading light accompanied by a crowd of villagers curious at two *gaijin* speaking Japanese—did they not know their own language?

After we were prepared to leave Odawara there was some little time before the moving trucks arrived. With nothing to do, I thought I would get a charcoal permanent. My sister-in-law had gotten one, and her hair looked soft and attractive in spite of the fact that the beauticians had substituted charcoal for electricity as a heating element. I made an appointment and was told to bring my own towels and soap or shampoo. I had long before used up my shampoo, so I made my own by putting odds and ends of toilet soap into a large jar and making a jelly by mixing in water. In the early morning I set forth with this homemade shampoo, feeling adventuresome and bold on my way to try my luck.

The parlor was filled with women waiting their turns. When I entered the shop the conversation stopped abruptly as though the ladies could not stare and talk at the same time. I could see the operator was nervous as, bowing low, she assured me what a poor thing she was but that she would try to do her best with her meager talent and hoped she would not burn me. At this, a chorus of reassurance came from the spectators indicating that she was *totemo jōzu* (very skilled). With everyone attending each movement the operator made, the hairdressing was begun.

All the women took the opportunity to feel the softness of my hair. Then, after a hand drying, it was rolled much the same as our electric permanents are, using a solution that smelled somewhat like fish and something of seaweed. The truth was, it was made of wood shavings, and how it came to emit such odors I cannot say. The charcoal had previously been broken up into tiny pieces which were now glowing red. The coals were put on the tops of clamps fastened into the rolled hair. Through practice, and doubtless a few disasters, the operator had learned how much charcoal would bake the hair and how long it would take the coals to burn out into ash. She used metal *hibashi* (tongs) to handle the hot coals, working swiftly and with precision. There was one thing certain, it was imperative that I sit absolutely motionless to avoid spilling the glowing coals into my lap. As I waited for my hair to dry, I could not help but think of the possibility of an air raid. I was trying to keep my nerve and assuring myself that no such thing would happen when the sirens began. The women fell silent and gripped their hands in their laps. We waited. Then the planes droned on, high up and away from us. The "all clear" sounded and the women settled back with relief to their gossiping, as hens after the hawk goes away.

As the operator began to remove the ash-filled clips, I held my breath. Everyone was silent again, watching the operator work. They could not have been more attentive had I been Medusa having my snakes arranged. The hair was unrolled, and the curls were elastic and radiant. A great "Ah-h-h" went up. Everyone chuckled and repeated "O *medetō* (Congratulations)" to me with genuine delight. And well they might have, for the permanent remained shining and curly for a full year.

Some of the women at the beautician's had babies on their backs, others carried their mending to the shop. Many times that morning the bell rang at the ration center down the street. If a woman was having her hair done, another would volunteer to go for her rations. There was much good-natured argument and gossiping and much talk of the coming air raids. Everyone was certain the raids would come soon. No one ventured the thought that Japan was steadily losing, perhaps no one needed to. As each woman finished with her hair, all would rise to bow and tell her that her hair was *totemo kirei* (very beautiful). She would always reply, "*Iie* (Not at all)." There were no dryers and each of us left with plastered wet heads. I wrapped a scarf around my head and left happily amid much bowing and waving.

Mako's tutor had given her a *bunchō* (Java sparrow) for her birthday. Now we had two pet birds to feed. Mako called him "Buny" to distinguish him from the canary "Daffy." We carried them with us all through the war and for several years after the surrender. Each time we moved, someone had to get them on the train unnoticed and remain composed when the two bundles burst into song.

Our trucks came and it was time to leave. *Sayōnara* again, to the neighbors and friends. *Sayōnara* (since we must say goodbye). *Sayōnara* and *o daiji ni* (take care of yourself). *Sayōnara* and *go-kigan yo* (forget not). *Sayōnara* (I leave a bit of my heart behind).

10

BAMBOO SPEARS

Wᴇ toiled up the long hill, through the tangerine grove, and around the slope to our tiny house with grandeur for its front yard. Once we stopped to rest along the way and listened to the girls singing as they picked the fragrant tangerines. The autumn colors were in flame, and Mt. Nangoyama was hazy in the distance. The sea nudged gently against the shore and the Isles of Izu. One of our friends from the Foreign Office who was helping us burst out, "Isn't it good to be alive!"

I found immediately that the house was not in any way equal to the magnificence of the view it afforded. There was no kitchen, only a bench outside in the rain or snow. The bathroom had water faucets but no tub. In Japan one moves his wooden tub as one moves other household belongings.

We were to share the big Japanese bath with our German neighbors. They were Jewish and in the bad graces of the Nazis in Japan and, like us, they were lonely. The owner of the three houses lived next to the Germans and we all were to share the large Japanese bath, alternating nights. Since we would have no

141

need for our bathroom I decided to make it into a kitchen. There was a tiny balcony, glass enclosed, overlooking the sea. There I put a bridge table and we ate each day looking out over the tangerine grove toward the bay and the peninsula.

The Germans helped me get settled. There was such an urgency about everything we did, an unspoken and ever-present dread of what we knew was coming. Two or three days after we arrived in Yoshihama a great formation of B-29's came overhead by way of the peninsula, just after noon. Three cities were bombed that day. The planes came in very high, great silver reflections in the sunlight. We ran out into the garden and watched. There seemed to be very little anti-aircraft fire. Our village sirens wailed all day. That was the beginning of a new pattern of living for us. There was no letup in the incessant wailing. When they stopped momentarily Terry remarked, "Listen to the silence." He frequently stood out in the garden and watched the planes go over. Once he said, "This is the beginning of the end." Everyone had to adjust his or her life around the coming of the planes or the threat of their coming. At first, the people felt a comparative safety on rainy days or moonless nights. They soon learned better, however; some of the worst raids came on rainy days and one of the most destructive took place during a heavy snow storm. Usually the planes came in over the Izu Peninsula and left over the Bozo Peninsula on the other side of Tokyo. Now and then that procedure was reversed and we would watch them leave after their missions were completed and their bombs delivered. For some time it seemed that the planes flew over our house about noontime. The Japanese expected this would continue and planned to be off the streets during the midday hours. But no pattern remained the same for any length of time. The planes came at all hours and one could not go on the streets without fear at any time.

As the people walked constantly with hunger they used to speculate on what kinds of food the pilots must have enjoyed when they returned to their bases. They talked of the ham sandwiches, Coca-Colas, and hot dogs that must be available at the American air strips.

One day at noontime when the planes were roaring overhead, Terry declared somberly to me, "Marrying me certainly put you not only in the teeth of war but also in the hands of slow starvation!"

I turned to him quickly and said, "If it were to do over, even knowing what I now know, I would do it again!"

He burst into sudden tears. Only once before had I seen him weep. We held each other in a tight embrace and clung together— then we smelled the odor of burning rice. I ran to the kitchen. Our lunch, the last rice we had in the house, had burned merrily to a crisp. Terry reflected that it was well that I would continue to choose starvation.

Our fuel situation became so desperate at Yoshihama that we had to go on foraging trips for sticks and pine cones. I found that the oil in pine cones makes them excellent burning material in the *konro*. One had to light the fire in the garden and when the cones were glowing red, if one stepped lively enough, one could manage to cook a meal before they burned out. Since we had no heat in our house, all of us would crowd into the tiny kitchen while it was still warm from the pine cones to get thawed out. That winter of 1944 was one of the coldest of the war. We were on a hill and constantly buffeted by the famous winds of Manazuru. I stuffed newspapers around all the windows and placed my screens against the walls where there were cracks. As long as I kept busy I could forget the cold, but there was no way to rest in comfort, no relaxing. A brisk walk in the open air did as much to warm us as anything.

For fear of the police, the anti-militarists had to be very quiet; yet, the police were not as severe as I have understood they were in countries held by the Nazis or Fascists. I knew of no alien wives having any trouble except one. She kept complaining constantly and denouncing the military government publicly. The *kempei tai* arrested her and took her to the station for a few hours, but they let her go with the admonition that she should be more discreet. The other alien wives were not at all displeased at this because she had been making it difficult for them by her constant carping.

Terry used to say of me to Mako, "Your mother is *nonki, nonki* (very carefree). Let's keep her that way. Do not speak to her of the danger." Taro always insisted I was more trusting of the Japanese than any Japanese would be, but I was more aware than they guessed—I knew why Kikuya had left so hurriedly.

She had announced that the country would be destroyed and she must be with her parents at the end. That was her excuse. The *kempei tai* had been questioning her from time to time about whether I did any writing. "Does *okusama* write?" She told me she had answered them, "Oh, no, because she can't write to her mother. She has no one else to write to." This was the truth of the matter. I wished to keep a diary but, whether I was as carefree as Terry thought or not, I felt it was too dangerous for one in my position. However, Terry did keep a diary in which he made entries almost every day. Just before Kikuya left us, the diaries had disappeared. I was certain she had been terrorized into taking them to the police and was then ashamed to remain any longer with us. How the loss of the diaries worried Terry! He had nothing in his notes that could have been used to link him with the cablegram to the Emperor but the close watch kept on him by the *kempei tai* was fearful.

There was no way to plan one's day. The unexpected became routine, and I could only try to take things as they came. Meals could not be planned for one never knew what rations were coming in. One unforgettable day the fishmonger's wife brought us thirteen cuttlefish, something I had never seen before. She offered to clean one for me to show me how and I accepted her offer gladly. I knew little enough about cleaning even the usual run of fish and the cuttlefish is very odd. It has a long black intestine that runs the length of the creature, and one breaks that intestine at his peril. I broke three before I learned. Then for a time we ate cuttlefish every day, three times a day. All we had to go with it was the citrus fruit that abounded in our district—oranges and tangerines. We ate so many of them that we developed what was known as "Manazuru" feet and hands; the palms of our hands and the soles of our feet became golden yellow.

Every anniversary of Pearl Harbor was memorable to us, as, indeed, to everyone in America and Japan—but December 7, 1944, furnished more than a reminder of calamity. The planes did not come over that day and the winds were not blowing in from the bay; we were left in a strange quietness. Suddenly there was a terrific roar, jolting everything. Another and another until the house was shaking with quick sidewise vibrations. I was terrified and could not move. Then I thought of Mako, playing in the orange grove, and I dashed out of the moving house. It was swaying so much I was hardly able to stay on my feet. Not until I reached the garden did I realize it was an earthquake. Our German friends and Mrs. Brasch's elderly mother had already arrived in the garden. They had been eating lunch and the white-haired old lady, pale and shaken, was still trying to put a crust of bread into her mouth. Terry came running and soon I heard Mako's "Mommie" and her delighted exclamation, "Oh, boy, some earthquake!"

We learned that the epicenter of the earthquake had been at the bottom of the sea off Miye Prefecture. Shizuoka Prefecture was also hard hit, and our village lay near the Shizuoka boundary. Tidal waves had washed away villages like ours located along the Miye coast.

We were almost grateful to the earthquake for the conversation it afforded us during the days following before the boredom of the daily struggle overtook us again. Terry became ill once more, this time with a high fever. Mako helped with the chores and I devoted most of my time to nursing him back to health, but he needed a doctor. It was virtually impossible to find a doctor; the only hope I had was of getting the village doctor, but he would not come unless I sent a horse for him. Where was I to get a horse? Terry got steadily worse, and when I was desperate I appealed to the Germans next door.

Mr. Brasch told me quietly, "I don't know about a horse but

I'll carry the doctor on my back if there is no other way." He could have done it; he was a large, muscular man of great determination. However, we managed to hire a farmer nearby to take his horse after His Excellency the village doctor and he arrived some time later in a blinding rain. When I went to the door to let him in, one would have thought that I was Old Nick's handmaiden. He crept past me like a little mouse, looking to the right and then to the left, wondering if there were more like me in the shadows. The blackout lampshades on our lights lent an eerie glow to the house and I longed for a toy spider with wire legs. But there was little time for such thoughts for the doctor began examining Terry at once. He asked my husband in a whisper,

"Who is she?"

Terry said, "My wife."

"Ah, yes, your wife, but *what* is she?"

That amused my husband, sick as he was, and he gave a shout of laughter. The startled doctor quickly wrote a prescription and said that Terry had pneumonia, that we must keep his room warm, and that he must have nourishing food. All these were impossibilities. I broke into the conversation to ask mildly,

"What kind of nourishing food do you mean?"

He replied, "Chicken soup, milk, eggs and stewed fruit, butter and bread."

I appealed to the Germans, who received special rations from the German Association. They promised to help. After a trip to Tokyo, Mr. Brasch told me he could buy butter but that I must buy at least fifteen pounds at one time. So I had butter to burn. We ate so much butter that we were really *bata kusai* (smelling of butter, an expression for foreigners).

Mrs. Brasch offered to take the prescription down to the *o kusuriya* (pharmacy) for me as she had to go to the village for her rations. When she brought the medicine back she was much amused. It seems the pharmacy was connected to the doctor's office and she had given the prescription to the doctor himself. The doctor realized she was not the same woman he had seen the night before at the home of Mr. Terasaki, yet she was a foreign person. I had told Mrs. Brasch about the doctor's visit, so she volunteered no information and left him frustrated and open-mouthed at her departure.

It was a month before Terry was fully recovered and he had to spend Christmas of 1944 in bed. I had one red candle, one can of strawberry jam, twelve pounds of butter, and two cups of flour, no sugar, and one can of powdered sage. I unpacked some of our Christmas decorations and we had a tiny tree. With the two cups of flour I made a cake, without using any sugar, baking it on my waffle iron. I used the whole can of jam for icing and decorated the cake with holly from the mountain. I made a stuffing with bread crumbs and butter, seasoning it with the sage. So there was a suggestion of turkey after all. The red candle gave us a real Christmas atmosphere and we were happy. Mako had asked Mr. Brasch to buy something for her mama in Tokyo and he bought a book at the second-hand store, Pearl Buck's *Fighting Angel.*

On Christmas Eve, after all our preparations were made and Mako and Terry had fallen asleep, I slipped out. The bright stars glittered in the sky and I heard the waves of Sagami softly rustling below. I heard what I at first thought was "Silent Night, Holy Night." I listened, rapt and nostalgic, for a few moments before I realized that it came from our neighbors' house. There was only a tiny gleam under the blacked-out windows, so I tapped gently on the door and they drew me in. Together we sang again the beautiful song that had come from the Germans originally. I sang in English and they sang in German, but our different languages expressed one meaning. We drank ersatz coffee and sat and talked far into the night, in whispers so as not to awaken the Brasch children.

Christmas day we spent in Terry's room; he was still in bed. He was able to sit up with a shawl around his shoulders and have his share of the jam cake. The strawberry jam was so sweet we did not notice the lack of sugar in the cake.

Early in January we were rationed horse meat for the first

time. I told myself there was little difference between it and beef and that if it was properly prepared it would be delicious. I boiled the meat for a long time, and then allowed it to cool. We sliced it thin, dipped it in *shōyu* (soy) sauce at the table, and ate it with rice, doing our best to keep our minds on "blue horizons." When Mako asked, "I wonder whose horse died," I wondered if war-time transportation were not too important for the government to slaughter any healthy horses merely to feed the people.

Terry began to mend and to regain his strength, thanks, perhaps, to the horse meat. Now he was able to take a short walk in the garden every day and to see those who came again seeking advice. Serious-minded young Foreign Office men—who probably would not have understood affectionate teasing any better than he—came to see how he was and to talk of the future. It was more than a sense of respect bred of the tradition of hierarchy or even shared political sympathies that inspired them to make the journey; they admired the older man and hoped to serve with him in the years to come. When they referred to him as *sensei* (teacher) they meant it.

I remember one idealist who spent the afternoon talking of the nature of man and government with Terry. When he left, he said with unmistakable fervor,

"*Sensei*, so long as my eyes are black you shall not want for anything which I can provide!"

Such declarations of loyalty were just what my huband's drenched spirits needed.

Our house was to be the meeting place of the next *tonarigumi* gathering. There were to be new instructions from the *chōkai* (town assembly). Our neighbors were farmers, fishermen, and a few families from Tokyo who had sought refuge there. I felt like an intruder among them and dreaded the meeting; but I had no choice and began to arrange for their coming. My rooms were filled with furniture and I had to move all of it into one room so as to make enough room for the people to assemble. It would have been simpler in a Japanese home, which would contain little furniture in the first place and where the *karakami* (sliding screens) could be taken out so as to make two rooms into one. I borrowed flat cushions for seating from my Japanese neighbors and set about making tea. Since we had some flour made of barley and wheat, I decided to make waffles and serve each member a waffle with honey. One of our friends had recently supplied us with the honey, and I knew our neighbors would think better of me for sharing it with them.

The honey reminded me of the time I bought some in Peking. There was a large specialty shop in Hatamen Street where one could buy all flavors of honey, fragrant jasmine tea, preserved ginger, and litchi nuts. As I looked over the display of goods, noticing that the honey was very colorless, I asked the clerk standing by if it was genuine.

"Oh, yes, Missy," he assured me. "Have got bee inside."

Sure enough, on closer inspection, I found a bee in every jar.

With silent promptness everyone arrived at seven in the evening. There is something about the dark streets and dark homes, conforming to blackout regulations, which induces one to speak in whispers or remain silent. Terry, pale and weak, received everyone with the traditional low bows on the *tatami*, and I bowed from the waist since that is as much as I can do with any grace at all, yet I felt silly standing while my guests were flat on their faces on the floor. Terry customarily explained that I, a foreigner, could not get down on the floor in the traditional Japanese bow. The guests invariably looked at me with tolerance and sometimes with a suggestion of scorn. Imagine a woman of my age so feeble! The Japanese bow is a lovely graceful gesture when performed by a dainty Japanese lady trained from childhood in all its niceties, but it is equally awkward and ungraceful when tall or stout people endeavor to respond in like manner. Most Western-educated Japanese realize the handicap of the foreigner and greet him with a firm handclasp or a small bow.

The *kumichō* called the meeting to order. There were two main items on the agenda. First, every person of adult age must provide himself with a bamboo spear of a certain length with which to meet the enemy when they came to invade the islands. I was so shocked by this that I sat in stunned silence. Terry said nothing. I urged him to push his cushion closer to the wall where he could have support for his back. They began to argue over the length of the spears and I was engulfed by waves of talk, most of which I could not understand. I thought of how these poor people would feel when they discovered how reckless their leaders had been. With docility and courage they were doing all in their power to stave off the inevitable, but it would come and they would know that they had never had the least chance to win.

When the spear length was settled there was a discussion of the evacuation plans whereby everyone on the coastline must move. We were to group at a designated area and march together under a leader. Terry was attentively taking down notes on all the *kumichō* was saying. Everyone's face was tense; they were more willing to fight for their homes than they were to leave them. There was bitter silence. Then Terry said,

"And where shall we march to?"

No one could answer.

I decided it was time to serve my waffles, and they were received with great interest and pleasure. My guests asked to see the waffle iron and admired its shiny chromium finish. Then they filed out, after much bowing. I knew they were still wondering where, with their bamboo spears, they would go when the marines landed in our midst.

As soon as they had gone, Terry said, "We must find a house or rooms in the mountains and leave this coast." Of course, he was right, for the coastline was being fortified, and we heard sounds of rapid building in the mountains behind our house. Nangoyama was swarming with soldiers.

One day a noncommissioned officer climbed to our house from the village, knocked on our door, and asked me for a glass of water. I went to the kitchen for the water. Handing it to him, I noticed he never took his eyes off my face. Even more significant, he accepted the water without a word of thanks. I felt uncomfortable. Finishing the glass, he handed it back to me saying, "*Mō ippai* (One more)." His suspicious gaze was steadily upon me.

Terry had warned me in such an emergency not to rely on my broken Japanese but to speak English, and when I went into the kitchen for the second glass of water I ran across the garden to the Brasch's. They spoke fluent Japanese. Mrs. Brasch came over and asked the soldier if she could do anything for him. She took him over to speak to her husband. He went without a word. Later he returned, bowed, and thanked me for the water.

Terry was greatly disturbed when I related this story to him. He and Taro had always said I trusted the jingoists among their countrymen far more than they did. He began to hunt for a new sanctuary in the interior and left in a few days with Taro for Nagano-ken, the mountainous prefecture in north central Honshu, the main island. Both were looking for a safe place for their families. Terry returned a few days later, weary and dejected. His search had been among the farmers and hill people wherever he heard of a house or a room or a shed. The "carpet bombing" of Tokyo on March 9, 1945, had sent thousands of homeless people wandering into the mountains for shelter and he could find nothing that was not already taken. I remembered the way our little orange grove shook on that night as we lay in our beds and listened to the deafening roar of the planes coming in over Sagami Bay headed for Tokyo. The wind had whipped up a great fire in the city, and people in some districts were surrounded by the wall of fire and burned alive. The skies around the city were red, and people in outlying areas knew a catastrophe had occurred.

One morning while we were having breakfast on our little balcony overlooking the bay, a submarine suddenly emerged from the water. We were startled that the water so near our village beach was deep enough for a submarine and amazed that the vessel should be there. The air-raid sirens began to wail and the radio told us the planes were coming over the Izu and Sagami Bay district. I thought, "This is it," but the underwater craft submerged just before the planes came in sight and the bay was smooth when the planes went over.

We learned of a vacant room in a farmer's house in the mountains of Nagano and Terry set off at once to see it. I feared for him to make such a hazardous journey in his feeble state, but there was nothing else to be done. I was really sick myself for the first time—my "hundred days cough" was nothing compared with this. I had taken a bad cold and it had gone into flu, so I went to bed. My depression and lassitude made life appear totally unsupportable. Mako was too young to do much of the housework alone, and Mrs. Brasch kindly came over to help her. I lay looking at the beauty of the land and sea and thought long black thoughts.

One night Mrs. Brasch went to the village and bought a *buri* (yellowtail fish) which she carried, under cover of darkness, to us. She was strong enough to come back up that hill with the sixty-pound fish strapped on a rack on her shoulders. We ate the fish voraciously and I began to feel somewhat better. When Terry returned in a few days, I was able to be up and about. I was glad he had not seen me so weak and unhappy.

One place he had found was half of a stable which we would have to share with a horse. At another place a farmer had offered two rooms on the condition that we would take care of his silkworms at their feeding time. Terry knew we could not sleep there because of the uneasy stir and clatter the worms constantly make. We had to remain where we were for the time being at least.

Many refugees were now coming through the village. They had no food but managed to feed the smaller children; the gaunt and wasted mothers, carrying fairly well-fed babies, struggled up the hill followed by bent old people riding pig-a-back on the shoulders of their sons. Some carried what few household goods they had salvaged from the flames.

It was during that blustery March that news reached us of "Baba" Kurusu, Ambassador Kurusu's only son. We felt very close to the Kurusu family. Alice Kurusu, Baba's mother, a beautiful and gallant person, was an American and for this reason our marriages had much in common. Speaking fluent Japanese, she was a brilliant hostess and a valuable asset to her husband's career. Kurusu himself was one of the most lovable of men; handsome, witty, and able, he was known affectionately as "Daddy" Kurusu among his close friends in Tokyo. They had two daughters, Pia and Jaye, and the one boy, Baba.

On their many trips they took the girls with them and put them in school in the country where they were posted, but they felt it was important that the son be educated in Japan and that his education not be interrupted. Alice Kurusu told me once how sad it was always to leave from the dock and to sail out into the bay while the one little boy waved goodbye from the shore. While the rest of the family was in Germany and Belgium and Italy, Baba remained. In military school he was very popular and intensely patriotic. When war came he was proud to fight for his country. But it remained his parents' wish that they might yet take him abroad to Europe and America.

He embodied a pride that reminded me of what Ambassador Sato's wife was reputed to have said to her small children when they evacuated Poland in 1939, making a dangerous overland journey to reach the *Terakuni Maru* at a neutral port. When asked how she "encouraged" the children, she said,

"I whispered to them, 'Remember you are Japanese!' "

When Ambassador Kurusu was sent to join Nomura in Washington in 1941, his family feared that members of the war party might attempt to assassinate him lest he succeed in making the peace with America that the moderates hoped for. On the day he left, Baba arose before dawn and drove him to the airport. All went well, and at the airport they were met by a number of officials of high rank who had gathered to wish the Ambassador Godspeed. Baba went aboard the plane with his father and returned the officers' salutes snappily, with inward pleasure that the navy "brass" should have to salute a mere lieutenant in the army. The rivalry between the two services was intense.

After the beginning of the war, Baba rose to captain in the Army Air Force. An aircraft designer and engineer, he had been frank in criticizing the overly academic approach of the Japanese engineers. His patriotism was beyond question so he felt free to speak of the superiority of Yankee design which he hoped one day to surpass.

The news of Baba's death was contained in the *Nippon Times* for Monday, March 5, 1945. Terry read it:

CAPT. KURUSU MEETS HEROIC END IN
COMBAT WITH ENEMY AIRCRAFT

Gallant Officer, Despite Mortal Wounds, Lands Plane
and Makes Report; Designing of Super-Craft to
Defeat B-29 Cherished Till Last

Succumbing to wounds sustained in a clash with the enemy ship-based planes that attacked Japan on February 16, Captain Ryo Kurusu, technical engineer pilot of the Inspection Department of the Army Aircraft Research Institute, and the only son of Saburo Kurusu, former Envoy Extraordinary and Ambassador Plenipotentiary, met glorious death in action.

Upon receiving information that enemy ship-based planes were over the Japanese mainland on February 16, Captain Kurusu left a certain air base aboard his favorite plane. Arriving over Yachimata, Chiba Prefecture, he met a group of 30 Grumman planes. He at once gave battle to the raiders and in a fight with eight of them, he shot down one.

Though he himself was hit by enemy bullets, he never once left the control lever. Putting forth the last ounce of his strength, he piloted his plane safely back to the base and made a complete report to the commander of the unit to which he belonged before breathing his last.

Unlike other test pilots he used to plan new planes while busying himself at the control lever of his own plane. With the wealth of experience gained in actual combat with other Japanese Army airmen against B-29's, he was thus able to work toward the planning of new crack planes for Japan.

That Captain Kurusu, up to the last, was mentally engaged in the planning of a crack plane, which in efficiency would be unlike any already in existence, is proved by the fact that his dying words were: "Planning! Planning!"

The death of Captain Kurusu, the first technical engineer pilot to die in aerial combat, is bound to stimulate to a great degree the entire world of aviation technique in Japan.

A certain lieutenant of the Army Aviation Headquarters, spoke to the press about Captain Kurusu as follows:

"I have no recollection of technical engineer pilots more faithful to their work than Captain Kurusu. It is to be regretted that even the screws which are designed in Japan do not compare with those made by American designers. The cause of this very deplorable state of things is that a large proportion of Japanese technical engineer pilots are incapable of piloting a plane.

"A screw made according to desk plan can have no soul. Therefore, it is not strange that a new plane using desk-made screws often tends to go wrong. Moreover, it is difficult to restore such planes when they develop trouble.

"Captain Kurusu from the first had no doubt on this point. His wish was to produce a plane which would outstrip the product of the brains of the B-29 designer.

"He used to say to his friends:

" 'The designer of the B-29 changed from a test pilot to an engineer pilot. In his mind he linked together the conceptions of fighting and designing. The result of his work, done in accordance with such a way of thinking, was the B-29, the Super Flying Fortress. I do not like to be beaten by that designer. Depend upon it, I will design a plane which will overshadow the B-29!' "

Terry broke off, tears in his eyes, "What a waste! What wishful thinking! Poor Baba!"

Then he read on, about the hopefulness of the "certain lieutenant" that Baba's example would not be lost on Japanese aerial technicians. The concluding paragraph concerned Baba's being born in the United States in 1919.

Japanese law requires that the dead be cremated immediately, but the officer in charge, knowing that Captain Kurusu had a foreign mother, ordered that the body be held for her to decide how it should be disposed of. Jaye, the dead man's sister, was in

Tokyo and went out to be with her brother's body. Kurusu was some distance away when he was informed, and he went by train to the airdrome. As a civilian, he had to make way for shipments of military personnel and it took him five hours to go from Tokyo to Tachikawa. When he arrived, he was ushered into the room where his son's body was lying. What thoughts of the mission of 1941 he must have held!

We wept for days. Terry repeated to me the Japanese poem of the death of a little boy who caught dragon flies by weaving an ever-narrowing circle about them with his fingers until they sat dazed and helpless. The mother sang:

> How far, how far, today
> Has gone my little
> Hunter of the dragon fly.

11

HUNGER IN THE MOUNTAINS

ONE of our friends from the Shanghai days wrote us that he was coming to visit. When he arrived he told us of his little *bessō* (summer house) in the mountains of Nagano Prefecture above Suwa City. Yes, we could have it; he wanted us to enjoy it and to take care of it for him during his absence.

Again we began to pack, this time under the pressure of making an immediate move. Mako's teacher stayed with me three days and we hired a Mr. Kato, a fisherman from the nearby village, to help with the heavy work. He was an able fellow and took charge of the whole moving operation, managing to send our belongings by rail on the last car allowed to carry nonmilitary freight. Our furniture and several trunks of household goods were left with friends for storage. Seeing the train depart so laden filled me with a wistful sense of abandonment and of last ditch desperation.

Everyone helped us. The Germans stayed up the entire last night before we left helping with odds and ends. Our Japanese neighbors cooked an *o bentō* (boxed lunch) for each of us, packing them with rice balls, roast dried fish, and pickled radish. We were up at dawn to breakfast at the Brasch's, and then we shouldered our packs, Mako carrying her two birds, I with the *o bentō* and all the neighbors trailing behind—the clack-clack of their wooden clogs echoing through the hills and across the waters of Sagami Bay. We turned around and looked once more at our little house nestled among the spring blossoms. Our eyes again beheld the majesty of Nangoyama, serene and aloof in the background, and we whispered *sayōnara* to the Seven Jewels of Izu. I have never known a more beautiful spot.

Our train coughed and sputtered, and with a mighty effort we were off. Our friends waved goodbye, running along beside the train a little way.

The trip was pleasant enough as the countryside was abloom with spring. Japan really looks like the old Japanese prints. There is that misty, elusive quality about it. As in Japanese art and poetry, the scenery suggested more than it revealed.

I was having my first experience eating with chopsticks on a moving train. From necessity our lunch was Japanese and eating rice balls with one's fingers is a very messy business, but the rice balls will also slip from chopsticks. The passengers around me made a delighted audience.

Our car was packed with travelers and one had to arrange his bundles and parcels so that the aisle was comparatively free for the standing people. At each station someone got on but it seemed no one ever got off. We had the same idea—survival— and were silent. A baby cried, *"Benjo, benjo* (toilet),*"* and when the mother realized she could not go through the car to the rest room she tried vainly to hush the child. The little girl wailed with more persistence. A woman suggested we all hand the child along over the seats and this we did, until near the end when the child let go and one resourceful passenger thrust her little bottom out the window. She was handed back, dripping, to her mother, but not a person laughed and we settled back again to the business of getting to our destination.

Mako was tired and dark circles had come under her eyes. I

knew she was frightened because she kept her trusting gaze directly on my face. She knew the trains were being bombed and had overheard that foreigners were not allowed on trains except by special permission. Every new conductor or railway employee would stop at my seat and ask to see my permit. Terry patiently explained my status and showed his Foreign Office card. Each time it was a relief when they passed on.

We were fortunate, however, and made the trip to Kofu without having to get off the train and yield our seats to the soldiers. This happened to others fairly often, and the hapless travelers sometimes had to spend days along the way.

At Kofu we changed trains. As we waited on the platform for our little *densha* into the mountains, we found ourselves suddenly surrounded by the dreaded *kempei tai*. Terry responded to their question, "Who's the foreigner?"

"She is no foreigner, she's my wife."

I could not avoid being reminded of the old joke, "That wasn't no lady, that was my wife." They wanted to know where we were going, how many pieces of luggage we had, and the age of the *okusama*. They put the information in their important-looking little notebooks and abruptly departed.

Mako and I took a walk along the station platform and I noticed a tall, distinguished Japanese who seemed vaguely familiar. He walked with a cane and I bethought myself that it was Prince Konoye, the former Premier and protégé of Saionji. Would we have been spared this if Roosevelt had agreed to meet him in the Pacific in 1941?

The wailing of the sirens began and I thought at last we were caught in a bombing. Kofu was a railway terminal of importance and was bound to be attacked sooner or later. Mako's anxious eyes pleaded with me not to let the planes come. Her long pigtails were swaying to and fro, and in each hand she carried a bird-cage. We walked in silence to where Terry stood guard over our luggage, heard the planes throbbing by, and saw them cast a shadow across the sun.

An unutterable sadness encompassed me that we should die

159

so near our refuge. A prayer escaped me, "God, don't let it happen."

The planes flew on. My knees went weak and I had to sit down. Two weeks later the bombers struck Kofu and devastated it.

Our *densha* came along and we hastened aboard amid shovings and pushings. Many of the people had been on foraging trips and had large rucksacks on their backs full of food. Often police boarded the trains and confiscated the food carried by the people; this was especially resented because one had to exchange some treasured possession for the food which the farmers would not sell for money. The farmers were tired of the refugees that poured from the broken cities, dirty, ragged and hungry, and the city people thought the farmers were turning the war into a profit-making scheme, exacting exorbitant prices for their produce.

Our station was Chino, where the *densha* stopped for only a few minutes. It was a scramble for us to get off and unload our luggage onto the platform before the whistle blew. Terry had engaged a charcoal-burning taxi for the climb up the mountain, a trip that took two and one-half hours on foot. We had written ahead to the resort hotel at the village of Tateshina for a room until we could get settled at the summer house.

Our taxi emitted a volume of smoke and fumes but slowly climbed the mountain. I felt sick from the fumes and realized our birds would die if we did not hold them out of the windows.

We must have looked strange on our arrival at the hotel, grim, covered with soot from the train and the charcoal-burning taxi, with two bird-cages swinging crazily from the windows. The villagers, astonished enough at this, immediately remarked at the foreigner. I knew I would remain the *gaijin* for the duration of my sojourn in their community. They were tolerant and rather patronizing, thinking I was a little "off," but they treated me kindly.

We slept three days, only getting up to eat our meals in our room. It was my first experience sleeping with the *kotatsu* (sunken fireplace with a coverlet). The maids laid out our mattresses so that our feet would be tucked under the quilt that covered the frame over the sunken area where the ashes held smoldering charcoal. In this way we slept warm all night but at the risk of asphyxiation if we got our heads under the covers. The fumes would render one unconscious in a short time. My feet became too warm, and I spent the night putting them out to cool and then tucking them back into the bed to be roasted.

We had a lovely room, with a balcony looking out over the snow-capped peaks of the "Little Alps." One thing I remember vividly about our room; one wicker chair on our balcony had a mountain-goat's skin spread over it. When one sat down on it the short horns would jab into one's back, and besides the horns I disliked the expression on Mr. Goat's face. I took the skin off, folded it neatly and covered the chair with a *furoshiki*, but invariably when we returned from a walk or bathing we would find the skin back on the chair. This went on during our entire stay at the hotel.

After we had rested we went up the road to our little house. Perched on the side of the mountain, it overlooked the valley toward the snow-capped peaks beyond. It was built in the Western style except for two Japanese rooms, and it was light and airy and convenient. There were six built-in bunks and a tiny bathroom—but it was completely unfurnished and we did not know whether our things would reach us or not. We had only our clothes and what we could carry with us. Wondering whether any furniture would reach us, we began cleaning the house, going up every day to clean and scrub and then returning to the hotel for the night. In less than a week the caretaker brought us the welcome news that our things had arrived at Chino after all; and we immediately asked him to have them brought to the house.

When the truck came puffing up the mountain with our belongings, a storm was brewing and large raindrops were starting to fall. The driver and his helper put our things, plunk, down by the roadside, refusing to carry them up the footpath to our house. They drove away and left us there with our few chairs, bedding, and trunks exposed to an approaching downpour. While we stood beside the road wondering what to do, we heard voices close by.

In the village of Tateshina there was a camp for young men who had been found physically unfit to enter military service. This camp was conducted by the government to rebuild health and teach the young men discipline and military life. They received extra rations and had expert medical attention. They were obliged to raise all their own vegetables and cut wood for the cooking and the making of charcoal.

The men from the camp came marching by returning from a wood-cutting expedition. One asked Terry, "What's the trouble?"

Terry pointed to our furniture and then to the gathering clouds and said,

"Don't you see? The end of the road; our things are to be ruined."

The noncom in charge immediately spoke up, "We'll fix that." He yelled to the boys, "Shall we help them?"

"Yes," they replied in a chorus.

There were about thirty of them and the job was quickly finished before the rain came. They suggested that each piece be put where I wanted it permanently. We put up the big bed, unrolled the rugs, and stored the trunks away in the storage room. They were greatly interested in me and very curious about the Simmons bed. The springs and inner-spring mattress caused considerable comment and each man had to have a bounce on the bed. We rolled out the *amado* (heavy wooden doors), locked the house, and walked back to the hotel. I thanked them all in my very best Japanese.

The next day we really moved into our house and spent our first night there. We soon had our rooms in order and we put our birds on the veranda where their song could mingle with that of the lark and the *hōjiro* (Japanese bunting). I placed my yellow Chinese lamp on the table, my wing chair near it, and my Peking glass flowers in a bowl and considered myself very lucky to have a place so homelike.

162

HUNGER IN THE MOUNTAINS

We had not been in our new home a week before we realized our biggest problem would be food. The farming district of Tateshina was more than two hours and a half on foot down the mountain. A day or two after moving in, we heard voices in our garden and there were eight young men of the group who had helped us move in, busily spading up our small garden. Terry went out and they told him there was still time to put in vegetables. We planted turnips, *daikon* (radishes), and beans. With much bargaining and two pairs of Terry's socks, we were able to procure potatoes for planting. We needed help and advice, never having raised anything in our lives except flowers. The soil was rocky and the stones we had to remove formed a huge pile. We worked furiously, having to stop often and rest because of our undernourished condition.

The bread that I had brought with me from Manazuru had been used up. We had no flour and were on a rice diet. We had dried soy beans, *shōyu* sauce, and butter, part of the supply I had gotten through the Germans. We had a box full of canned goods but we were saving this against the approaching winter. Our rations consisted only of rice and sauce, and now and then some dried fish. The fish had such a hideous smell that I could not endure the thought of our eating it, hungry as we were. I threw it out to the voracious little field mice who scampered across our yard, their lean bodies showing every rib. Our rice ration was delayed each month so that there were as many as ten days to two weeks when every family had to forage for something to fill in. We learned to chop carrots, potatoes, or turnip tops to boil with the rice. The Japanese called this gruel-like stew *zōsui* and ate it with much complaint.

For breakfast we had boiled rice mixed with soy beans fried in butter, and we drank black tea without milk or sugar. I had about a cup of sugar and one one-pound can of Klim powdered milk that I had been saving to use in case of further illness. Breakfast was the meal that I minded most. The only food I used to long for was corn flakes. I had never been particularly fond of corn flakes but breakfast had always been my favorite meal and the thought of a cereal came repeatedly to mind. Enough toilet soap was another thing I missed. In my dreams I was always in a large department store with shelves and shelves of toilet soap and corn flakes.

Before our little garden began to yield anything green to eat we used to search for wild edible greens. Our neighbors showed us the ones we could eat safely. We found that the wild onions, a cross between garlic and our garden variety, were very tasty but they were so small that they could only serve as seasoning. As I am very susceptible to insect bites, I always wore long-sleeved shirts and slacks, or *monpe*, and a scarf over my head when we went searching for mountain vegetables. I seemed to have a talent for putting my hands on crawling things and half of the time I was crashing down the mountain, fleeing in terror from centipedes or snakes.

On one of these trips, far up on our mountain, we came upon a wild clover field and its discovery was one of the most enchanting experiences of my life. Its fragrance permeated the air. We could hear the hum of insects and the laughter of a waterfall nearby. Behind us along the horizon rose the jagged, snow-tipped peaks of Nagano's famous mountains. Mako and I sat down with Terry in the midst of that clover and gave ourselves to the day. Far down the valley the air-raid sirens wailed but up there it did not seem to matter. We returned that evening to our house almost empty handed but in good spirits. This reminded me of one of my friends in Tokyo who had searched the shops endlessly for a bit of food. Not finding any, she had bought half a dozen roses. When her weary husband, coming home in the evening, remarked on the beauty and fragrance of the roses, she said, "I am glad you like them; they are what we are having for dinner."

The only vegetable that seemed to thrive on our mountain ledge was the turnip. We ate not only the turnip but the leafy top. The Japanese are very fond of simply-cooked greens and, having no supplies, I could cook only in their manner. They wash them and cook them in a pot with the lid fastened tightly, using only the water that clings to the leaves. Afterwards the vegetable is cooled, drained, chopped into intricate shapes, and usually garnished with shredded bonito. We saved our butter for breakfast and there was never enough *shōyu* sauce for seasoning.

The three of us were growing much weaker. I had lost my physical energy and suffered from a mental lethargy which made me very forgetful. When one starves slowly, it is not a spectacular thing, a great yearning for food and craving to eat. One is content to sit in the sun and do nothing; one even forgets that there is anything to do. One loses control of tears and lets them roll unheeded down one's cheek. It took me at least forty minutes to an hour every morning to comb my hair. My arms ached if I kept them up to my head for more than a minute or so. I had to stop and rest several times before I was finished. Mako's hair was another chore. Her long pigtails reached almost to her waist, and since she could not do them herself and I was unable to do them for her, we finally had to cut them off.

A very fine doctor, who was suffering from high blood pressure, lived in the village. When he evacuated from Tokyo, he had brought his supply of medicines with him, keeping it buried against the day when our mountain retreat might be bombed. In Japan one often receives one's medicines from the doctor. He usually has a large supply on hand and has his own dispensary connected with his office. We found that the doctor had Vitamin B Complex shots and I began taking them every day.

I had been taking the shots for about a week and was beginning to feel somewhat stronger when Mako awoke from her sleep one night, crying with pain. She had a fever and was suffering intensely. Terry had to go down the mountain at midnight carrying his little *chōchin* (lantern with a candle) to get the doctor. I was in a terrible state of anxiety as Mako wept with the pain which she said was "all over." I felt helpless and fearful, fearful of what would happen if my only child should be seriously ill so far from a hospital.

The two men with high blood pressure had to trudge up the mountain in the darkness with only the flickering light from their lantern to show the way. Terry told me that the tiny light from our little house looked like a small star strayed from the heavens. I waited with Mako until I heard the voices of the men approaching. The ailing doctor was exhausted by his climb and had to rest before examining our little girl. His hands were trembling violently as he adjusted his stethoscope.

He told us that Mako had either typhoid or dengue fever. The next twenty-four hours would tell the tale. The thought of typhoid was a shock. In her undernourished condition she would have little chance to fight it off. The doctor gave her a shot to ease the pain and told me how to care for her. He promised to return next morning soon after breakfast. Terry left again to accompany the doctor, lest he fall along the way.

Mako had dozed off with the sedative and I sat near her looking at her thin little face. Marked by hunger, overwork, and illness, it was dreadfully mature for a twelve-year-old. I closed my eyes and imagined her riding a pony across a green field, her hair flying and joy in her face. I saw a swimming pool and Mako lazily slipping through the water with the sun smiling down at her. I saw a circus, with elephants, a calliope, a high-stepping clown, ice cream cones, and boxes of sweet popcorn with treasures inside. Those are the things a child needs. I prayed that night, "Oh, God, don't let her die before she has seen some beauty."

When Terry returned, he tried to encourage me by telling me that the doctor thought that by morning he would surely find that Mako had dengue fever. He had told Terry that it would not be as serious as it would be painful and that it should not last more than a week.

The next morning, I opened the can of powdered milk and began to use the last bit of sugar. I had a small bottle of vanilla flavoring and one of lemon, so I made milk shakes flavored with first one and then the other.

The doctor arrived to find Mako racked with pain and delirious. He diagnosed her sickness definitely as dengue fever and began to treat her accordingly. At this I relaxed a bit and devoted myself to making her as comfortable as possible.

166

We played make-believe and I acted out plays for her. We had read over and over again all the books and old magazines in the house—even the old *New York Times* we had used for packing at White Sulphur Springs. We enjoyed the book review section and tried to fill out the stories of the books. We made lists of new books we wanted when the war ended. We read poetry—Mako loved Poe's "The Bells" and learned to recite much of it. She lay there in intense pain, saying over and over, "The ringing and the dinging of the bells."

Depressed by the close quarters of our little house, I went out while she slept one afternoon to the bare ledge at the side of the building. There, near enough that I could hear Mako if she should awake, was a moss-covered rock on which I liked to sit. The sky was clear and at first I could see far into the deep valley below but, inevitably, the white ocean of clouds appeared and began its habitual, silent advance up the slopes. It approached stealthily nearer and nearer, nothing could withstand it; implacably it came on, filling the hollows and shallows of the land. As I watched, a distant witness, it came upon a farmer peacefully chopping wood far below. Without pause, it moved over him; the glinting blade of his axe disappeared and the farmer was gone. Only opaque nothingness remained. Now it had taken the lower hills, blotting out their color as if all the warmth and joy of the world was to be forever absorbed in its dull white mass. About its shores, tall trees stood for a moment against the onslaught, then without a sound they too yielded. Submerging all things, it rolled effortlessly on and reached the base of the cliffs below. The cliffs began to melt into the all-embracing host, which inexorably reached higher until only the peak of our hill remained, a tiny island encircled by a sea of white. In a few moments more of unequal warfare it would overwhelm the island as it had reduced everything below. The all-engulfing mist would then conquer our little house and the desolation would be absolute. A sense of urgency drew me up from my seat and I made my way back to the sick room before the clouds should reach the house.

I do not know how the days went by but in a week our child

was better. On the first day she sat up, I retired to my room and and a good cry. Sometimes tears can bring joyous relief. I bathed, powdered my face, and brushed my hair before going out on my small balcony to watch the splendor of a Tateshina sunset. The gold and red sky blazed over the mists, and here and there one could see smoke rising from a *konro* being freshly lit for evening rice.

The weeks passed but we hardly noticed. We were continually busy and could never relax. We had to go down to the village for our rations twice a week and it took us at least an hour to climb back up our mountain with the heavy rice strapped on our backs. Charcoal was hard to get so we cooked our rice in the garden with twigs and leaves. A crude stove was all we had, and on rainy days cooking was a heartbreaking chore. I finally managed to cover a small table, which we had on our tiny back porch, with tin by beating tin cans flat and tacking them down with my precious supply of tacks from Woolworth's, bought so long ago in Washington, D.C. I put the stove on the table and was able to cook the rice on rainy days without getting soaking wet.

More and more the authorities called on the people to give time to the war effort. Someone had found that fuel for airplanes could be manufactured from the resin of pine trees, and each family in the countryside was required to extract a certain amount of it to be turned over to the local *chōkai* (town assembly). Terry and Mako were called to that duty but their efforts resulted in the smallest amount of resin collected by any family in our neighborhood association.

Terry had always been opposed to the whole idea of a *kamikaze* corps, saying that if a country had to use such methods to continue, it should give up. The pine-tree tapping for fuel also depressed him, and he kept muttering, "How long, how long?"

Our little garden had started to yield green beans and a few *daikon*. We were especially proud of one perfect *daikon*, and gave it a place of honor in our living room. We admired it until it became too shrivelled to eat.

168

HUNGER IN THE MOUNTAINS

The air-raid sirens let us know that American planes now flew over Nagano more frequently. One day we heard that Matsumoto, a city in our prefecture, had been bombed. We also heard by the grapevine that the Japanese army had planned its last stand in the foothills of Nagano. One discounted three-fourths of what one heard, as a fresh rumor skipped about every day. Our newspapers came irregularly and the static in our mountains made it almost impossible to hear news broadcasts. But we knew that the cities of Japan were being bombed steadily and even in our remote village what at first was a trickle of refugees became a flood.

From our mist-covered hill if one stopped and listened to the quiet, one could almost hear the blood flowing throughout the warring world, gurgling like the little mountain streams that ran down the slopes. It may have been a good thing that our daily lives were so taken up with keeping alive. Starvation was always near and threatening, although we continued each day to stave it off. I thought of the "Song of Hiawatha" and the three unwanted guests in the wigwam of the old Nokomis who fastened their hot eyes on the lovely Minnehaha. We felt those eyes and were just able to keep our unwanted guests in the shadows.

One morning we were awakened by a young boy knocking on the *amado*. When my husband unlatched the door and pushed it back, he found it was the son of one of our neighbors. The boy told us that his mother had died and, because the crematorium in the village had closed for lack of fuel, the family would have to cremate the body themselves. Each family in the neighborhood association was asked to donate wood for that purpose. The body had to be carried to the town at the foot of the mountain to be cremated. I remember seeing the little procession start off down the slope carrying the corpse of the dead mother and the wood with which to burn her body. I could not understand why war-time expediency would not allow prewar regulations to be shelved so that the poor body could find a grave on the mountainside overlooking the valley. We later heard that the wood was so soaked by the recent rains that it would not burn.

169

I was saddened that those pitiful children were prevented from doing a last service to their parent.

To revive my spirits, Terry told me the story of a funeral that later became known all over Japan. It concerned a man who refused to eat anything but the official rations. He slowly starved while his family begged him desperately to eat food they had bought on the black market. He preferred death, and when he died they had his body burned in a cremation casket which they purchased—on the black market.

This ironic incident probably should not have made me feel better, but somehow it did. It was like the remark made to one who justifiably complains of hardship for which there is no cure, "Cheer up, things are a hundred times worse than you think they are!"

The refugees were called *sokaijin* (escaped to the country). A friend of Terry's furnished a remarkable example of someone very much *sokaijin*. He was a wealthy person who had collected Chinese art for many years and had a fine home furnished with beautiful carved furniture which he had painstakingly collected during a long sojourn on the mainland. His library contained many ancient scrolls of the T'ang dynasty in China, a period which the Japanese had regarded with awe for centuries. This gentleman had been forced to move repeatedly, and each time he was forced to pack away his delicate curios, his scrolls, and his carved furniture. They were not easily packed, and much care was required to ship them from one place to another without doing considerable damage. As it was, exercising every precaution that money and love could afford, a few mishaps occurred each time a change was made. On the first move this connoisseur had transported his possessions out of Tokyo and to a small suburb, then in a few months farther inland, then again, and yet again. In the early summer of 1945 he came to visit us at Tateshina in high spirits and announced happily to Terry,

"Terasaki-san, I have very good news. You know all my things that I have been moving and moving all over Japan? Well, they are all gone. A bomb hit my house and burned them all. I don't have to worry with them anymore. Only this small vase is left, and I have brought it to you so I can move freely once more!"

There is, I guess, such a thing as a spiritual "second wind."

I was getting weaker steadily, and the symptoms of malnutrition were becoming more evident day by day. Mako was thin to the point of emaciation, and the ribs stood out pitifully on Terry's once stocky chest. We had no energy beyond that needed to prepare our rice and keep our house and ourselves clean. My finger nails were almost gone, and I had to bandage my fingers to keep blood from getting on everything I touched.

Our Japanese bath had been built to burn *rentan* (synthetic coal) and coal, so we could not burn wood to heat the water. Although there was a public bath at the hotel for Terry, for Mako and me the public bath was out of the question. We managed with sponge baths and a kind of bucket shower. Later, Terry arranged with the hotel owner, by paying an extra fee, for Mako and me to bathe a half hour before the regular opening time. The owner would sit cross-legged like a big Buddha at the entrance and tell the customers, "Don't go in now, the *gaijin* is bathing." At this signal, everyone would rush to the windows and gape in at "the foreigner." Finally Terry prevailed on the owner to say simply, "The bath is not open yet." Then the crowd would wait docilely until the word was given, "*Dōzo o furo* (the bath is open)."

All our spare time was taken up in searching for food, or for people who had food to sell. How happy we were one morning to see Mr. Okura, an old friend from Karuizawa, arrive suddenly with a rucksack on his back! He had been walking for more than three hours and had been on a train that was bombed and machine-gunned. He had lost the way back to the train, and when the attack was over it had gone on without him. He had stumbled into a barracks for evacuated children and in the darkness had blandly climbed into bed with a little boy. He told us of their mutual astonishment upon awakening the next morning.

Our guest brought bread, flour, butter, and jam—and news of the outside world. We sat up most of the night as he talked of

171

Karuizawa and our friends there. He told us for the first time of the persistent rumor that Japan had sent out peace feelers.

Adoringly I held the loaf of bread in my hands, poor little loaf of black bread that it was, and we felt joy again. Not only did Mr. Okura bring news and food but he delivered a fat letter from my dear friend Hélène who had moved to Karuizawa. She told of life there where most of the foreign refugees had gone to escape the intensified bombings of Tokyo. Food was getting scarcer at Karuizawa also, but since the government gave special rations to foreign nationals, Hélène had fared better than we. However, they had not fared so well that she had not written, "Our children are healthier now as we have *daikon* again."

Mr. Okura had been on Terry's staff years before when he was Chargé d'Affaires in Havana, and we spent a second evening talking of Cuba and our life there. We spoke with warmth of the Cuban people, of their music, gay but with an undertone of sadness, their optimism and gusto. We saw Mr. Okura off next day with the hope that he would get home safely.

We had alerts very often, and now and then we could hear vague rumblings in the distance. The war was getting closer. More and more people were toiling up our mountain, heavily laden, searching for relatives or friends to give them shelter. Some of them had large burns on their faces and arms, and others, more severely injured, were carried on the backs of the men.

The rice ration was being held up more frequently, and we heard the devastating news that a large warehouse full of rice had burned and in its place we were to be rationed *kabocha* (pumpkin). It was like being told to eat squash instead of bread.

I continued to have vitamin shots, and soon Mako and Terry joined me. The search for food was never ending, and there were trips to the village for our rations, which made up in bulk what they lacked in food value and variety. Our potato crop was a failure. So was our corn crop. We had turnips every day and occasionally some green beans.

I made a kind of johnnycake from Mr. Okura's flour as long as it lasted. I put salt and water with the flour and mixed it into a dough. After pinching off a ball of dough, I would roll it flat and pierce it with a fork and bake it over the charcoals in a frying pan. It was tough and tasteless but we thought it delicious. We used to plan the days around "johnnycake days." I used to make several at a time and pack them in old coffee tins so that we would have two or three days' supply on hand. One day, hungry and exhausted after working outside all day, I made tea and decided to serve one johnnycake each. Mako asked in a small hungry voice, "Mommy, may I have one more?" I could not refuse and with choking voice declared, "Have all you want." We had an orgy of johnnycake as we gazed across the valley and over the jagged lines of our mountainous horizon. The next day we had to return to our *kabocha* diet. It was our last bread of any kind until the war ended.

Terry had been giving English conversation lessons to a young man who had been rejected for military service because he was tubercular. They had their conversations outdoors because Terry was afraid for the student to be near Mako and me. I frequently paused in my housework to hear their voices speaking in English and I realized how hungry I had become to hear my own language spoken. One day the young man arrived with a gift for me, and when I opened it I found with delight it was Dickens' *Tale of Two Cities*. I sat up all night reading it again. I believe that I missed reading matter almost more than I did food. Perhaps the *Tale of Two Cities* had a peculiarly strong appeal. It somehow strengthened me to live again the days of the French Revolution; I could understand, now, the terror of people forced to eke out their everyday existence against a backdrop of chaos. It came home to me that my experiences were more of a commonplace in history than I had thought.

The newspapers carried only victory stories and such headlines as, "Japan girds herself to give a knockout blow," but there were few people who did not know that Japan was almost at the end of the road. We discussed this with no one, as the *kempei tai* had agents everywhere and people were being questioned every day. Some of them were being sent to prison.

The meeting at Potsdam had taken place. The Japanese press was allowed to print the Potsdam Declaration with some deletions. Everyone was reading it and the discussion of it was welcomed as a little change in our monotonous routine.

Our own little private war with hunger and physical weakness continued. We had to think of the coming winter with its freezing weather high in the mountains. We realized that we must get a stove to burn the wood that we must saw each day and stack around our house. But first we needed to secure a saw.

We thought of the carpenter who did odd jobs for us and from whom we had secured a few vegetables and sometimes an egg. We had nicknamed him *"Hokane,"* (Mr. Ain't that so?) as he had a way of evading a direct answer to any question. He would roll his eyes to the ceiling, moan softly, and say, *"Sa-a-a."* After a long wait and much rolling of eyes and soft moanings we would finally get an answer of sorts. Perhaps he could help us obtain a saw. It took us three days with scores of cups of scalding green tea and much dwelling on all our deficiencies before we were able to arrange the business at hand. Think of all that metal just for one family's use! But he eventually promised to do his best and left after many bows and moanings.

After a week, his best was good enough for our purpose and we stood around admiring our new possession. If there is anything good to be found in war, it is the deep sense of gratitude that one feels on acquiring a much-needed thing that once was commonplace.

Mako could hardly wait until morning to go out and slay the forest. She spent most of the evening polishing and admiring the sharp teeth of the saw, putting it into its case and taking it out again.

Bright and early the next morning she was up and full of enthusiasm. She announced that she, and she alone, would provide wood for our heat in the cold days ahead. She wanted an *o bentō* (boxed lunch) and a rack to fit on her back for carrying the wood. She wore an American cowboy shirt, a cowboy hat, a pair of *monpe,* and Japanese rubber-soled shoes. With her precious new saw strapped to her waist and her rice balls and pickles snug in the *bentō bako* (lunch box), she set off with instructions not to go beyond calling distance.

Her mother, looking at her with compassion, burst out, "Mako, I have a hunch that some day we'll all go together to the opera. We'll buy you a red velvet gown to wear to it." (A red velvet gown was the epitome of my childhood dreams.) A long look passed between mother and daughter and, with a warm-eyed smile, she set out.

The morning passed swiftly and lunchtime was at hand. I had tried to keep my mind on my household routine, but as noontime drew near I decided to look for my little girl. I was sorry she had such hard labor to do and I wanted to tell her so. I crept up the mountain and stopped short as I heard Mako singing at the top of her voice. I could not see her at first but soon discovered that she was sitting high among the branches of a tall tree. She had eaten her *o bentō* there, and now was singing her exultation to the mountains and the trees. I slipped back down the path without speaking.

Daily she went about her task, and in a short time one whole side of the house had wood stacked against it. She was reading *The Scarlet Letter* in the evenings and we often read aloud to each other from the *Oxford Book of English Verse*. Her favorite evening entertainment, however, was to hear me talk about my childhood and school days.

My symptoms of malnutrition were becoming more pronounced, and as I walked around my house I sometimes had to hold to chairs for support when the spells of dizziness would strike me. I had to lie down often to rest and I learned to get up very slowly from bed or from a sitting position—otherwise, I "blacked out." Once I fell against the wall, cutting my lip. We did nothing unnecessary and only waited.

The doctor told Terry that I must have some nourishing food as the vitamin shots that he was giving me were not enough to keep me out of the second stage of malnutrition. He suggested chicken. He might as well have suggested humming-birds' tongues.

We knew that our "Mr. Hokane" now and then had an egg to spare. He must have chickens! We sent word to him by the grapevine route and when he came a few nights later, we began the long and tedious negotiation for a chicken. Terry said at the time that full diplomacy had to be brought to bear and he believed that never in his life had he been more alert to the use of persuasive words. The carpenter said, yes, he and his wife had an old hen past her laying days. He would talk to the *okāsan* and see if she could be persuaded to sell her. The hen in question was a fine white hen and the *okāsan* was rather fond of her. On and on for a long afternoon the discussion continued, while the mist swirled around our house.

A few days later Terry showed signs of an unnatural fatigue and could not stop yawning. Knowing his blood pressure was very high, I feared a cerebral hemorrhage and put him to bed. He seemed to be almost in a coma as the day wore on, and by evening I was terrified. There was nothing for Mako and me to do but go down to the village for the faithful doctor. I was too weak to start out alone and anyway I needed Mako to interpret for me. I was afraid to leave Terry alone high up on our ledge but there was nothing else to do. We lit the candle in our little *chōchin* and left, disappearing into the night. The mist enveloped us and we crept along, minding never to get off the path as we could see only a step or two ahead. The flickering candle cast long shadows which seemed to jump and dance a macabre fandango. I had to rest every few minutes, but after hours of darkness we neared the house of the doctor. At two o'clock in the morning a shuttered and sleeping Japanese house seems like a fortress bulwarked against the night. We beat with our hands against the wooden *amado*. The doctor's wife's voice came to us with the customary, "*Hai, hai* (Yes, yes)," and I sank down on the steps to wait for her to pull the doors back. She awakened her husband. He knew by my face and said simply, "*Ikimashō* (Let's go)."

The three of us inched our feeble way up the steep mountainside. Mako, stronger than I, walked ahead with the *chōchin*. The doctor, himself ill, had to walk with care and I brought up the rear. At last we reached our house to have the door opened for us, surprisingly, by our friend the carpenter. He had arrived late in the night with our much sought after black-market hen. I asked him to wait. After a swift examination the doctor said that Terry was on the verge of a stroke and since he had no medicines for that, we would have to "bleed" him as an emergency measure. He gave orders for boiling water and towels. The lights were so dim that Mako had to stand near the doctor with the lamp in one hand and the doctor's flashlight in the other. We forgot about the carpenter during our grim business until at length a muffled exclamation brought him to our attention. The sight of blood had made him deathly sick and he had covered his face with both hands. Now and then he took an agonized peek between his fingers. While he sat dismayed in the dimly-lit room, the burlap sack in which he had brought the hen began with slow jerks to move across the floor. Of a sudden I realized I had fallen into uncontrollable, almost hysterical, laughter. Mako was shouting with me, and for a few moments we could not stop. The doctor, unmoved, gave us a frigid stare and waited for us to pull ourselves together. Terry's eyes had a twinkle in them as he whispered, "You couldn't help it, could you?" He was given an injection to make him sleep and in the early dawning light the doctor left.

We paid the carpenter and acquired one frightened white hen. I could see at once why the *okāsan* had a fondness for her, and Mako began pleading with us not to kill the hen. She named her "Henrietta" and fed her our few meager scraps. I promised to keep Henrietta at least until she was fatter; feeding her added to another very real problem—bird seed for our two songbirds. The supply was getting lower and lower. Frantically, we asked everyone we knew; they looked at us with dull, uncomprehending eyes, "No bird seed? Isn't that too bad? We have no milk for our babies. Why don't you eat the birds?" The bizarre news that the *gaijin* wanted bird seed for her pets was spread about quickly and one day a farmer came up our mountain with *awa* (millet), a tiny grain suitable for birds. The price was high but it was worth it. We had had only a teaspoon of bird seed left. By this time, Mako had grown very fond of Henrietta and would take her out walking on a leash. To augment her diet, Terry would catch dragonflies which he would hold above Henrietta's head and she would jump like a dog to get them. Mako's life was so bare of fun or companionship that we could not bring ourselves to put Henrietta in a pot. It is no wonder that the village people considered us a strange family. In desperate war-time, here was a hungry family scouring the countryside for bugs to feed a hen that goes out walking on a leash and paying an enormous price for seed for two birds in a cage. I knew the doctor certainly took a dim view of my sanity. Vitamins, indeed!

Mako one day brought a letter to her father on her return from the daily trip to the village post office that told of the strange bombing of Hiroshima. The letter was from a newspaper-man, an old friend of many years. Of course, he did not know that it was an atomic bomb but he did know it was something extraordinary. He added as a post script, "As yet we know of no defense against this new and terribly destructive weapon." We discussed this all day and remembered that years before in Shang-hai a European Buddhist monk had told us one evening that he foresaw a bomb so powerful that it could wipe out an entire city—a bomb that would change the course of history, that would create an era of fear of total destruction of civilization. At the time we had thought the monk was mad, but on this August day in 1945 we remembered his predictions and were afraid.

Terry and I were constantly talking it over. Believing much of the talk of the *Yamato* spirit, I thought that Japan would fight until the entire country was destroyed, the Japanese people broken and almost extinct. Terry disagreed and insisted that among Japanese statesmen there were realists who had a true love of country and the welfare of the people at heart. I remember asking him once how he thought the Japanese government should ap-proach the Allies, through Russia or Switzerland. His reply was quick.

"Never! Go to the United States directly, and lay our cards on the table. Americans are good sports, and if we are direct and sincere, it saves time. The Russians should have no part in it."

The very next day when Mako returned breathless from the village, panting from her run up the hill, with the news that Russia had gone into the war against Japan, Terry looked at me and said, "Now the change in world politics will be swift and ruthless. Japan is beaten already. Russia has only come in for the kill; the Four Horsemen will ride across the night." Underneath their despair the Japanese felt a smoldering resentment against the Russians.

We learned that the Americans were dropping leaflets that were masterpieces of insight and knowledge of the Japanese, of their poetry and psychology, their love of nature. Few Japanese got to read them for the military had given orders to turn them over at once to the nearest police box and not to repeat what was written on them. Yet the contents of the leaflets were passed by word of mouth and even far up in the hills we had learned of the messages. It had been reported that the Emperor himself picked up one of the leaflets in the palace garden.

It was August 15, 1945. We struggled through breakfast, a bowl of rough cereal (a kind of oatmeal) with salt to season it. While we were drinking our tea an excited, urgent call came from the entrance, "Terasaki-san, Terasaki-san, *ohayō gozaimasu!* (Good morning)." Terry and Mako rushed to the door and were told that orders were for members of the entire *tonarigumi* to assemble at the home of the *kumichō* because the Emperor, for the first time in history, was to speak over the radio. The speech was scheduled at 10 A.M. I heard the clack, clack of the messenger's wooden *geta* as he went on to the next house.

Terry dropped into a chair. Mako and I went up to him. Clasped tightly in our three-way embrace, he sobbed, "It is over; no more bloodshed, at last, at last, my poor country!"

I told him, "I'm sure it is not surrender. His Majesty will only tell us to fight on to the last man and die."

Mako spoke up, "I don't want to die."

Terry, looking gently on her, said, "The Emperor will not waste his time to reiterate what others have said. He will say something different."

As Terry was still weak from his illness, I told Mako to accompany him to the house of the *kumichō* which was farther up the mountain. Feeling that I, the *gaijin*, had no place there, I announced that I would remain at home. I told Terry that if it was really surrender, on returning he should lift his hand as he came around the corner on the high crest where I could first see him. Otherwise there would be no sign. I watched them as they walked slowly across the garden, around the bend, and up until they were out of sight. Alone, I wanted to cry out. There was no sound but the "dree, dree, dree" of the *semi* (cicada) and then the "coo, coo" of the mourning doves. All my thoughts were with Terry. His bitterness was two-fold. His country was defeated in a war that he had never believed in. A needless war. He had not been himself these past four years. His previous life had been one of hard work, contributing steadily to the cause of Japanese statesmanship with ability, energy, and optimism, always without display. Pearl Harbor had shaken him radically and for these four years he had been a sick man. His wretchedness was the measure of his quality; he felt boredom at this enforced leisure to the extent of his fine intellect and his frustration was fed by nobility of spirit. Now, perhaps, he could return to his work.

I looked across the beautiful valley, watched the sun playing with the shadows, and hoped that if we had to die it would be here on a mountain in Nagano.

After a timeless wait I moved out onto our little porch where I could see the high crest in the bend of the road. Our two birds kept up a smart conversation from their swinging cages, responding to the chant of the *semi*. A snake, startled for a moment, made his way across a large flat rock and lost himself in the tall autumn grasses nearby. First to the horizon and then up to the bend in the road went my anxious gaze.

Terry appeared and raised his hand, little Mako silent beside him. It was peace.

180

12

BEARING THE UNBEARABLE

I RAN down the path to meet my husband and child and the three of us walked hand in hand back to the house. We were silent.

Later in the afternoon Terry told me of the broadcast. Most of the twenty or so people who composed our *tonarigumi* were women and children; there were only two or three elderly men there and Terry; even the *kumichō* at whose house the meeting was held was a woman. One woman, her right leg bandaged to the hip, had fled the heavily bombed Kanda district of Tokyo with her grandchildren and her daughter-in-law; another woman in her forties had brought her five children to our mountains from the city. A few farm people from the region surrounding Tateshina were there. The children were afraid, awed and quiet; they kept close, huddling around their parents.

All were grave and solemn with unspoken wonder at two things: How would the Emperor's voice, which they had never in their lives heard, sound? What was their final destiny which the voice of the *tennō* would reveal?

They sat and listened intently when the high-pitched and quavering voice began. Leaning forward with brows furrowed and heads cocked to one side, they concentrated upon the sound. There was an eeriness about it, the way the people strained as if they were deaf, for the voice was loud enough and distinct; they heard the words easily as their future life or death was announced —but they could not understand. The Emperor spoke in Court Japanese and only Terry could comprehend.

As Terry translated and they grasped the sense of what was being said, that it meant surrender, the bandaged woman began to weep—not loudly or hysterically but with deep sobs that racked her body. The children started crying and before the Emperor had finished, all his people there were weeping audibly. The voice stopped. Silently the old men, the women, and their children, rose and bowed to each other and without any sound each went along the path leading to his own house.

The Emperor had told his people that he could not bear to see more of their suffering. He asked them to "bear the unbearable" and "suffer the insufferable," and to go about their daily tasks quietly and obediently, without bitter recriminations among themselves. With their traditional respect for authority the Japanese were able to hold together and simply wait until they were told what to do.

For a few days, a strange calm seemed to envelop us. A preoccupation dulled the reality of the routine jobs we had to do; we felt an expectancy, waiting for we knew not what. Many people climbed up our mountain to see us, and one enterprising *kumichō* asked me to talk to the women of his association on "Present Trends in America." I declined, telling him that I had had no news of home since the war started and had read no publications of recent date—I knew no more of the trends in America than he did. I did tell him, however, that I was sure the Americans were as happy as the Japanese that the war was over. The request surprised me, and I was to continue to be surprised at the turn of events just after the war. All the bitterness I heard expressed was

182

directed toward the military of Japan and those members of the civilian government who had actively helped the war party.

I had expected to hear of mass *harakiri* but it turned out that I was much mistaken. There were suicides, but nothing on the scale I had feared. The only group to suicide that I knew about was composed of certain officers who had unsuccessfully attempted to interfere with the Emperor's broadcast; others acted as individuals. The Chief of Staff, General Sugiyama, shot himself in his office, and upon hearing of his death, his wife donned her ceremonial kimono and took her own life in the traditional short-sword manner. The War Minister, Anami, also died by his own hand. In apology to the *kamikaze* dead, their commandant, Vice-Admiral Onishi, killed himself. He left a message which was printed in all the newspapers and widely read by the people:

> I speak to the spirits of the *kamikaze* boys. You have fought well. You have my abiding gratitude. You have died as Human Bullets, convinced of final victory which did not come true. I wish my death to express my regret and sorrow to you and to your loved ones left behind.
>
> To you young men living now in Japan:
>
> I shall be happy in the Beyond if my death will show you that any reckless action will only worry the Emperor. You must carry out His Majesty's wish. Bear the unbearable and do not lose pride in being Japanese. You are the treasures of Japan. Hold tight the *kamikaze* spirit and use it for the welfare of Japan and the peace of the world.

There was a stunned apathy on the faces of the people in the street. Everyone was starving; few had the physical stamina even to express their thoughts coherently. The people were shabby, hungry, and often physically unclean, being without fuel and soap for the bath that is the daily necessity and pleasure of every Japanese. There was sadness in every face and a kind of tired relief. They waited for what they had to face and seemed resigned to it.

One morning we heard a roar of planes and rushed out to our little veranda to see them. They were American planes. After they circled many times over the prisoner of war camp not many miles from our village, we saw that they were dropping colored parachutes of food-stuffs and medicines for the prisoners. Guiltily we wondered if one might fall near us. We sat all day watching them with streaming, tear-drenched faces. Terry, gripping my hand, wept for his destroyed land, and Mako cried to see her father and mother together in tears for the first time in her troubled life. For several days the steady roar of the planes continued as they dropped what looked to be veritable flower gardens of multicolored crates. So, it was final, the war was really over.

Mako's thirteenth birthday was at hand and we had nothing to give her, although I knew that the following year things would be better. I opened two cans from our stock saved up for the winter. I had a kind of Japanese gelatin and, with a can of peaches, I made a molded dessert. Then, feeling very reckless, I opened a can of salmon. We were to have a feast. Mako's principal gift was our promise that the hen, Henrietta, would live, and that if we moved back to Tokyo we would take her with us. In added celebration Henrietta proceeded to lay an egg. A beautiful, large, white egg, a luxurious, gladdening, remarkable thing. The first fresh egg for us in months. We three went out to bow formally to our hen for her bounty and it seemed to me there was a gleam of satisfaction in her henly eye. Now, we not only had a can of salmon but an egg to go with it. Mixing it all together, we had the means to cook salmon patties. Merrily I put on earrings, Mako wore a white dress, and Terry donned a red tie. The war was over. White clothing had been forbidden during the war because it was too easily seen from the air. When Mako put on white it was like a ship turning on lights again after running blacked-out since 1941.

In the midst of our festivities, we heard shouts and a hacking noise. We rushed to the door to see what was causing all the commotion and to our horror saw a young man brandishing a sword, yelling and striking every tree along his way. I was frightened and Terry closed the *amado*. Finally the man went on his way. We never found out who he was or why he was acting in this manner. I suppose he was meeting the defeat of his country in his own way. However, he had spoiled our day, and we soberly finished our peach mold and salmon patties.

At first the wild rumors of American depredations were astonishing. Mariko would return from the line of housewives at the rationing queues with the most shocking reports—where the women would be hidden to escape the oncoming rapists, and the like. We did not explain to her precisely what that meant but assured her that my people were not really to be feared. It turned out that the rumors had little substance and when news of the actual conduct of the American troops in Tokyo filtered back into our mountains to replace the ignorant though understandable fears of the people, I was greatly relieved. Many people came to tell us of things they had heard. They had all been apprehensive before the arrival of General MacArthur and the American forces, and they asked my husband what he thought the Americans would require of the Japanese. I remember very well one man saying to Terry, "Terasaki-san, do you think we will all be required to bow down before each and every American soldier?"

Terry replied,

"If so, I shall be the first Japanese to crack my forehead on the pavement. After all the Chinese in Shanghai and Peking that I have seen forced to kowtow before the Japanese soldiers, I hope to do the same with dignity."

We looked for a way to move back to Tokyo. Our doctor had urged Terry to try to find a place there for us to live because he did not believe that we could survive the rigors of a Nagano winter in our underfed condition. We required no urging. Terry was anxious to go back to assist in working out an occupation of mutual cooperation; I was anxious for Mako to make up for the time she had lost in school, and I needed again to see my friends, to talk women's talk. There were only peasant women nearby and I was starved for feminine companionship. Mako and I were great friends and without her I could not have kept alive my steady hope for the future.

Terry made plans to go to Tokyo to search for a house. He

185

had a friend who owned two or three houses that had escaped the fires and had told us we could have one of them. The friend warned us that it was occupied and there would be some difficulty getting the occupants to move out. Then there was the problem of ways and means to get our belongings together and back to Tokyo. I had household effects in five different places in Japan. It seemed a hopeless task at first. There was the doctor, climbing our mountain every day to give me life and substance with his hypodermic, urging us on, "Go on to Tokyo. Mrs. Terasaki is an American and her own people will see that she gets adequate food and medicines. Don't wait until cold weather." Mako did not want to move. Tateshina meant home to her. It was all she had to cling to in a world that for four years had offered her no security or safety. She felt at home in our house and had made friends of the trees, the scenery, and the pleasant, simple folk who lived around us. Another move meant new vistas, and for adults in that world of September, 1945, new vistas were uncertain and frightening. How could we expect a child to be less fearful than we? I told her that she would be able to go to school, have friends her own age, and there would surely be new books to read. And above all, we would have all our things together once again and we would make a home for ourselves. Over and over again she asked,

"Will it be safe, Mama? Will it be safe?"

Mr. Shigemitsu wrote Terry about the surrender:

"It will be my unhappy destiny to sign the first surrender in our nation's history."

The letter shocked my husband into realizing that the time had truly come to begin again.

Terry packed a rucksack, putting in rice and *shōyu*, for in Tokyo one could not eat in a restaurant or even in a private home without giving rice to the owner.

We watched him go down the mountain, lucky to have gotten a ride on the back of an oxcart, and my heart welled up with love for him. I watched the lumbering, slow-moving oxcart until it was out of sight, cut off from me by the mists and shadows, and I raised my head to smell the wind with its autumn fragrance. Already the air was cold, and we knew that by the middle of October the leaves would be down and the air would be freezing. There was much to do. We had already begun to use our little *kotatsu* and spread a quilt over it to snuggle under in the mornings and cold evenings. We were alone, high on our mountain with neighbors no nearer than the village. I must not forget to fasten each door and window snugly and to bring Henrietta in against the night. We must wait for Terry's return hoping that no Japanese would want to take revenge on us for the defeat of his country. We were helpless. The most formidable means of defense in the house was a golf club.

A great silence set in. Loneliness is, after all, a silence. We had nothing to eat but the rough oatmeal with salt and a few cans of salmon. There was nothing to add to the salmon and we ate it cold. There was the ever present *kabocha* but it did not agree with me. I was afraid of becoming ill, so I did not eat it. But the oatmeal was warm and filling, the hot green tea was good, and under the quilt we could warm our toes.

Mako went down to the village every day to the post office to get the *Nippon Times*. I read that General MacArthur had arrived in Japan, that the surrender had been signed on the *Missouri*, and that demobilization and disarming of the Japanese forces were being carried out swiftly. Instead of requisitioning food-stuffs as the Japanese had expected, the Americans brought their own food and made some surplus Army rations available for rationing to the needy Japanese. Prince Higashikuni, a near relative of the Emperor, had been made premier to facilitate the surrender; since he was a member of the Imperial Family his authority would be unquestioned by the Japanese people.

I was eager to get back to Tokyo and observe how things were going with my own eyes. I knew that Terry, with his devotion to both countries, would be able to do much toward mutual understanding, if given the opportunity. My eagerness was increased one afternoon when Mako brought me a letter, my first with the name and address in English in many years. It was

187

from an American soldier, the youngest brother of an old friend
of mine, who had gone to the Foreign Office to ask about me.
A friend there had told him that I was safe and had given him
my address. The letter told me that my family in America were
all alive and well, and that he would write to them about me as
soon as he received my answer. I wrote him a long letter, asking
him to tell Mother what I would have written directly had the
mail service been restored at that time. I knew how my mother
must have worried throughout the long years of the war and
what it would mean to her to know that we three were alive.
The soldier and I exchanged several letters and I finally received
one telling me that he would soon leave for America. He sailed
from Yokohama just before our arrival and I missed seeing him
by only a few days.

While Terry was away, Mako and I spent wakeful nights; we
heard strange voices around our house. Once someone shook
our wooden doors and we thought he would force his way in.
Perhaps it was some kind of prank, a terrifying one. God knows
we were helpless—a woman and a child alone far from any occupied house. If anyone really wanted to enter the house, all he
had to do was break the glass of the kitchen door at the back.
We lay there wide-eyed and trembling. I had told Mako that
if we heard glass breaking, she was to hide herself behind the
sliding doors that fitted into the wall paneling. Each night when
the prowlers arrived, I lay in my bed thinking not only of our
personal safety but of how easy it would be for them to get in
and carry off our neatly packed suitcases and all our possessions.
Loss of one garment in a defeated and destroyed country can be
an extremely serious thing.

This state of affairs continued for the entire week that Terry
was away in Tokyo, and by the time he returned Mako and I
were in a state of mental and physical collapse. We had both lost
more weight and were nearly exhausted. We had engaged our
carpenter to help us pack during the day. That tedious, trying job
plus our sleepless nights and our poor diet had reduced us to
pitiable scarecrows.

Terry had a house! Not only had he found a house but he had two packages of air-raid biscuits. He said he had inquired of two G.I.'s ("What's a G.I.?" I asked him) about the length of skirts in America. He assured me that my skirts were quite in fashion. Imagine the expression on the faces of two battle-worn G.I.'s when asked by a Japanese gentleman getting on the train in the wilds of Nagano, "What length are American women wearing their skirts this season?"

Terry told me that he thought we should take a Western-style house which he had located but that he had also found a small Japanese house in case I preferred that. He told me that the Japanese house would not be too satisfactory. It belonged to one of his friends who had rented it to a businessman and the businessman was using it as a home for his mistress. It appeared that the concubine did not want to move and the businessman had no idea of returning to his legal residence with his wife and children until he had to. It occurred to me that Terry was probably overemphasizing the difficulties out of his notorious love of comfort, of Western beds and Western fixtures, and I told him I thought we should take the Japanese house because the Americans would be requisitioning Western-style homes first. Terry pointed out that it would be both absurd and embarrassing for us to attempt to live in a house with the businessman and his girl friend, but I insisted that we should take the Japanese house in spite of the complications.

Terry acceded to my wishes and began thinking about moving. He had located a truck belonging to a friend of his and had obtained the use of it to transport our household effects. Not knowing what restrictions might later be clamped on trucks and other transportation, we thought we should move at once and laid our plans to descend upon the *geisha* and her patron. Terry told me that the house had seven rooms, and we reasoned that if we could not force the people to move we could take the two upstairs rooms for the time being.

There was still much heavy packing to do and we had not the strength to do it. I insisted that we go through some of the

189

trunks of official papers which we had been carting around all over Japan with us and get rid of things we did not need. Terry was far from orderly about these matters. When we would move, he would take the papers piled high on his desk, dump them in a trunk, and mark it "important." That was his packing. He agreed we should lighten the load and we started on the musty trunks. It took us all day; each thing we picked up was a poignant reminder of the past. I remember a letter of protest from Secretary Stimson, written to the Japanese government about the bombing of Chapei, outside Shanghai. The Japanese had taken the position that they were destroying a Red ammunition dump and their security demanded that they risk the deaths of people nearby to destroy it. Stimson's letter stated, "The civilized world is horrified at the bombing of innocent people." One could not help but wonder if he had felt the same way at the atomic bombing of Hiroshima and Nagasaki. The rumor was that the Japanese had already opened negotiations for peace through the Russians and that the bomb was dropped on Hiroshima as an experiment, not as a military measure. It was reported that the bomb dropped on Nagasaki was used simply to see what it would do in a mountainous area.

Terry had written to Mr. Kato, the fisherman in Yoshihama, and had asked if he would be willing to make the trip to Nagano to help us move. We had no word from him and as the weeks passed we gave up hope of getting him. Then late one dreary November evening as we sat huddled in the living room close to the *hibachi* that was our hearth, we heard a joyous shout at the door. It was Kato—all decked out in the uniform of a private in the Imperial Japanese Army! He joined us near the fire and I gave him tea. How good it was to hear him gripe about the army! It seemed he had been drafted a few months before the surrender and had been sent to the island of Oshima for duty. With weary anger, now and then relieved by an almost tolerant cynicism, he told a story of hunger, lack of munitions, and poor leadership. He said the war ended just when he had decided that his bones would be picked clean by the birds. He had been returned to

Japan and had arrived at his home a few days after our letter had been delivered there. Stopping for only a short time with his family, he had come on to help us. The large rucksack slung over his shoulders was full of fish and vegetables, and after telling us of his adventures he began, with an industrious matter-of-fact air, to prepare the food for cooking. Next day he inspected the whole house, inquiring about every piece he remembered from Yoshihama. I knew I could shift much of my task onto his shoulders.

Mr. Kato was one of the most unselfish and pleasing people I have ever known. He was kind to me, as one human being to another. With almost no education and no experience with "foreigners," he accepted me and never seemed to think I was strange in any way. His simplicity and humility were not untouched with dignity. He felt no bitterness over his country's defeat, dismissing it with the statement, "We lost—now we must change our ways." I used to sit near him, making lists while he packed, and we talked of many things. Somehow he understood my broken Japanese and was patient with me when I could not understand everything he said. Sometimes we really got into deep water and had to call Terry or Mako to interpret for us.

He wanted to know about democracy. I launched into a somewhat self-conscious and platitudinous discussion of "government of the people, for the people and by the people," the Declaration of Independence, the Bill of Rights, and freedom of religion in America. I felt myself floundering but he saved me by his questions. The thing that impressed him most in our Declaration of Independence were the words "the pursuit of happiness."

"What did you say? Would you please repeat?"

"I said, 'Life, liberty, and the pursuit of happiness.' "

"Pursuit of happiness! Pursuit of happiness! Does it mean what it says?"

"Yes, it means letting everyone alone as much as possible to do what he enjoys, not interfering unless the government has to protect someone else's happiness."

191

"Pursuit of happiness. I like that. It is not the same as the Imperial way, is it?"

I thought of all the Mr. Katos of Japan and hoped that the American occupation forces would have better answers to the searching questions that would be asked. The defeat left the Japanese in a spiritual vacuum. A literate, virile people, eager for knowledge, they would not be satisfied with platitudes, however high sounding. I thought of the story of St. Francis Xavier and his conversation with Yajiro, the Japanese interpreter he met before going to Japan. St. Francis asked Yajiro if he thought the Japanese would be drawn to Christianity. Yajiro replied, "You come to Japan, Father, and teach us. We'll listen and we'll watch you."

Mr. Kato solved the problem of Henrietta by making a special box for her to ride in on the truck, and finally we were packed up and ready to go. But the trucks did not come as soon as we expected them. Day after day we waited and heard nothing. We had reduced our living to a kind of camp life because we wanted to be able to leave immediately. Mr. Kato roasted a pumpkin in the ashes of a wood fire in the garden. Overnight a chill had come in the air, and the fire was cheery and comforting.

The morning after we arose to view a new landscape. The autumn scene of the day before had vanished. We awoke to see thin, black trees sharp against a winter sky. We had been told that the leaves in Tateshina would fall suddenly and all at the same moment. No beautiful, long autumn days with russet leaves gently falling. The suddenness of the one great disrobing of all the trees was somehow shameful.

As the days went on we became very restless. We frequently sat on the sunny side of the house in the warmth while Mr. Kato caught up on his sleeping and Mako did watercolors of the magnificent view. The whole silent countryside seemed to be waiting. There was a blue haze over the mountains from the charcoal kilns being fired. Many a *hibachi* and *kotatsu* would be warmed by the charcoal from those kilns.

After two weeks, the truck came slowly up the mountain with

the driver and the loader beside him. We spent the last night at the hotel in the village going up once again to our house to see our things loaded. There was lots of room on the truck so we piled in the wood that Mako had cut and three bags of charcoal. At last came Henrietta and her feed sack, and they were off, carrying with them a letter in English:

To whom it may concern:
Please allow this truck to go through to Tokyo. It is loaded with household goods belonging to Mr. Hidenari Terasaki and his American wife, Mrs. Gwendolen Harold Terasaki.

Signed, Gwendolen Harold Terasaki.

They were not questioned along the way and made the trip in record time.

Again goodbye to another little house where we had lived. We had suffered much in this one and had expected perhaps to die in these mountains. We looked back with misty eyes and boarded our charcoal taxi, again holding our birds outside to avoid the fumes. Always it is sad to say goodbye but sadder, I think, in the evening when the sun is sinking. We looked back until our car turned the bend.

The hostess of the hotel at the Chino station, where we spent the night, brought our meager dinner on small lacquer tables, setting one down before each of us on the low table. Then, folding her legs under her in the traditional style, she busied herself in serving our rice. I sat fascinated, watching her dip the dampened wooden ladle into the steaming rice, first lightly turning it up from the bottom so that each grain would stand out and assert itself. Terry always called this process "worrying" the rice into action. Then, still with the same light, deft touch she scooped up enough to fill the rice bowl. Never too much in the bowl and never any stray grains on the rim. Then the bowl was placed on a tiny tray and served reverently. I looked at her calm pale face and wondered what thoughts lay behind that composure.

To make conversation, Terry asked her how she had managed

193

through the war. Almost casually she replied that until her husband was killed in a raid on Tokyo, she had been able to get along even though her two sons were at the front. When last they were heard from, one of them was in Manchuria. She had never received one line from the other after his departure. The thing that had broken her was the destruction of her house, situated near the railroad tracks; it had been torn down just a few days before the surrender to prevent the spread of fire from the tracks, which had been under special attack near the end of the war. She had moved her belongings into the tiny room in the hotel where she slept when she was not on duty.

She paused and offered the lacquer tray for an empty rice bowl to be refilled. Again that light twist of the ladle and the fluffy steaming rice was in the bowl, again the smiling bow and the passing of the tray.

Up early the next morning, we waited, shivering, in the musty station filled with charcoal fumes. Never at my best early in the morning, I felt especially glum with the heavy Japanese breakfast inside me. Terry had urged me to eat even the sour, cold *umeboshi* (pickled plum) which, surprisingly enough, is dear to the palate of all Japanese. It is supposed to refresh one's spirit but it has a distinctly humbling effect on mine in the early morning.

The station master, a courteous little man wearing thick glasses and white gloves, was very much interested in our two birds. He asked what we fed them and, finding they ate *awa* and that we had great difficulty in getting it, he said,

"If you will kindly wait a few minutes while I run home, I will give you some *awa* for your birds."

Away he went, racing along in the gloom, almost invisible except for his white gloves which were *de rigueur* for all station masters in Japan. We saw our train coming in and looked anxiously for him up the street. Thinking he would not return, we were busily stowing away our bags and bundles on the train when our station master, very much out of breath, puffed up to us, waving

194

a large bag of bird seed triumphantly. Again, "*Sayōnara, sayōnara. Arigatō gozaimasu* (Thank you very much)." We were off.

The awful hush, the stillness of the people on the train was something new. The passengers were silent, looking sorrowfully out the windows, musing deeply to themselves. Before the war ended, there was bustle and confusion and much talk; now the passengers were bewildered and uncertain. There was a listlessness and a general lack of energy, but no fear. The American troops had been in Japan long enough for news to have filtered back into the most remote districts that if the Japanese observed law and order and carried on their duties, they had nothing to fear.

As our train stopped at the many stations, I peered out the window to try to catch my first glimpse of American forces, but I did not see any occupation troops until our train neared Tokyo.

As far as my eyes could see there were signs of destruction. Great shells of buildings and burned trees were outlined against the sky. The vacant, bare patches one realized had been residential sections where incendiary bombs had erased the wood and paper houses. I saw people walking on sidewalks around a block devoid of buildings; how neatly the sidewalk skirted the emptiness! Many people had salvaged metal and stone to build rude shelters; some were living in dugouts. The shelters were placed where their former homes had been. Here and there were mounds covered with rusted metal that resembled nothing until one saw a gaily-patterned kimono drying in the wind and realized the mound was all that was left of home to someone.

Not having left my mountain top for six months, I was worn out by the time we reached Tokyo. So weak had I become that when we got to the station and I stepped off the train onto the platform, I went down to my knees. Immediately a great crowd of curious people surrounded me, and Terry and Mako had to fight our way through to a place for me to sit down. We rested and had a drink of tea, and after awhile I was able to go on. We were all three burdened with rucksacks and suitcases, and Mako, of course, had her two birds. We had to stop to rest many times. Dust was thick on the sidewalks and the roadways were littered. Where was beautiful, sanitary Tokyo with its clean streets? I had thought the people in the mountains looked underfed, but they were in robust health compared to the hungry human beings I now beheld.

We plodded on. I noticed the veins in Terry's forehead were swollen and throbbing. There were dark shadows under Mako's eyes and she stumbled under her heavy load. We turned a corner and Terry pointed silently to a little house behind a spreading pine tree.

We eased our bundles off our backs, brushed ourselves futilely, and Terry rang the bell. A pretty woman with a huge white Chow dog came to the door. She invited us in, dusty bundles and all. We were ushered into the *seiyōkan* (Western-style room) and asked to wait for the master of the house. I looked around. I had subdued many houses in many countries since my marriage but something made me feel that this house was going to subdue me. It betrayed the dreariness common to houses where there is no permanence in the relationship of the occupants. We waited.

Tea was sent in, served with a sweet Japanese candy made of wheat and red beans. We could hear voices in the rear and when the head of the house finally came in it was obvious that there had been a quarrel. He welcomed us and said that, owing to a delay in getting ready to move, he and his friend would have to remain longer. They had cleared the two upstairs rooms and he hoped we would not be too uncomfortable. The public bath, only four blocks away, had recently reopened so there would be no difficulty in bathing. All very vague and a bit too hearty, I thought. Terry replied that this would be a satisfactory arrangement until the truck arrived with our things. Then we would collect all of our stored household goods, and he was quite sure that they would have to leave since our belongings would completely fill the house. A box of K-rations was produced by our reluctant host who then took us over the house. A house has always been a challenge to me, especially a difficult house, but as I tried to visualize my things in it, this one awoke no response, only a sense of hopelessness and despair. I was tired with a fatigue that went to the bone.

Carefully I saved the tiny envelope of powered coffee in the K-ration box. I would have that and the package of crackers and the preserved butter for my breakfast. It was a comforting thought. I fixed a bed and we went fast asleep; without even waking for the *o bentō* we had saved for dinner, all three of us slept through until the next morning.

Then began a month of living in the tiny rooms upstairs. Our meals were prepared after the regular meal hours so that I could be alone in the kitchen. One never knew when one would come face to face with a strange man in the halls, bathroom, or wherever. One washed oneself in fear of interruption and I began to feel like a scurrying rabbit. The one thing that kept up my morale was the memory of the human beings I had seen living in tin houses and in underground hovels.

Two days after we reached Tokyo our truck arrived from Tateshina with everything intact, including Henrietta, who was windblown but otherwise no worse for wear. There was dismay on the faces of our co-occupants but I knew that compared to what they would feel after our entire belongings were thrust upon them this was nothing. They sacrificed another room in which to unpack our things and this became a pattern. Another truck load, another room, until finally they had to go. The man went back to his wife and his friend went I know not where. I salved my conscience at literally shoving them out by telling Terry that it was, after all, a good moral deed.

On November 14, our wedding anniversary, I went in the truck with the driver and the loader across Tokyo to my former house in Meguro to gather up the last of my possessions. I sat between the two men and we bumped along at a meager pace to avoid the bomb craters in the streets. On and on we drove through the desolate city. There had not yet been time to clear the rubble and it was lying just where the bombs had left it. There is a peculiar hush over a burned city and people automatically speak in whispers, so as not to disturb the dead, perhaps.

I began to cry, fighting my tears to no avail. The loader reached over and patted my hand in sympathy, murmuring, "*Kawaisō okusama* (Poor Madame)."

We had to stop now and then to cool the antique engine of the truck. Each time swarms of children, seeing an American face, would climb all over the truck crying, "Chocolate *chōdai*, chewing gum *chōdai*." I was sorry that I had no sweets to give them as the G.I.'s did. I remembered how the American sailors had taught the beggar children in Shanghai similar English phrases. The most successful beggar, a boy of about five, used to be across from the Cathay Hotel; he chanted,

"No momma, no poppa, no whiskey, no soda, I all same bastard child."

Our dishes and glassware had been buried in the garden and these had to be taken out of the boxes in which they had been stored away; the damp ground had caused some of the goods to mildew. Many people had used sealed tin boxes to bury clothes in and the garments survived in fairly good condition, but those who packed their things away hurriedly found them almost unusable. Valuable curios and jewelry were often put underground and some people buried large safes.

It required the whole day to finish packing up our belongings. The large box of Mako's dolls that I had kept for her seemed a part of another world. The little Shirley Temple doll that she had loved, the yellow curls all matted together, the peeling foot, and the missing arm, was part of the life of a carefree and happy little girl. How would I ever be able to make it up to her or to the other children of the world who had walked in the same shadow?

Again we crossed the city, this time in the twilight amid the scuttling leaves and a wind that whistled by, searching for trees that were gone. The noise of our truck was somehow out of place and one felt almost ashamed to be alive in a city where so many had died.

198

When I got home, I found Terry waiting.

"You look so tired, my beloved wife."

"We'll all feel better after some tea," I replied. "Let's go in and sit down."

After we had taken tea, Terry said,

"I have not forgotten what day it is. I searched all over Tokyo; do you know there is nothing to be found anywhere? But I did get this."

He handed me a package wrapped in festive paper and carefully tied. I opened it to find a peanut roaster!

"Maybe someday we'll have peanuts, too," Terry remarked wryly.

The house was bulging. I could not see my way clear to conquer the confusion. We hired a maid, a young girl from one of the northern provinces, by the name of Yoshiko, who jumped every time I spoke to her. She did not even know how to cook Japanese food and my husband found it a great joke that an American woman should be teaching a young Japanese woman how to cook Japanese-style dishes. The house was in very bad condition. Panes of glass were missing, doors would not open, and the pump in the garden would not work. But it was ours and I knew we were most fortunate.

We had brought a few bags of charcoal with us, and the glorious wood that Mako had sawed added to that would help to warm at least one room. The first winter in Japan without heat had given me frostbitten feet which left me crippled every year, at times unable to wear any shoes and at others only the biggest Oxfords I possessed. Usually during the coldest months I suffered from chilblains on my hands.

We had a tiny sun porch and since the entire house had southern exposure, we could do very well without heat of any kind on sunny days. I had inquired of every shop and of everyone I knew to learn of a stove for sale. But I had no luck, nothing made of metal was to be had.

After putting my Chinese rugs over all the *tatami*, I hung what curtains I possessed, together with bamboo screens, over the windows to keep out the wind. I put *hibachi* in each room, but there was never enough charcoal to fill them. We kept two or three blankets and an afghan folded on the couch in the living room to wrap around our guests and we kept serving them hot tea. The only place we were ever really warm was in bed, fortified with large copper hot water bottles. We slept in sweaters and bed socks and, determined still to read in bed, I wore woolen gloves to keep my fingers from freezing. I never sat down for a minute without putting a fur cape over my shoulders and a blanket over my knees. We wore slacks and *monpe* in the house and Terry had fur-lined house shoes.

Soon after the Americans landed in force a rumor was spread that there was a campaign on to exterminate the Japanese through poisoning. There had been much Soviet propaganda that the Americans were not feeding the Japanese as they should; one remarkable placard at the Tokyo station read, "If the Russians were giving us food, they would give us rice instead of sugar." When the rumor of the poisoning reached our neighborhood, some of the women came to me about it. I discovered the reason for the rumor and had a meeting called at the local *tonarigumi* whose leader had told me the Americans are "trying to kill us." I got a can of the "food." It was canned heat, Sterno; I had them cut a hole in a can and showed them how to use the Sterno to cook rice or make tea. How awed they were to see me strike a match to it! The cans had "poison" written on them, and the Communists had said that they were labeled in this manner so the American troops would not eat the contents. Fuel was scarce, and when the people understood the use of the Sterno they were grateful to have it.

We were afraid. The occupation authorities had disarmed the police and no Japanese were empowered to enforce law and order. Since the Americans could not provide police for Japanese civilians, bands of robbers were about, pillaging, robbing, committing barbaric crimes. One such gang, well armed and riding in a truck, went to a house in our district early one dark morning and systematically looted it of all its belongings, furniture, clothing, the woman's jewels, everything. Without a gun or anyone to call for help, the outraged occupants could do nothing. Desperation swept the community, and a meeting was held, and something like the *posse comitatus* of medieval England resulted. Every home was to have a cowbell to ring when the robbers approached, then everyone in our *tonarigumi* was to take up the hue and cry and fall upon the bandits, overwhelming them by force of numbers. So it was that my husband began sleeping with a cowbell. We even put firecrackers in the garden, rigged up like booby traps to explode when an intruder steeped upon them. The looters never tested the device; all that happened with the firecrackers was that one of the stray dogs that Mako had taken in struck one with his nose and was killed. As soon as they could, the Americans re-established law and a semblance of order, and the bandits were stopped. By then the Communists had started organized agitation and Koreans flooded into Japan, like the carpetbaggers descending on the South. They made their living on the black market and wore arm bands saying "Allies," in big letters. Their smuggling operations and general belligerence created a problem and reflected badly on the occupation forces. One day one of them came up to me on the streets; greeting me like a politician, he put his arm around me and said, "Hello, *Amerikajin*. We're friends!"

I stepped back, horrified, and said in Japanese, "Take your hands off me, *Chōsenjin!*"

He faded away from me with a great "Ahhh!"

The Communists made many mistakes. One of the worst was to attack the Emperor in a joking way, attempting to ridicule him as a myopic, funny little man of no ability. They were desperately attempting to prevent the occupation from being peaceful and constructive, and no one knew what violence they might attempt. The Communists who had been imprisoned or sent into exile by the Japanese were set free and brought home by the occupation. They staged many demonstrations. One such noisy, banner-waving exhibition took place in front of the Palace. The agitators had done their work well, and the screaming and shouting throng seemed to the nervous police to be on the verge of starting a riot. Then, in the midst of the clamor and excitement, the crowd went silent and, as one man, bowed low toward the Palace gate. A limousine bearing the Empress of Japan had emerged and was moving slowly across the moat. The Empress acknowledged their bows as her car turned out of sight. The mood of the crowd had changed and, unable to regain their enthusiasm, they soon dispersed.

A few weeks after we had gotten settled someone poisoned our dog, Chubby, using a substance that worked slowly and left him to drag himself into the library where he sat staring at the marble Buddha my husband had bought in Shanghai. He gazed on the Buddha fixedly for several minutes and the maid told us he was praying. Realizing the dog had been poisoned, we called a veterinarian to look after him, but the doctor told us Chubby could not live and we agreed that he should be put to sleep. The doctor bowed low to the tortured little dog and said, "*Gomen nasai* (I am sorry), Chubby-chan." He thrust the hypodermic into the dog's side; Chubby sighed and was dead.

Yoshiko suggested that since the dog had been making his peace with the Buddha, he should have a funeral befitting a Japanese pet. Terry agreed we might do this so long as he was not expected to have any part. We had a friend make the arrangements with the temple and on the appointed day we went to pay our last respects to our little friend. We sat on the *tatami* facing the altar where the large statue of Buddha looked over us. Chubby's body was placed on the altar at the foot of Buddha. The priest presented a banner with the name "Chubby-chan, beloved pet of the Terasaki family" printed in ink. Dressed in formal vestments, the priest intoned the sutras, ringing the bell each time. He rang the bell loudly in order that the Buddha would bend his ear lower to hear the prayers of the little dog. We walked forward on our knees to burn incense. The last words of the priest were, "To Chubby, beloved pet of the Hidenari Terasaki family, may he find his peace in the western hills."

Then the dog's lifeless form was put in a box and we went out to the animal cemetery in the suburbs of Tokyo to bury him. There was a brief ceremony and Mako threw in the first dirt to refill the grave. A large memorial stone stood nearby dedicated to "Tama, beloved cat of Prince and Princess Takamatsu," and we saw fresh flowers which people had brought to adorn the graves of their pets.

I was relieved to see that Mako did not cry at the funeral, and I realized she had developed the Japanese attitude toward showing grief. I have always thought these people repress grief at their own misfortunes too much although they show sorrow readily when it is for someone else. At their funerals the body does not lie in state; in place of the body a picture of the person is displayed. Incense is burned and mourners bow to the picture and to the family of the dead. The widow and family sit while the mourners pass and bow, and they must not cry. I remember the first time I went to call to sympathize with a friend over the death of her youngest child. She came into the drawing room, smiling and calm, and we talked of many things. I could find no opportunity to mention her bereavement. After serving tea and little cakes, she took me through her garden, pointing out each of her loved plants and blossoms. I left, feeling awkward and clumsy. The next day I received a charming note from her, thanking me for my call and "taking your precious time to give me solace in my loss." Although the trait may produce an unhealthy repression through years of control, it often has grace and delicacy.

Years before, I had been advised by a White Russian that it was a wise course to hoard small denominations of money against postwar inflation. Happily I had remembered this bit of information from one who had experienced the financial disaster that now was the lot of the Japanese. I had saved a trunkful of paper fifty-cent pieces and, since our investments in Japanese bonds and insurance companies had been lost, this helped a great deal—both financially and in my morale. The government called in the *yen* but as my adviser had told me, it did not bother with the small denominations and they retained their value. For several months we were able to pay all our expenses from the little trunkful of paper money.

When it was expended, we joined most of the Japanese in the process of selling our remaining belongings for food—"onionskin living." This mode of living was aptly named because the sale of each prized possession did indeed bring tears. We sold many of our things, regretting to part with all of them with one exception. Terry had purchased an accordion for Mako before the war, and I sold it for 35,000 *yen*. Terry felt that bargaining was mean and beneath respectable persons, and he had insisted I sell at the original offer the buyer made, 15,000 *yen*. This seemed reasonable enough, even with the inflation of the times, since we had only paid 1,500 for it, but the buyer wanted the accordion to play for the American soldiers and he had plenty of money with which to pay. He had made the mistake of bringing it in his pockets and I could see from the bulges that he meant to have the instrument at any price. Terry was always a little ashamed of me for bargaining as I did; but I thought my people in east Tennessee, a section where close trading was not unknown, would have felt otherwise. We used the money from the accordion for food of which my husband partook heartily.

13

GOYŌGAKARI

JUST before the surrender the Japanese had asked if the Potsdam terms meant that the Emperor would have to abdicate. The Allies had replied in the negative, adding that his status would depend in the long run on the will of the Japanese people. The occupation policy now was to make use of the authority of Hirohito in organizing Japanese cooperation, a wise course. It was necessary that there be an official liaison to advise the Emperor and to meet with him and MacArthur, someone who knew the languages and customs of both nations and who would be trusted by both. Yoshida, who was now Premier, chose my husband for this position.

It was a great surprise to us both. The first I knew of it was late one night when Terry sat on the edge of my bed happily reporting the events of a busy day. As usual he had ignored the doctor's orders and had come upstairs.

"Gwen, you awake?"

"Uh-huh."

"I've got something to tell you. I have been given a position by Mr. Yoshida. I am to be *goyōgakari*—that means liaison and adviser for the Emperor. I've already called on all the officers and officials. They are very nice and friendly—and, I've found a cousin of yours."

Yoshida had told Terry that he wanted him for the job, but first Terry would have to call on the occupation officials. High on the list of officials which Yoshida handed him was the Secretary-General of the Allied Council, General Bonner Fellers, who was also one of the "Bataan boys" and Military Secretary to MacArthur. Terry called on General Fellers at once.

"How do you do, General Fellers. My name is Terasaki."

"I am pleased to meet you, Mr. Terasaki. Won't you have a chair?"

Terry sat down in the chair across the polished desk from the General. "I have been told to call on you. I have just been appointed adviser to the Emperor."

Being accustomed to a more obsequious type of Japanese, the General remarked, "So you've been *told* to call. That's not very flattering!"

Terry saw the General's ire, but there was no retreating now. "I am sorry. But after all, I could have no other reason to be here."

"What makes you think you're the man for the job?" snapped the American.

After a pause, Terry said slowly, "Well, first, Mr. Yoshida thinks I'm the man for the job. And, secondly, next to Japan I love the United States more than any country in the world."

"Why do you love the United States?" asked the General suspiciously.

"I was posted there—it was my first post. I went to Brown University. I had many friends there. I come from a family that has always been frank and outspoken, and I like the Americans because they are so direct and at ease with people. And, besides that, the most important thing, I have an American wife and she has helped me understand America."

Suddenly interested, the General asked, "Where is your wife at present?"

"She is here with me in Tokyo. She came back to Japan with me when the diplomats were exchanged."

"Good God!" The General leaned forward in his swivel chair. "Well, if you have an American wife who has followed you through the war, I think you qualify for the job, Mr. Terasaki. Here, have a cigarette. What was your wife's maiden name, may I ask?"

"She was a Harold," replied Terry, lighting the cigarette and taking a deep puff.

"You don't say! I have some relatives by that name. Not very close, but relatives all the same. Where is she from?"

"Tennessee."

"Really! This is the most astonishing thing I ever heard of. Mr. Terasaki, I think we must be some kind of cousins-in-law!"

And the following evening Bonner had us to dinner at his apartment in the American Embassy.

Each day thereafter Terry was to be at the Palace for consultation with the Emperor and to go with His Majesty when there was a meeting with MacArthur. He was called for by a chauffeur at the wheel of an Imperial Household limousine, a canvas-topped Rolls-Royce dating from about 1930 which the G.I.'s stared at and which we knew affectionately as "the cement mixer."

A few weeks after his appointment, I learned indirectly that Terry, like all Japanese, was using the freight elevator at occupation headquarters. This was a matter of some resentment and I spoke to one of MacArthur's aides at the first opportunity.

"I don't want him riding on that elevator where they carry freight and everything else—he is sick!"

The Colonel was taken aback. "Why, I didn't know he was riding that elevator. He doesn't have to—he's got a pass."

It was my turn to be surprised. "Oh, forgive me, Colonel, I misunderstood; I knew the Japanese had to take the freight elevator and I didn't know he had a pass."

Armed with this knowledge, I urged Terry to be sensible, use his pass, and take the passenger elevator. He was disappointed that I knew about the pass.

"After all, I am Japanese, Gwen—I didn't want to take any advantage."

"But you are a *sick* Japanese—certainly you won't be worth anything at all to your country dead!"

In response to my insistence, he started using the other elevator, but he remained shy and self-conscious about it.

Speculation concerning the new constitution, trade policies, Formosa, and just about everything centered on the meetings between General MacArthur and the Emperor. As a diplomat's wife I had learned the habit of self-containment where official matters were involved, but I was long out of training and when the headlines screamed that war with Russia was near and editorials asked whether Japan was again to be a battleground, I could not restrain myself.

"Terry you had a long conference yesterday—so that was it! You must have discussed this. You know all about it!"

"My dear wife, I did not discuss it!"

"But you *know*, you translated it all. The three of you know!"

Terry smiled warmly and said,

"Please bring me some tea in the study. I wish to examine the Chung Yao."

I was dismissed. How I wanted to be in on the secret! I took him the tea and then sat down in the living room to see what I could read further in the *Nippon Times* and the *New York Herald*. The telephone rang almost at once and Yoshiko, the maid, said it was for me.

It was another newspaperman. They called constantly, both the Japanese and the Americans. Pretending to make friends, he asked his questions indirectly. When we could find no mutual friends from Tennessee (he knew someone from Memphis—they always did), he asked,

"What did your husband have to say when he got home?"

I could not convince him that Terry told me nothing I ought not to know, or even a lot of things I thought I should know. I had to be pleasant and banter with him until he understood. I told him,

"Oh, he said 'I'm very tired.'"

Laughingly, the reporter persisted until I offered to have Terry come to the phone and tell him himself. No, he did not want to speak to Terry. He thanked me and said goodbye.

It happened constantly. After a few weeks the older reporters got so they would not bother, but any time a new reporter got a position in Tokyo and learned that the liaison had an American wife he would dial my number.

When I told Terry about the calls, he was amused. He told me,

"I am just an instrument in this case."

As the months passed into the spring of 1946, I found a number of friends from the United States were arriving in Tokyo. They would get in touch with us through the authorities and come visiting. We told them where to shop and what week-end trips to make to see the beauteous and historic Japan. They shared the luxuries of the Army PX and commissary with us. I also began receiving boxes from home, and with the food coming to us from these sources together with the fresh vegetables now obtainable at the Japanese market places, I became interested in having people to dinner again. I wanted to do this for Terry even more than for myself. Nothing pleased him more than to play the host. He loved to mix the drinks, suggest the conversation—to look around at a pleased and animated group of his friends and think he had promoted their happiness. Some of the spirit of argumentation we had known in Shanghai came back. Terry enjoyed putting people of loudly opposite views next to each other, giving them both a drink, mentioning the matter in dispute, and then siding with first one and then the other with great merriment. Sometimes when he had a particularly intelligent and interested listener, he would draw him away into the garden to talk with great intensity and emotion about Japan and America.

After dinner, liqueurs were served with coffee and the talk continued in serious vein. At length, when it seemed to go on almost too long, I would interrupt and focus Terry's attention on his curios or some object of Japanese art. This was about the only way to get him off a hot political tirade. Relaxing, he would go to the *todana* and remove one of the delicate *hinoki* (cypress) boxes. Then, he would sit cross-legged in the center of the room and very lovingly, one by one, untie the gay *furoshiki* from the box and take out a scroll, a vase, or a small cup. With great ease he would tell his assembled guests about the piece he held in his hands. A calm would come over him. It was as though our furious world of postwar Japan, the Palace, headquarters—all the tensions and suffering and pain of life—had faded away. In our little sitting room, we thought of the joyfulness of these exquisite things and were glad they had so long survived the troubles of men.

Terry had a capacity for seeking out eccentric people who amused him—artists and poets, people with odd backgrounds and training who were interestingly different. Over the years he accumulated a startling array of such people.

One in whom my husband took pleasure was an expert swordsman. He came to our house as a guest and entertained us by throwing pennies into the air and striking them with his sharp blade which he drew from its scabbard with lightning speed. I could not avoid exclaiming in English,

"I do hope he is not bitter about the war."

After a long performance which ended with his slicing a newspaper with the keen edge of the sword, the swordsman took his departure, bowing to Terry and saying in good English,

"I have had a most pleasant stay with you and your gracious family. Good evening."

Another who struck his fancy was a three-hundred-pound faith healer who always came at mealtime. He was a survivor of Hiroshima. When the bomb was dropped he was awaiting his *shōsen* (tramcar) at the railway station and had fallen unconscious into a drainage ditch. Sometime later he awoke. The siren was stilled, the planes were gone, and there was only emptiness where the station had been, but as he related it to us it appeared his greatest concern was that his clothes had been burned off. He arose and ran to his little house four miles away. When he got there his surviving child did not recognize him for his skin was a livid black. Having no medicine, he put potato juice in a mixture made from tea leaves on his burns. His wife and one child had been killed along with almost everyone he knew. He wondered why he had been spared. He came to think that the homemade remedy he had concocted had saved him and believed that he had been endowed with special curative powers and had a mission to perform. That was how he had become a faith healer. I remember his face, covered with keloids and scars from the after-effects of the bomb. He did not understand why he could not cure his sterility but thought that when his faith was pure and strong enough he would overcome that, too.

The doctors had ordered Terry to avoid all strenuous sports but permitted him to take up archery as being only mildly demanding. He did so with enthusiasm, virtually with fanaticism, or so it seemed to me when he brought his archery teacher home eight days running to lunch with us.

We also entertained a number of diplomats and several American army people we had known in Washington and elsewhere. So the months passed, and it was Christmas.

During the holidays we had a party for some close friends from both Japan and America. Terry was in an exuberant mood that night. I remember he took one Air Force colonel off into a huddle in the den expounding and expostulating as he used to do with the Chinese in Shanghai. How pleased I was to see him his old self—vibrant and magnetic again, with an infectious interest in life, with a renewed faith in himself and mankind. He was smoking again and that was a sign that he was either better or worse. He had given up smoking when things were as usual—I knew he was better. He spoke with the Colonel about many things, about Chinese art (how astonished the Colonel would have been to know that Terry learned much of what he knew of this subject from the Norwegian wife of a German consul) and they launched upon a friendly but warm debate on freedom of trade. Terry proposed this as the keystone to recovery and peace in Asia, telling the Colonel, a Republican from New England, at his

faintest protest, that Cordell Hull was the American who understood those things.

Later, after dinner, Terry took another officer and his wife in
to see his curios. He took a stone Buddha he had gotten in
Peking in 1940 from the glassed-in cupboard where he kept it
and as he was sitting down on the floor he seemed to lose his
equilibrium; he kept going over backwards until he was lying
flat on his back. The Colonel reached over and pulled him up.
Terry laughed that he had had too much to drink, but I noticed
how he had paled.

Mako and I were in the living room a day or so later when we
heard the old Rolls-Royce that brought Terry home from the
Palace creak to a stop outside. We stood at the door to welcome
him home and Mako asked me, with the innocent cruelty of
childhood, as she saw her father coming up the sidewalk to
the house,

"Is Daddy drunk, Mother?"

He was walking with an odd shambling motion peculiar to
one whose sense of balance has been disturbed. I rushed out to
him and took him by the arm. He pushed me away, a little
brusquely I thought, and said,

"I'm O.K., Gwen, just a little tired."

I looked at him closely, he puzzled me so at times! Sometimes
he wanted to be consoled when he was feeling ill—sometimes
he might be very sick but would become irascible at the first show
of solicitude, as if he meant to forget his illness. I decided to
telephone the doctor and it was well that I did. Terry had suffered a brain spasm.

For six weeks he remained in bed, fretful at the enforced
inactivity. He seemed to recover at the end of that time and
the doctor said he could return to his duties.

Our house was located in Nishi-Ogikubo, a suburb of Tokyo.
It was a great distance for Mariko from there to her school but
we could find no other place and knew we were lucky to have
a house at all. The Communists were constantly clamoring of
the violence they intended and causing frequent riots. For this

reason someone always went with her; when the maid could not go, I went. When I could not go she rode in "the cement mixer" with Terry and he dropped her off on his way to work. On the way to school with Mako we passed an army post and saw the Negro soldiers feed the children. They were not allowed to do this, but they habitually found that they did not want all their bread when the hungry little faces pressed against the wire enclosure. One by one, they would put part of their food into a large sack, taking up a collection to distribute to the long lines of women and children that soon learned to form near the barracks. This was done on such a scale that the commanding officer was hard put to keep his back turned.

We lived undisturbed for several months in our little Japanese home and began to enjoy it very much after we had it to ourselves. The American home which Terry would have chosen had been taken almost immediately by the Americans, and it was toward the middle of 1947 when they first began to show interest in Japanese houses.

One morning the maid told me that there was an American officer outside, adding contemptuously that a Japanese interpreter was with him. The interpreters were often hated for coloring their translations. I told her to have them enter. In marched a big colonel with a mustache and the air of a football coach about to give his losing team a half-time lecture. I could not resist telling him he was in a Japanese home and should remove his shoes. He pondered this a moment and then did so, but he kept his cap on until after we had talked for some minutes. The interpreter had presumed to enter without taking off his shoes either, but the maid had fairly screamed at him,

"Take *your* shoes off, too!"

The Colonel wanted to know about the house and how many people lived there. With a knowing air, he asked me if I was from the South. I told him yes and thanked him for asking, saying I was afraid I might have lost my accent. He was uncomfortable; he was acutely conscious of the hole in his sock which seemed to cause the eagles on his shoulders to shrink. He showed interest

213

in our furnishings and asked if we had any more in storage. I told him it was all in the house. When the maid brought tea, he demanded,

"What's this stuff?"

I told him it was green tea and that it was automatically served as the custom of the country. It was then that he finally took off his hat. He asked me how long I had been there and I told him since 1942.

"I'll be damned!" he declared.

He stomped through the rest of the house and then announced that they were not taking any Japanese houses unless they were Westernized. I was relieved to hear this and more relieved when he left. I knew of some houses which had been taken where the new occupants had painted the interior woodwork, some of it centuries old, with Kemtone, to the astonishment and dismay of the original inhabitants who were still on the premises, being permitted to stay in the teahouse in the garden.

Once at a party, a friend of Terry's from the Imperial Household was invited to see a beautiful inlaid table which his host, a lieutenant colonel, thought was very old. The Colonel asked the Japanese as an authority whether it was not around a thousand years old and, "Isn't it a beaut?" The Japanese gentleman assured the Colonel that it was indeed near a thousand years old, it had been made in Japan, and it had been in his family over five hundred years.

Regulations were tightened later and such happenings ceased with the requirement that Americans who had Japanese goods must also have a bill of sale. This led to an amusing incident involving a sale between a Japanese family who had been moved into a little teahouse and the new occupants of their home. The officer's wife was interested in acquiring some of the curios owned by the Japanese. She sought out the Japanese wife and offered some clothes for the objects, but the *okusama* would not part with them without consulting her husband and so informed her. When the husband returned to the teahouse that night, he was met by the officer's wife who announced that the exchange had been agreed upon and offered him used army uniforms in consideration for the curios. The Japanese told her:

"I am sorry, but you see in Japan the wife has no right to sell anything without her husband's consent. I was not here when it was discussed. I do not wish to sell."

He kept his antique scrolls, his lacquer bowls, and Imari cups.

Of course, many a G.I. was induced into what amounted to buying the Brooklyn Bridge and I suppose when things settled down the Japanese held their own rather well. A lot of trading went on. The Japanese had become acquainted with the Sears, Roebuck and Co. catalogue; they were so delighted with it and the beautiful world it promised that they ran the price up to 5,000 *yen*. That catalogue was probably the best propaganda the American forces had.

On one of those bitter, gusty days of early March in 1947, Terry was leaving the Palace to attend a conference at the Dai Ichi Building. He was helped with the venerable great coat that he had bought at Brooks Brothers in New York a decade before; he wound his muffler tightly around his neck and went through the hallway to the door, moving slowly and relying on his cane to help him along.

As he emerged he caught sight of an oddly familiar figure alighting from a taxi on the street below. The man was of medium build and carried himself with military erectness; as he turned from the cab he started briskly up the steps and his handsome head of snow white hair came into full view. It was Stanley Jones, whom we had not seen since early December nearly six years before. The two men recognized each other at the same time. They fell into each other's arms and stood on the steps of the Palace weeping.

As soon as it could be arranged, Dr. Jones and Terry met for dinner. With profound wistfulness they talked of the past, of what could be done to help Japan recover, and of how to prevent a recurrence of the tragedy they had so nearly avoided. Terry informed Jones that the Emperor had told him that if he had received the cablegram from Roosevelt a day sooner he would have stopped the attack. What poignant memories my husband and his American comrade shared that night! Then Dr. Jones was off on his mission to the mainland of Asia and Terry, much heartened by the visit, went back to his post at the Imperial Palace.

The two other Terasaki brothers were also busy. Taro had spent the months just after the war's end on an extensive lecture tour, explaining to his countrymen what they must do and what they might expect of the Americans. He declared that they had made a grave mistake in signing the Tripartite Pact and had been misled into destroying the natural friendship with the Americans and British. He told them the Americans would treat them fairly and they must obey. Later Yoshida appointed Taro Vice-Minister of the Foreign Office. Now he was in office again and in a higher position than that of Director of the American Bureau which he had resigned in 1941 when Prince Konoye's government fell.

Taira, youngest of the three, was now thirty-one years old. He had not been caught up in the vortex of Japanese politics along with his elder brothers. A quiet, somewhat remote lad, he had grown up alone in a boarding school. Deciding to be a doctor, he had studied medicine at Imperial University.

In 1941, when he was twenty-six and had just finished his internship, he was called into service. He looked a little odd to us in the naval lieutenant's uniform, wearing white gloves and with a sword at his side. In contrast to his upbringing which had been quiet and removed from the crowd, his war-time experience had been harsh, violent, full of recurrent danger and rescue. He was, at one time or another, assigned to the medical unit aboard some seven ships—each of which was sunk by enemy action. Yet when Taira spoke of "the enemy," in that friendly, enthusiastic way of his, it seemed almost an abstraction, and I could never accustom myself that it was my people whose planes and ships had brought death to his comrades and destruction to those graceful cruisers and destroyers upon which he had served. I could not imagine harming my polite, mild-spoken brother-in-law.

Taira was now at a nearby hospital, working sixteen to eighteen hours a day. He shared with the average Japanese medical man a dedication to his profession such that he was content, or very nearly content, to live on a cramped scale and work very long hours in the overcrowded hospitals. Few of them have automobiles and most doctors walk, ride a bicycle, or take the *shōsen* to go to work or on their rounds to people's homes. The American doctor's scale of living would astonish all but the minority who have developed a special clientele of wealthy Japanese and foreigners.

The practice of medicine had been socialized in Japan and the doctors were assigned places of duty, types of work, and were told the standard charges to make.

Taira disliked socialization for many reasons. It made it difficult for him to specialize in stomach surgery as he desired and forced him to do his studying from midnight into the early hours of the morning. But he was amazingly jolly and looked forward to having a small clinic of his own after the country began to make a substantial recovery and things had changed.

He worked Mondays through Saturdays and on Sundays he came to be with us. During the week he had no time to be lonely but he enjoyed being with us on the week end. He enjoyed Mako, especially; their rapid Japanese flew back and forth so fast I understood nothing. Most of his stories of the war were told cheerily to Mako, who delighted at them and imitated his enthusiasm in retelling them to me.

Taira told Mako about the war at sea, about the great waves in typhoon season, about the way the water leapt up when the bombs splashed near the ship—how the sailors, bounced from their gun stations by a bomb falling inboard, would fly into the air ten or fifteen feet, fall with a thud to the steel deck, and then drag themselves back to the anti-aircraft gun to try again at the next plane. He told her, while her black eyes shone with tears, of the battle of Manila Bay in 1944. They got the news that the planes were coming from the radar post early in the morning and all hands took their battle stations. As they stood there watching the stars fade and dawn come, little dots of destruction appeared from under the far clouds. A bet had been made as to how many there would be. Taira counted three hundred and then gave it up, saying with a shrug, "What's the point of counting beyond the first three hundred?" Then the planes were overhead and the jangling din of exploding bombs, straining propellors, machine gun and 20 mm. fire began. The ship was in shallow water and could not be maneuvered to escape the rain of bombs. Mako pressed Taira for the number of planes it had shot down and Taira said he heard it had accounted for eight. She wanted to know, with a child's curiosity, about the arms and legs Taira had amputated in the ship's hospital, but Taira told her instead of how he had gone topside when the ship was sinking. He ordered a sailor to go to the rum chest and break out the whiskey so it could be passed around for the crew to take into the water with them. The sailor made his way across the tilted deck, past the dead, the wounded, and the twisted apparatus of the ship, and returned to say above the noise of the battle that the chest was locked. Taira said,

"I don't care if it is locked. Break it open!"

"But, Commander, it is against regulations to break open a locked chest!"

"God damn it, the ship's sinking! Do you want that whiskey to go to the bottom of the bay? Break open that chest and bring the whiskey here at once!"

The whiskey was preserved, and as the ship went down some of its survivors leaned back in their life belts and drank a last toast to it with Haig & Haig Pinchbottle.

Taira had lost most of his possessions, books, statuary, instruments, pictures, and letters; and it was his standard excuse for years afterwards when he could not find something that it must have been among his stuff that went to the bottom of Manila Bay. When Terry asked him for a cigarette or a match that Taira could not produce, he would say,

"That go to the bottom of Manila Bay, too?"

Taira told us how a submarine taken at Yokosuka was towed out to sea after the surrender by an American destroyer to be sunk. The Japanese crew asked for permission to pay homage to their vessel before it was gone, and the lieutenant commander in charge of the destroyer gave them permission. The Japanese who went aboard the sub to open the pet cocks took a spray of cherry blossoms and tied it to the conning tower; then, as the vessel sank slowly out of sight, its former crew stood at attention, saluting until the cherry blossoms were engulfed by the inrushing water. The Americans turned their backs and did not watch.

After the battle of the Philippine Sea there were no ships left and Taira had shore duty at a large hospital near Yoshihama. The hospital was filled and jammed with suffering people and Taira drove himself trying to help them. When he got a few hours rest, he came to me once at our house at Manazuru. He told me he had nothing to use for the injured; he had no bandages, no penicillin, no plasma. There was little he could do. Those imploring eyes of broken men and women and children who trusted him to do what he could not were more than he could bear. Several months later he asked for a transfer and in July, 1945, he was sent to Kure Naval Base. He was there in August when Hiroshima was bombed. He went immediately to the stricken city, the first medical man to reach the city from the outside. With a crew of fifteen nurses and soldiers, he worked for a week with only a few hours sleep to care for the thousands of maimed and tortured people. Then he was ordered back to Kure to care for the wounded who had been sent there.

While Taira was staying with us during the Easter holidays he went out one night and did not return until around 3:00 A.M. I was frantic because there was some danger in one's being on the streets at that time of night. Roving gangs of teen-age hoodlums called *furyō* were about; people were being robbed, shot, and stabbed almost every other night on the dimly lit streets of Tokyo by these desperate youths. Terry and Mariko were asleep in their bedrooms but I could not rest. I sat in the living room and waited. Taira had been a favorite of mine since I had first seen him on the dock at Yokohama and Terry had told him to say "How do you do"; he was only a few years younger than

I but I felt almost a mother to him. When he did not come I went to the kitchen and made myself a cup of tea. Then I returned to the living room and resumed my vigil. A little past three I heard snatches of song outside on the street and, creeping to the window and drawing the curtain, I caught sight of a group of five or six raggedly-dressed young men in their late teens or early twenties. They were drunk and reeling. They had their arms across each other's shoulders and the whole line of them, which stretched nearly across the road, staggered from one side to the other and threatened to collapse in a pile in the gutter. Watching them anxiously I caught sight of Taira. He was in the middle and singing with the rest. I raced to the door and shouted to him to come in. After some hesitation and confusion and bowing all around, he left his companions, came slowly up the steps, and into the house.

My fears for him had gotten a strong hold on me and before I realized it I scolded him violently for scaring me like that, for coming in drunk and disheveled after a brawl in the streets. He stood there with a look of patient disbelief on his round face for a while; then he slipped by me and went to his room muttering a thousand apologies.

He told Mako and Terry the next morning (he was up and away before I awoke) that he had been attacked by the gang who wanted to rob him. For several minutes he kept the pack at bay, inflicting painful injuries on two or three in the process. When they saw how well he defended himself, the ringleader shouted that he fought too well to be robbed and they should all be friends. Taira assented quickly and it was mutually agreed that they should repair to the nearest bar to celebrate their mutual heroism. There they had gone at around midnight and toasted each other until nearly 3:00 A.M., when Taira's money and the money the *furyō* gang had somehow acquired was exhausted and they were all thoroughly inebriated. Then, they had left together, with the gang escorting him safely home.

Terry and Mako thought it was vastly amusing, especially that I should have pounced upon the triumphant hero upon his return.

14

DEMO-KURUSHI

THE Japanese had adopted the English word "democracy" with the occupation, and the American efforts at what in the official language was termed "democratization" of the country evoked from them the devastating pun *"demo-kurushi"* (suffering from democracy). Few Americans, be it said to their credit, failed to enjoy the humor in this expression—and for those who knew Japanese it was uproarious. Under these circumstances, it would have been extraordinary indeed had the Japanese felt much liking for MacArthur at the outset of the occupation. Although they came to feel quite differently with the passage of time, their original reaction to MacArthur was one of intense dislike.

They resented his treatment of the Emperor the first time he was required to call. The picture taken of this meeting was widely circulated throughout Japan for the purpose of illustrating who was the new boss. It showed His Majesty, his short, slight figure respectfully clothed in full morning dress in the presence of a casual, unimpressed MacArthur who wore no blouse, was tieless, and stood aloof with his hands in his pockets. The Japanese understood the intent of the picture but thought "the dignity was with the Emperor." The contrast reminded me of the surrender at Appomattox.

It was not only the Japanese who sympathized with their Emperor on that day. When the little man came under escort in the big limousine to the American Embassy and got out to meet MacArthur, he squared his shoulders and marched toward the guards at the entrance. He had brought his personal physician with him, so little did he know what to expect.

As MacArthur's Military Secretary, Bonner Fellers was at the entrance to receive the Emperor. As His Majesty approached, with his doctor and the chamberlains, Fellers extended his hand to him. The Emperor took it gladly and the two men shook hands on the steps. General Fellers told me later he could not restrain himself; he stood there and thought, "My God, the humiliation!" Upon returning, the first thing the Emperor asked was, "Who was the man that put out his hand to me when I went to the Embassy?" Terry was pleased to be able to say that General Fellers was a relative of mine. The Emperor sent Bonner a photograph signed in English. It was fitting that the gift came as a surprise, for Bonner's act in greeting the Emperor had also been unexpected, the spontaneous gesture of one moved by the Emperor's example to his people of "bearing the unbearable."

MacArthur and the Emperor became friends. The General would put his arm around the smaller man in a fatherly attitude during the course of their frequent meetings—he recognized that the Emperor was acting in good faith, doing all he could to cement relations with the conquerors. I wonder how it would have been had Hirohito acted upon Sir Winston Churchill's dictum that in defeat one should show defiance to one's enemies.

Once, the Emperor asked if he might tour the country and MacArthur granted permission. The Emperor had seen little of his country, being confined by custom and protocol very closely to the Palace. His people had seen even less of him. There was a superstition that if one looked on his face the radiance would be blinding. When he had approached in the past the guards would yell, "Bow your heads, Their Majesties are going by." It happened to me once and I have always wondered which member of the royal family went past in the carriage.

Rigid and unyielding tradition bore down heavily upon all members of the royal family. The children were taken from their empress-mother at birth and reared separately in their own quarters near the Palace; they could not live with their parents or each other. Terry wished that the royal children might have a more normal family life and Mrs. Vining, who was brought from America to educate the Crown Prince, Akihito, wished for a change—at least that the children might live together—but it was too much against orthodox tradition. Such had been His Majesty's childhood, living in his own small palace, brought up by a chamberlain and a staff of retainers, paying formal visits to his brothers and parents, seeing them as his family only during brief vacations at the summer palace when they lived together.

When he was permitted to go among his people freely for the first time, it was as though the Emperor had been liberated. Terry accompanied him on one trip. Immense crowds choked the line of travel as they went by auto through the villages and towns and cities of Japan. The people would surge toward the car, cheering, tearful in their joy to look upon the *tennō*. An old lady held up the photo of her lost son for the Emperor to look at, saying, "Look upon him, look upon him, I beg you. He died for you!"

Terry was deeply moved—he had never fully realized the pervasive love his people felt for the Emperor. When Terry first received the appointment, he told me that he went into the Palace as a blank piece of paper to see what the man there would write upon it. The man wrote well.

Once Terry asked him,

"What was the happiest day of your life, sire?"

The Emperor described a trip to France he had taken when he was Crown Prince. The chamberlains clustered around everywhere, making arrangements, clearing the way, doing all things. The Prince had never used money in his entire life. He became separated at the railroad station amid the confusion and proceeded to walk alone through the gate leading to the trains. A ticket agent had shouted to him, "Hey, bud, what are you doing going through there without a ticket!"

That had been one of the happiest days of his life. On that same trip in Paris, he had enjoyed going shopping for himself for the first time.

Like other Japanese—including my husband—the Emperor came to admire MacArthur. The General had a gift for the splendid gesture. This was strikingly illustrated early in the occupation. He went about in public without guards and even went to meet Mrs. MacArthur when she landed without any escort. It was reported that she asked where the M.P.'s were and he told her they were not needed. Japanese by the thousands took note of this and thought with pride that such trust was something for them to live up to.

When Terry first started going to the Palace he was careful to observe all the details of proper etiquette when in the presence of the Emperor. He would take off his shoes at the entrance way, after the Japanese manner to achieve cleanliness in the house and show respect, replacing them with slippers provided for the purpose. But Terry was a heavy man with high blood pressure; when he was at home he was careful not to bend over or exert himself in any way, and it was difficult and dangerous for him to lean down to change his shoes. He was seeing the Emperor every day and after a few calls he said to him, "Sire, let's dispense with that. I'm too sick and it takes too much time." The Emperor assented. They also cut short the formalized greetings, instead of the elaborate bowing and the crossfire of formal questions as to everyone's health, Terry would tell the Emperor, "Good morning, sire"; the Emperor would bow and say, "Please sit down," and that, quite sensibly, was all there was to it.

As a courtesy to Terry, I was invited to have audience with the Emperor and Empress. How excited and nervous my husband was! He was a member of the Imperial Household and if his foreign wife did not carry the thing off correctly everyone from the chamberlains to the scullery maids would know him as the man with the *gaijin* wife who knew no manners.

I was carefully instructed as to the procedure. The ceremony would be formal and brief. I should approach and bow to each of the ruling monarchs, answer their questions, remain standing and watch the chamberlain on the Emperor's right for my cue to depart, and in departing I must back out and not turn my back on Their Majesties.

At 10:30, the appointed hour, I was dressed in a beige linen lace dress, gloves to the elbows, buff colored shoes with high heels, a brown pillbox straw hat, and a string of pearls. I waited in the anteroom with my anxious husband. He patted me on the back when I was announced. I thought of how a football coach sends an untried but eager substitute in to replace the injured star.

On entering the royal presence I found them standing in front of a gold screen. They appeared happy and pleased to see me. I bowed at the entrance to them both and then to each side, first to the Emperor and then to the Empress, and each of them shook my hand. The Emperor asked me to sit down. I was so engaged in following the beautiful Japanese the Empress was speaking that I hardly noticed this shattering of precedent; so far as I know no other woman had ever been invited to sit down on such an occasion. One would ask me a question, which the chamberlain would translate, and then my reply would be translated.

"You have been married a long time, we understand, and have been a great help to your husband."

I replied that we had been married since 1931 and I had tried to help. The Emperor then said,

"I am very grateful."

The Empress asked me about my mother and where she was. When I told her that my mother had heard nothing directly from me for four years, tears flooded into her eyes. The Emperor said he had been told that I understood the Japanese very well, and he expressed admiration that I should have remained with them during the war. I said I had wanted to prove that an American woman could bear as much for her family as the Japanese women could. The Empress said I had surpassed them.

The chamberlain to the Emperor's right was shuffling uneasily.

225

I saw him catch the Emperor's eye and almost imperceptibly His Majesty shook his head.

The Emperor then asked if I had been treated very badly by his people. I was glad to answer. There were so many instances of unusual kindness shown me. I told him of a woman who, a month or so after the surrender, had come alone across the entire width of Tokyo to bring me two rolls of bread wrapped in a newspaper because she knew I had not had bread for months— no, his people had not treated me badly.

The Empress asked about Mako and told me Terry had shown her the child's picture. She wanted to know how serious Terry's illness was. I told her he was sick but that he had to be working now. They asked about my house and the Empress was especially interested to know how our daily lives were carried on. The Emperor asked about Bonner Fellers. Then the chamberlain, growing restive again, nodded to me and I executed my withdrawal, moving backward without turning around.

Many times Japanese had told Terry and me with some wistfulness that it was a rare and precious thing, our romance. "Not many Japanese ever have a chance to have a romance like yours!"

But it occurred to me that the royal couple was an exception to that unhappy rule.

I saw the Empress several times after that. Once, while Mako and I were walking through the gardens of the Palace we heard someone say, "The Empress is coming!" We stepped back off the path. There was the Empress in a purple kimono strolling with her lady in waiting. She saw us and started toward where we were, a happy smile on her face, but the lady in waiting said something low in her ear and they passed on, the Empress turning to look again and again. As they passed, I bowed and was amused to see Mariko bent almost double, her tall thin body resembling a croquet wicket. The lady in waiting had reminded the Empress that there were many people in the gardens and that if she spoke to us she would be obliged to speak to everyone.

Sometime later I sat next to the Empress at a luncheon at the Palace.

"Oh, I saw Mariko-chan!" she exclaimed joyously.

She displayed the most avid curiosity about her and wanted to know what I did each day, from the time I got up, in the way of keeping house and shopping. We were still talking when it came time to leave. The Emperor and Terry were going to walk to the gate together and they were waiting on us. His Majesty stood at the door of the dining room silently demanding that we come on, and I thought that a husband's impatience was a part of my daily life that I need not explain.

George Atcheson had been on the *Panay* when it was sunk in 1933 by the Japanese, and he had witnessed Japanese atrocities in Nanking. When it was learned that he was coming out as adviser to MacArthur, a feeling of dismay went through the Japanese who knew him. We had been acquainted with him in Washington, over the telephone, at least, but we too feared he would be too hard on the conquered.

Soon after his arrival in Tokyo he came to call, saying he wanted to meet the woman whose voice he had known over the telephone in Washington. How embarrassed we were that the house was frigid. We wrapped him in a blanket and set a *hibachi* at his feet. He looked like an Eskimo but he never got warm.

Terry discovered our mistaken opinion of Atcheson first. He came home one evening, flushed in the face and with the vein at the temple pulsating. Mako and I took him into the warmest room we had, removed his coat, and brought tea as we always did. After one cup his spirits returned and he wanted to laugh with us. It seemed Atcheson had given him a large heavy object about the size of a squash and asked that it be presented to the Emperor. It was some part of a whale and from the first successful whaling expedition since the surrender. Terry knew nothing of whales or what this bone might be, but he appreciated Atcheson's good will and his efforts at rebuilding the fishing industry. He knew the Emperor's hobbies included the study of marine life.

Feeling extremely silly, Terry presented himself at the Palace with the gift wrapped in papers. He had to tell his secretary not to put ribbons on it.

"Sire, I have something for you. A gift from Mr. Atcheson. I don't know exactly. . . ."

"Oh, thank you! What a fine specimen! The middle ear of the blue whale. Convey my thanks to Mr. Atcheson," and Hirohito examined the bone excitedly.

From this and many other things we perceived that Atcheson was a much larger man than we had thought. He was firm with those responsible for Japan's folly but he was compassionate with the people—not the indiscriminate and overly-righteous avenger some in his place would have been. As time went on our friendship grew warmer and, as he noted happily, the house grew warmer, too. We had found a woodburning stove and it kept the living room and dining room comfortable.

George made trips to and from the United States at intervals, and on one occasion as he was leaving he asked me if he could do anything for me. I told him gleefully that he could bring me a new dress. I gave him the size and admonished him to have his wife do the selecting.

Shortly he returned and telephoned us to come over to see what he had for us. I suppose he had broken all the rules in flying back with such a large satchel bulging with the dress, shirts for Terry, some liqueurs and cigarettes, and candy for Mako. The bags of the diplomats are not inspected at customs. Anyway, Terry went over immediately to pick up the haul.

He had seen Atcheson and was just leaving with the satchel, about to get into "the cement mixer," when two M.P.'s took hold of the bag and told him to get in their jeep which had pulled up behind the limousine. They furnished no explanation, hustled Terry into the rear of the jeep with two other M.P.'s, and went bounding down the road to the stockade. Terry's dazed chauffeur had no choice but to drive back to the Imperial Household alone, leaving his master in the hands of the Americans.

At the stockade headquarters the satchel was opened and its contents examined with knowing, satisfied eyes by the M.P.'s.

"Unh-huh, two Arrow shirts, American shirts, where did you get *them*, bud? One carton Camel cigarettes, they were not made in Japan, were they now, bud? Where did you get them? And candy and a dress for the girl friend, eh, and all made in the States. All right, what black-market dealer did you get them from?"

At each question Terry tried to explain where he got them. He asked repeatedly that he be permitted to call George or that they place a call to verify his story. They would not permit him to call nor would they call themselves, doubtless thinking the story too absurd to be worthy of checking. Terry took a grip on himself, knowing the great danger if he should become angry. His mental state was quieted when a Negro M.P. gave him a letter in Japanese from his "girl friend" to read. The author of the letter, it soon appeared, was not the lady she might have been and was, regrettably, one of what the soldiers called the "pon-pon" set. The letter grew more and more lascivious with each line. The white M. P.'s huddled close to hear the contents which their colored comrade in arms had ordered their "gook" prisoner to translate. Terry read slowly and with painful emphasis until the Negro muttered, "O.K., that's all, that's good, thanks, don't read no more."

But Terry insisted that there was more and it was important. He continued to read to the raucous enjoyment of the audience. When he had finished, the Negro took the letter, thrust it into his pocket, and sat down in a corner some distance away.

Terry was permitted to use the stockade latrine, but when it seemed to his captors that he was staying there too long, they went in and slapped him on the shoulder, "Hubba hubba, bub!" In vain did Terry search his vocabulary of Brown-learned slang for the meaning of this, but he got the general idea and returned to the grilling. The questions began again; from his pocket they took his fountain pen given him by Dick Buttrick and they wondered at his brown felt hat, with the inscription inside, "Roma, Italia." They did not know how he had come by any of it but were sure was not telling the truth. He wondered wryly what would happen if he told them in addition to the goods made in the States he had an American wife—could he explain where he had gotten her?

He was picked up around five in the evening. At ten he was allowed to call the chief of the metropolitan police of Tokyo, a personal acquaintance, who was permitted to take him into custody overnight with the agreement that he be returned in the morning.

I was notified that Terry was spending the night out and only learned the next morning what was going on. I ran the six blocks from our house to where Major Harris lived; he was the nearest American whom I knew who would help. When I got there, around nine in the morning, the Major was having coffee and reading the Sunday paper. He was unshaven but announced, as he put on his blouse, that he would not shave, he looked tougher without it. At the provost marshal's office we interviewed a bored sergeant who said, "Oh, that case. He's already released."

We went to George Atcheson's. In a violent rage, which the State Department reserves for the army on such occasions and is returned by the army on others, he telephoned the head provost marshal. The general said the M.P.'s had orders to pick up Japanese who had American goods—regardless—that it was not their fault. Atcheson insisted they should have checked the man's story. Finally the general agreed. Terry was angry because they had kept the fountain pen which was not in the satchel.

Later that afternoon, George appeared at our door with the satchel and the fountain pen. Terry said it was all for the good because the regulations were changed thereafter and the M.P.'s were instructed to verify the story of any Japanese they picked up about articles in his possession.

It was a pity men like George were not in charge of the war crimes trials. There should have been such trials and a purpose could have been served by them, but they failed miserably the way they were carried out.

General Tomoyuki Yamashita, "The Tiger of Malaya," was the first. He was brought to trial in Manila in October of 1945 before a military commission. The charge against him was not that he ordered or condoned the atrocities committed by troops under his command (at the time the Philippines were being re-invaded by the Americans) but simply that such atrocities were so widespread that they must have resulted from his failure to effectively control his troops. At the time of his trial, the Japanese public was not yet willing to believe that a Japanese general would have participated in such atrocities, any more than the American public would have believed a West Pointer could be guilty of such an offense. They thought he was being tried for defeating the British in Malaya. The Japanese had made a movie of the surrender there which showed the British general truculently attempting to state the terms of surrender and Yamashita striking the table with his fist and declaring,

"Enough of that. We will have no more talk like that at this table. I will make the terms!"

To the populace that was the crime of which Yamashita stood accused—putting the white man in his place. We learned that the General himself had much admiration for American soldiers and was supremely confident that they would not see their antagonist on the field of honor sacrificed to political propaganda and the spirit of vengeance.

Yamashita had been popular and a strong rival of Tojo, such a rival that for a while after his victories in Malaya mention of his name was forbidden in Japan. Tojo sent him to the Philippines to bury him from public view and people were arrested for wondering aloud what had become of him. This had aroused much sympathy for Yamashita, especially toward the end when Tojo had resigned and made a shameful failure of his suicide attempt—dishonoring his people to behave with so little dignity as to fail at *harakiri*. How could one with so little ability have run the government?

The Commission which tried Yamashita was ordered to disregard the usual rules of evidence and it proceeded with the trial so hastily that the accused had little time in which to defend. The officers appointed to defend him worked diligently and, upon his conviction, took the case to the Supreme Court of the United States, which upheld the conviction in a split decision. The dissents were strongly worded to the effect that Yamashita's rights were grossly violated and that the procedure used in his conviction would support the punishment of the vanquished by the victorious under most any circumstances and regardless of his personal culpability.

When Yamashita was hanged his dignity masked any fear of death, any humiliation at the ignominy of the public spectacle, and any astonishment that the Americans would execute their adversary in battle.

Later, as the soldiers came home and corroborated the stories of brutality and oppression, public sentiment underwent a great change. People began to realize what fools had been made of them. They saw the parallel between their mistaken certainty that their forces had treated prisoners decently and their mistaken certainty that Japan had been forced into the war—they saw that the military party had not been responsible to them in either respect. The average citizen had never known much about the previous barbarities of Japanese soldiers at Nanking for which Itagaki was taken as a war criminal. The revelations about Nanking and later outrages during the war came as a dreadful, sickening surprise. The people now realized also that while their government had been faced with very grave problems in the period before the war, the solution attempted by the militarists was wrong both morally and practically. It had increased the evils it was meant to cure to a grotesque degree. For had not the result strengthened the old enemy, Russia, which was now repossessed of territory won by Japan in the old war, and were not Formosa and all the empire of islands gone? What chance had they ever had? Granting the valor of her sailors who sank the Allied cruisers off Savo Island, did the admirals really calculate that the war could be won without the staggering losses of the Coral Sea and Midway? Did they suppose American shipyards could not replace American losses threefold—whereas the Japanese yards could not begin to rebuild the sunken warships of the Imperial Navy? How had the government thought the millions of tons of merchant shipping were to be replaced? Did they think that the American submarines and bombers would not sink their freighters by the hundreds? Not until it was over did the people have opportunity to judge these things—then it was clear that the miscalculation had been enormous. A war spread over thousands of miles of water from Attu to Guadalcanal could only be a test of which country could produce the most planes and ships; and the industrial might of Japan did not even remotely rival that of the United States. The conclusion reached in the syllogism based on these premises was obvious. What solution should have been sought was less obvious but there could be no doubt but that the government had done the worst thing possible.

Looking now at themselves more carefully than they had ever done in their history, the Japanese perceived not only the fanaticism of the militarists but also their own great ignorance in having trusted them. The people's disillusionment penetrated to the marrow. In natural consequence, a public scapegoat was sought and readily found in all military people of whatever rank. Everywhere the returning veterans were treated with resentment and contempt. There were few who did not indulge in the indiscriminate bitterness. My husband was one of these few; possibly because he had realized what would happen from the start, he said nothing further against the militarists after the inevitable defeat had come.

Had the trials proceeded with dispatch at this time and the ample proof of guilt of some of the accused been presented before neutral judges, most Japanese would have cheered the results. It was tragic that this did not happen. Too many were tried and the delays of the law were multiplied and persisted in from month to month and year to year so that judgments were not reached until 1948 and 1949. Terry was gravely disappointed that the trials did not succeed in the propaganda effect intended and thought it unwise that the particular political appointees sent out from the United States should have been chosen to match wits with some of the best brains, evil or not, of the Japanese nation.

Mako and I witnessed Tojo's trial. The people would have lynched him themselves had they had opportunity. He had betrayed them into the war and perpetrated the cruelties that had abased his people. He was despised for having failed at suicide, thus permitting the Americans to nurse him tenderly back to health to stand public trial. There was a saying expressive of the people's resentment at such awkwardness, "Going to be another Tojo, not even able to kill yourself?"

The American prosecutor did not handle his examination of the former premier well. He postured in front of Tojo, jibed at him, and tried to outwit him. He referred sarcastically to the change in the educational system, the abolishing of Ichiko and other Japanese schools, and asked Tojo if he had not kept the Education Ministry under his thumb when he was prime minister, and if it was not much improved by the democratic rule imposed by the occupation. To this Tojo pointed out calmly that he had been in prison for the past two years and was in no position to know how well the Americans were succeeding. There was general laughter, joined in by American officers among the spectators.

The prosecutor called Tojo "Mr. Tojo" and asked him if he was aware that he was only "Mister" and no longer "General." "*Mochiron* (Of course)," stated Tojo.

At one point in the translation where Tojo had replied, "I didn't have enough understanding," the interpreter put it in English, "I didn't have enough virtue." The gallery, who had suspected Tojo might be somewhat short on virtue, was greatly amused. Tojo blurted out, "That is not right, it is not translated correctly!"

Once he leaned over to tie his shoe and sighed; the microphone amplified a loud noise out of the groan, "*Yaa, dokkoi sho* (Oh, me, oh my)," and again the audience was amused.

General Homma had been tried in Manila for the death march of Bataan. He pleaded that he did not know what was happening and had not ordered or condoned the offenses. He was a big, fine-looking man who had spent sixteen years in the British Army after graduating from Sandhurst. Before the war he had tried to divide the army and avoid the approaching conflict. Many of the army officers were his followers and with luck he might have succeeded.

I was told this story by an American officer. He said that

Mrs. Homma was flown from Japan to Manila to be a witness at the trial. She was a small, gentle lady who knew nothing about the issues in which she had to play a part. A WAC was ordered to stay with her, see her to and from her apartment, and guard her against the Filipinos. The WAC was bitterly resentful at such duty and made a point of showing her hatred to Mrs. Homma. For several weeks they were together constantly, at the trials, in the apartment, and going back and forth.

When Mrs. Homma was called to the stand she could only state that the General had been good to her and exceedingly kind to their servants, while her accused husband sat bolt upright and stared straight ahead, never once looking in her direction.

When the trials were over, Homma gave her several letters to read after his death. He wrote her to carry on, that after all he was a soldier and a soldier is dead from the moment he goes into the army, that she should consider his passing as an inevitable loss of war itself.

Mrs. Homma was flown back to Tokyo before her husband was executed. On the way, the heating system on the plane failed and the WAC, who had become very sympathetic, got out an army blanket to keep her charge warm. She took the blanket to Mrs. Homma and unfolded it. The General's lady glanced up at the big U.S. printed on the blanket and shook her head in refusal. She sat quietly in the bucket seat and nearly froze before they descended to land.

Soon after, her husband refused to be helped and walked un-attended to the stake to face the firing squad, remarking that he did not wish to be blindfolded, he was not afraid of guns.

There was an execution every few days now although no one was permitted to know in advance who would be next. The widows were not permitted to have the ashes of their condemned husbands because the authorities thought this would foster nationalism again. One night our little girl awoke with a scream, and when we went to comfort her she told us she had been dreaming that a man was being hanged in our garden.

We had fears for many of our friends, but most of all for Mr.

Shigemitsu. The Americans, British, and Dutch appeared to have no charges against him, but until the purges should be over we were anxious for his safety.

The day before the Class "A" defendants were to go on trial, Terry came from the Palace and told us that Mr. Shigemitsu was a defendant. He wanted me to understand that it was at the request of the Russians who were pushing for convictions of everyone who had served in their country; we had been correctly informed about the American and British intentions.

Terry would not attend the trials but Mako and I did. Along with his goddaughter I watched Mr. Shigemitsu hobble in, disdaining earphones, assistance, or any defense. His American lawyers, appointed by the court, read affidavits from Churchill, Grew, Sir Miles Lampsdon, and others. Terry told us nothing could be done to get Shigemitsu to fight the charges, that even these affidavits had been sent unsolicited.

Mr. Shigemitsu was convicted and sentenced to seven years in prison.

The last thing he told me was, "Don't feel too badly, Gwen. I can rest and read and write. If this will help deter future wars, I am all for it."

Many who were not prosecuted by the Americans were convicted and punished by the Japanese public. One friend of ours was a colonel when the war ended and, of course, he was purged from holding office by the Americans, but he was punished more severely by the Japanese. They had come to regard the military as responsible for all their ills, and the ills were grievous. Even our friend's son no longer wished to associate with him, as the father stated, "He is very much oppressed in my presence." The ex-officer could not get a job and returned to the country to work as a farmer, doing the jobs he had done when he was a boy. As he said, his countrymen considered him a "useless person." He had been one of Homma's peace party group and the American forces eventually found use for him in the section on Japanese history. They called him "Colonel" and he began to regain his self-respect.

15

THE BROKEN HEADSTONE

TOWARD the end of 1947, my husband began to show further signs of the toll his work was exacting from his tired body. His face was red and the vein at his temple was showing violently each night when he returned from work. We redoubled our efforts at getting him to rest completely once he was home. In February he collapsed with another stroke.

Ashen faced, he lay in bed, Taro and a coterie of young friends about him. The stroke had paralyzed one side of his face and his tongue was so twisted that he found it easier to speak in English than in Japanese. For several weeks he remained in the hospital, then he was allowed to come home to have bed rest for an additional period. I took the first cherry blossoms in to him. This was a great mistake because, when he looked at that symbol of quick death at the peak of one's powers and beauty, he could no longer control his despair and, for the only time in all his long illness, he broke down.

Two months in bed and he was able to get up and go out again. It was more difficult than ever for him to walk, but in time his face returned to normal except that his mouth remained slightly twisted. No one but Mariko and I noticed it except when he spoke, but then it was as though he were trying to speak from one side of his mouth. Errors began to appear in his English speech that he had never made before.

One of our friends from America brought me two pairs of shoes to give to Admiral Nomura. Taking the shoes, I journeyed with them across Tokyo to the suburb where he lived. I was eager to see him again.

Just before Pearl Harbor he had called us once at home. It was unusual for the Ambassador to call a subordinate except on business, and I told him I was sorry but Terry was playing golf at Burning Tree. He said he didn't want to see Terry, he wanted to come to see me. I told him I would be delighted.

He came in and spun his hat toward a chair, a trick of his; it hit exactly in place, to the great delight of little Mako. He sat down and we talked. He said:

"I've been thinking of you. You know I have been busy."

"I imagine you have, Ambassador Nomura."

"It must be terrible for you, your country and your husband's country in a serious dispute and you unable to do anything. I just brought you a little present to show you how much I think of you. You are a fine and a brave woman."

He took out a box of cultured pearls. I could have wept. They were Mikimoto pearls. I said,

"Ambassador Nomura, you sweet thing!"

"Say that again," replied my delighted guest, and I did so with fervor.

Then he asked if I liked to cook, to make fried chicken. I asked if he wished to come to dinner one evening. He told me,

"You know, Mrs. Terasaki, I am very lonely. My personnel do not invite me. I know how they feel. I am very lonely. How about tomorrow night?"

So he had come to dinner and eaten my fried chicken. Terry was astonished and deeply pleased at the visit. He and the Admiral talked for hours at the failure of understanding and the irresponsibility of the war party which had led us to the brink of an unnecessary war. When I insisted we change the subject, they talked about movies; Nomura was very fond of movies. Driving his car and going to the cinema were his chief relaxations. He drove every afternoon around Washington. The waitresses all knew him, even after long absences, partly because he took three helpings of ice cream.

It took me all day to reach Nomura's residence in a suburb. He had moved there because his home had burned down in Tokyo. When I arrived he greeted me in an open shirt and sleeveless sweater. He took me to his study and showed me many interesting things, letters from American naval personnel he had known, curios he had picked up all over the world. He sat down, took off his slippers, and tried on the shoes.

"Oh, they fit!" he said. His feet were too large for the sizes carried in Tokyo stores; he weighed about two hundred pounds and stood six feet. He tried on both pairs and began wearing one of them at once.

"You fine, brave girl, to come out here with these for me."

I had always wanted to ask Admiral Nomura about his careers. He had been president of Peer's school, where the children of the nobility went, he had been Admiral of the navy, and had served as Foreign Minister and Ambassador. I asked which he preferred.

He looked at me with a warm smile and remarked,

"Just plain schoolteacher."

We talked of Terry and his work, the future of America, and what the Russians would do. It was very late indeed when I got home.

In the fall of 1948, on orders of his doctor, Terry left for a short rest at a warm spring near Miyanoshita. The Emperor's physician was personally attending him since a fall that he had had in the Emperor's presence. Terry had been away only a day or so when Mako suddenly developed the symptoms of appendicitis. It was strictly against the rules for her to go to a military hospital since she had no status as a dependent of American personnel. However, I had never relinquished my citizenship or quite agreed that Mako was a foreigner so I immediately set out to see if I could get special dispensation for her. Japanese hospitals were dreadfully overcrowded and short on supplies.

I asked George Atcheson if something could not be done, inasmuch as the child had an American parent, and he said he would intervene for her. I was especially thankful because Terry would not have to know of her illness if the hospitalization was handled in this way. George asked me about Terry; he had heard of his falling. He suggested that Terry be examined by MacArthur's personal physician, Colonel Kendrick—not that the Emperor's doctor was not equally capable, but simply that two examinations might be more thorough than one. I agreed to this, of course, if we could get Terry to assent.

I was never able to do anything toward repaying George Atcheson for his supreme kindness. Soon after I had spoken to him about Terry he was aboard an airplane which crashed into the Pacific enroute to the United States. A survivor told me his last words as the plane plunged toward the water were, "It can't be helped."

There was no way of preventing news of this tragedy from reaching Terry. When he heard it, he went out to the resort at Sagami Bay and waded in the sea, a gesture of homage typically Japanese.

Mako was installed at the Army General Hospital. Although the chart at the foot of her bed showed her name, her Japanese parentage, and that she had no right to be there, no one seemed the least concerned on that account. The nurses and patients alike were very kind to her. Her appendix was removed and she recovered quickly, spending her time in bed sketching strong faces of old men and women weighed down by the war.

I had no time now to be concerned with her predilection for tragedy as a subject for her paintings. Terry had returned from the hot springs and I had to try to coax him into the further medical examination George Atcheson had suggested. I told him first of Mako's illness and recovery to perfect health and extolled the abilities of the occupation medical staff. Then I advised him that the fullest diagnosis of his own condition could be had from the same physicians. He did not resist the suggestion and agreed to go, commenting only once that it would not do any good.

He visited the hospital several days while all manner of tests were run on him. Perhaps the X-rays and microscopic examinations, one of the marvelous tests, would reveal that the illness was curable.

Sometime later, after the tests had been completed and studied, a doctor (a captain) telephoned me. Terry was sitting nearby when I answered the telephone.

"Yes, this is Mrs. Terasaki speaking."

"I've called to tell you our opinion about your husband," a harrassed voice said, "and in sum, Mrs. Terasaki, I'm sorry to have to tell you this, but your husband is going to die—when, I cannot say. He may live a few years—he may die tomorrow. He will have another stroke which will eventually kill him. Of course, he should eat lightly, give up smoking, and not overexert himself. Goodbye, Mrs. Terasaki."

With Terry at my side waiting for the verdict, I continued speaking into the telephone—

"Yes, doctor, I'll tell him to be careful—not to overeat, not to smoke—yes, doctor, he'll live for years—I'll tell him."

As soon as I could slip away I raced to Dr. Kendrick's office. I sat there in a fit of trembling until I could see him. He told me he was sorry the Captain had been so abrupt; the Captain was so overworked at that time that he could not help being unceremonious. Colonel Kendrick told me he knew I wanted to know the facts and he showed me an X-ray of Terry's heart. It was enlarged to twice the size of a normal heart that was shown me in comparison. It was hopeless; Terry had an advanced state of hypertension and the medical world could do nothing for him. He would live a while longer and he would die; there was no way to know how long it would be, but it would not likely be more than a year or so. He might as well continue his work but

241

should be careful of his diet, stop smoking, and all the other things we had heard so often before.

Terry was told to take certain medicines and to follow a prescribed routine of treatment. He meekly agreed. At times he seemed to know it was hopeless but at other times he would tell me he felt much better, that it was only a question of time before he would be well.

"It is a question of will, Gwen, of having a strong mind. I shall get well! I have so much to do and we have so long to live together, to watch Mariko and the future."

I tried to believe he would recover. Doctors had been wrong before. If I could not believe he would live, how could I go on? I shrank before the prospect of long empty years of remaining alive without his force and purpose beside me. I thought of all the famous people who had been given only a short span to live and had survived to achieve a great place for themselves and live to a very ripe old age.

As the months passed and Terry remained weak and unsteady, he began to be interested in all kinds of unusual treatments, some of which seemed to me more than a little superstitious. He did not slow down at the office or let up on his official duties, and the doctors said probably that was wise, but he did do some remarkably foolish things in his desperation to recover. I suppose no one knows the desolation of physical debility like a person who has been athletic and bold, who, for instance, has played golf and tennis and swum miles in the sea off the beach at Atami. Terry went to a healer who stuck pine needles into him, who put a counter-irritant called *o kyū* on the back of his hand and then set fire to it, scorching a circle of flesh. *O kyū* is often so used in Japan and the practice sounds more shocking than it really is, or so I told myself. Terry also resorted to leeches, horrible things that sucked until they fell away from his inflamed skin, tumescent with his blood.

He fell into the habit of going to the movies for relaxation at times when he was not permitted by the doctors to work. His eyesight was growing weaker, so he would see only half the movie one day and time himself exactly to see the remaining half the next day. Mako found in him her constant companion, anytime she wanted to go to a movie he was ready to go with her. The three of us went to "Treasure of Sierra Madre" together and Terry insisted on seeing it to the end; he remarked that it was one of the best movies he had ever seen.

Taira confirmed to me what Colonel Kendrick had said. We spoke of Terry's health constantly. Once I mentioned to him the stiffness that had come in the little finger of Terry's left hand while we were interned at White Sulphur. Taira became intensely interested and asked that I tell him exactly when I first noticed it, how long before the finger was well again, and everything I could remember. He told me the stiff finger might have indicated a slight stroke and that the chances were it had been caused by the shock of Pearl Harbor.

Terry's illness had, when I realized it, been obvious ever since Pearl Harbor. His manner had undergone a great change from the moment the war had begun. He sometimes complained, not seriously but rather casually, that he felt as though something were pressing in on his head, as though he might be wearing a lead cap; he tired easily and became depressed at the least difficulties. For a time during internment I was almost ashamed of him, so limp and dependent had he become, so dispirited and remote. Gradually, though, he seemed to recover; when he was looking for a house for us, when he was meeting with the group for postwar planning during the war, or when Mako would speak polished Japanese to him, he would seem to take a new breath and determine to see things through. At other times it was as though reality had become unbearable for him and he lived unto himself, guarding the remaining strength he had like a hibernating animal until he could again take part in the shaping of things. The attack of pneumonia at Yoshihama and the two periods of hospitalization at Saint Luke's for high blood pressure had taken their toll.

He would not tell me how he felt and I did not speak of it often. There seemed little to be done about it and I wished to divert

him. As the weeks and months passed, I felt more often the pang
of anxiety when the vein at his temple stood out, swelling extraordinarily just beneath the surface of the skin into a huge knot.

He had ceased any strenuous exercise and tried to stop smoking in accordance with the doctor's orders. We took walks each
night at twilight around the park, Terry going slowly, leaning
on his cane, with me at his side. Mako was growing up and rarely
went with us anymore. She preferred to stay at the house with
her paints ·or her books and occasionally made trips into the
country with her young friends. Terry seemed worried about
her, he wanted her in America where she could forget some of
what she had witnessed since, as a child of nine, she had left my
country in 1942. But there seemed no way for her to leave Tokyo
unless I went with her and, of course, I could not leave.

Christmas, 1948, was less austere than the past holiday seasons.
We had a huge tree that the maid had arranged to get for us
through the black market. It stayed up until the middle of January.
I became so fearful it might catch on fire that I had it removed
to the alley while Terry was at the Palace one day. He hated to
have the Christmas tree removed, wanting to keep it as a symbol
of the season—it was like his inability to sleep the night before
Christmas or before his birthday.

Since the New Year was beginning, we planned to go to the
Terasaki tomb. For the past three years that we had been back
in Tokyo the visit to the cemetery had been on our minds. We
had put it off and put it off, knowing the cemetery had been
bombed. Now, it appeared the time had come, and we laid plans
to make the trip that week end.

On Saturday morning we took the train. It ran for miles to
the suburbs of Tokyo, past empty, charred remains of homes
and the makeshift hovels which were unchanged since September,
1945, past new buildings recently erected, and past the rubble
of the bombings. It seemed there were sections where reconstruc-
tion was proceeding apace and other sections where nothing had
been done since the surrender.

We knew what the park would look like and dreaded to see

it. Terry had spoken often of his father, both before and after we were married, and I felt a great kinship with him. The elder Terasaki had been a handsome man, distinguished and gallant and something of a "plunger" in the export-import business. He was sometimes very wealthy, sometimes quite poor, but always willing to take a gamble. Terry adored him and venerated his memory as symbolic of the best of Japan. Often I had heard him remark when some business at hand had been very trying:

"Oh, for more men like my father—where is the Japan of my father?"

It was a cold, clear day. The air was sparkling and we got off the *shōsen* before our stop so we could walk the rest of the way to the Akasaka district. Terry stopped to gaze at a grove of burned-out trees, and we slowed our walk. Then, motioning to a devastated spot that had once been wooded, Terry said in a choked voice,

"My mother and father lie there. We must find the spot."

The destruction was complete. The lovely old temple had burned and in its place stood a crude shack. We called and knocked on the door—no response. When we were ready to move on, an old nun with a shaved head drew back the sliding door and bowed. Her dim old eyes were unknowing until Terry spoke.

"Ah, Terasaki-san, *shibaraku de-gozaimasu* (It's been a long time!)" she cried and then was silent.

That moment twenty years of our past went through my mind. Terry had brought his bride to his parents' tomb when he first took her out to Japan. As a proper Japanese son he wanted to introduce his young wife to them. He taught me how to pour the water on the stones, using the tiny bamboo dipper, three times for each stone. Then the sticks of fragrant incense and the three bows upon leaving. We returned to the cemetery each time we were ordered to a new post and again after returning to Japan. Before Mako's birth we went there to inform the grandparents of the expected child. It had been four years after Mako was born in Shanghai before we got back to Tokyo. We took her to

245

Akasaka and her little hands held the dipper and her little fingers touched the match to the incense.

I knew we were all three thinking the same thoughts. Abruptly I asked the nun,

"Are you alone here now?"

She told us that the other nuns were dead. Bombs and the privations of war had taken them. She added,

"I want to see all the graves made dignified again—then I'll seek my peace in the western hills."

We began our search, Terry poking with his cane through the rubble, searching for headstones. We picked up each stone or slab with characters on it, looking for the name "Terasaki." On and on we searched and I knew he was getting very tired. Then, his face despairing, he turned to me and said,

"It is no use—there is no tomb, now."

I said brightly, "Terry, let's stop and eat our *o bentō*. I'll ask the nun to brew us tea. After a rest we'll start again."

We found a flat rock to sit on, opened our lunch boxes, and ate in silence. The nun's steaming green tea brought color to Terry's face and I felt my spirits rise. I said,

"Terry, we are only feeling sorry for ourselves. Your father's spirit is free and he is forever in your heart."

Terry replied, "We Japanese are always closely associated with our dead—that closeness is an inspiration for us. In a way we do not actually accept death at all—it is so tied up with this great thing we know as life."

I sat longer, considering what he had said. Then he spoke again,

"When we do homage at the tombs of our beloved dead, we show them we know that in many ways they are earthbound and still a part of our lives here."

We arose. The old nun came and showed us a map of the cemetery that she had drawn from memory. Following her directions, we concentrated on that section where the tomb appeared on her crude map.

A shout went up! Terry had found a memorial slab—jagged and cracked through the center. The "Tera" had been blown off but the "saki" and a date remained. I ran to him. He had removed his hat and stood rubbing his hand over the cold stone. The nun produced incense and its purple, sweet smoke rose in the air.

Terry took me in his arms—how slight they had become—and I heard him whisper,

"Gwen, I know I will never be well again. Now wait and listen! I cannot recover. It will soon be over for me. Therefore you must take Mariko and return to your country. You understand, that will be best!"

I wept. I clung to him and looking over his shoulder raised my eyes to the sky and the gaunt, barren trees.

Time passed and we put off making a final decision concerning my taking Mako to America. Her welfare was always foremost in our minds. We wanted our daughter to finish the year's schooling before we left. She was attending the Tokyo Joshi Daigaku (Tokyo Woman's Christian College) taking English, history, and American and English literature courses. Because it was so difficult for one to get around and the occupation forces had taken over most of the amusement centers, we and our friends were without means to provide the youngsters much diversion. When not in school, Mako spent almost all of her time at home sketching, painting, and reading tirelessly. One morning I suggested to Terry that she should do some Japanese-style painting. I was disquieted by the faces she persisted in doing. He asked the famous critic, Mr. Suma, for the name of a painter who could give her instruction in Japanese landscapes. A man was duly chosen and he introduced Mako to rice paper, Japanese ink, and other materials she had never used. He looked at what she had previously done and reported excitedly to her father that she had real ability and a style of her own that might be affected if he should teach her. Terry was inordinately pleased but not sure how much of this was flattery. We had never taken Mako's painting seriously, she had had no lessons, and some of the faces she drew in a frenzy of intense and brief activity. It was some of these that her teacher thought best. Terry asked me what I thought.

"Gwen, was he just saying that to please us? Do you think my little Mari-chan has done anything unusual with her fussing around with her paints?"

I could tell him no more than that I supposed the teacher knew best—after all, Mr. Suma had recommended him.

The next thing I knew Mako's enthusiastic tutor had arranged for her works to be shown at a gallery in Tokyo along with art done by other Japanese painters, living and dead. Terry was like a child with a new pair of shoes and he bragged about his daughter—a most un-Japanese thing to do.

"Oh, Gwen, have you seen this magazine? Look where it says, 'Terasaki, Mariko, a fifteen-year-old genius.' That's my Mariko! And she is having her things shown with the famous ones!"

"Mr. Suma is such an extravagant person—how generous of him to say that!"

Terry told all his friends and it amused me how he tried to bring every casual conversation around to painting so as to remark,

"Oh, by the way, have you heard about Mariko? She is showing some of her paintings at the gallery this month."

One entire day he spent at the showing at Ueno Art Gallery. After a cursory glance at the other works, he sat down near the corner in the right wing of the gallery where Mako's two pictures hung. One of them was a mountain scene in black and white, the best of the few landscapes she had done. The other was a picture of an old man, a person reduced by fear and crushing disaster to a whimpering animal—she called it "Lost." Terry stationed himself near these pictures all day long, listening to the comments of the spectators who came in groups to stand and gape.

"Some mistake," they would say. "It was not done by a young girl. Too strong. It was done by a man."

"They were done by my daughter, Mariko," said the man sitting there with the cane.

THE BROKEN HEADSTONE

How glad Terry was to see his friends that day!

For her part, Mariko, who had conditioned herself to expecting the worst, was overcome by it all and was walking on air. She followed the crowds around to hear them exclaim over her works. I saw her there (the whole family was there) on the second day of the exhibition, standing tall in the midst of some Imperial University students, in happy anonymity, listening to what they said. One of the students remarked that the landscape could not have been done by a Japanese. Mako allowed herself a slight smirk as she overheard them examining the nameplate and determining that maybe after all it could have been done by a native. She would stand close, then back up, craning her head this way and that, scrutinizing the pictures along with the others. She listened in silence as they wondered aloud what medium she had worked with, and she was watching when one furtively touched the painting and informed the others, "*Kurepasu* (A chalk-like crayon)."

Soon after, an art magazine carried one of Mariko's paintings on the cover. It was entitled, "Grief," the portrait of a bowed old man, leaning forward with a hand over his eyes. How many copies of the issue her exultant father bought I do not know, but we had no friends that he failed to present with a copy.

In June of 1949, six of her paintings were shown in an all women's exhibition in Tokyo and she took one of the first prizes with a despairing countenance she called, "Aftermath."

Mr. Suma did a magazine article on her, referring to her exceptional talent and quoting her remark to the painter who had discovered her ability to the effect that she was not sure she would find in America the beautiful subjects he had suggested she would—it was Japan that she wished to paint, "The beauty of the people's suffering." Mr. Suma and other Japanese took very well to that observation.

Japan was changing fast. The MacArthur constitution had converted it into an oriental Switzerland, a pacifist nation, by fundamental law at least. Cabarets in the American style had sprung up, where girls in Western dress—many of them from the Yoshiwara district which the Americans had closed—danced to Stateside "beebop" with the Yankee soldiers and sailors. American slang enjoyed great vogue among the *mobo* (modern boys). With amusement and concern we watched the merging of our national customs. Intermarriage was becoming common and not infrequently one saw the bridegroom dressed in *yukata* (cotton kimono).

With all the veteran government servants on the purge list, an amateur Japanese Diet came to power. A number of women made their unaccustomed appearance there and the socialist representation grew; the Communists, who had been sent into exile before the war by the Japanese and were returned by the hospitality of the Americans afterwards, enjoyed a number of seats. The result was very nearly chaos. The Diet had never reflected the dignity of the Japanese, but now it was bedlam. I remember the disgust with which my husband answered me once when I inquired if that was a baseball game on the radio. "No, my dear, that is the Imperial Diet in session."

One day I started across the booming city to visit friends who lived in Meguro. The *shōsen* had just passed when I reached the station and while I waited for the next, a train carrying repatriated Japanese from Russian camps in Manchuria came in. People in the crowd held up big photographs of their sons and husbands, missing in Russian hands now for four years, imploring the returning men piteously,

"Please, have you seen him? Private Ichiro Suzuki. He was with your division. Please, look! Have you seen my husband?"

A few of the returning soldiers carried red banners and behaved with coldness toward their weeping families. In time, I knew they would be like the rest of the returning "reds." They, too, would grow pinker and pinker and finally throw the red flag away as they settled back into their own lives again.

A boy of twelve and his mother stood near me in the crowd. I heard her tell the child,

"Stand by me, son, do not get too near the train. Your father will be here. I know he will be here. This is the right train. I am sure of it."

As I regarded them, a man in his late thirties in the uniform of a sergeant in the Japanese Marines came out of the mob and approached, a grave look on his countenance. How the woman's face lit up!

The sergeant drew near and bowed. The wife bowed low, then drew the boy up, and presented him. Boy and father bowed to each other.

"Wait a moment, I must dismiss my men."

He turned to loose his pack. The boy stepped quickly to him and took it.

With military curtness the father muttered, *"Arigatō* (Thanks)," and, as he turned to address the squad of men who had lined up behind him, his wife moved near him and took his tunic firmly in her grasp.

"Go home, fellows. I am proud of you, go home now and be at ease!"

They saluted and bowed. *"Sayōnara, sayōnara!"* I saw the whites come in the knuckles of the woman's clenched hand where she held the edge of his blouse.

Then they were gone, leaving me wondering at their manner. Yet, would it have been better in San Francisco and a G.I. had wept, "Oh, my darling wife, words cannot express my joy at this moment"?

How does one greet a son who had grown up while his father was away at a distant war? My Latin friends had always thought my Teutonic restraint remarkable, but what would they think of the Japanese way? I knew the son would have been humiliated had his father touched him in a public show of affection. Perhaps, when words will not suffice the silent way is best, to speak to the boy as though he were one of his father's Marines, saying with the abruptness of command, *"Arigatō."* Intimacy may lie in avoiding inadequate words, in conveying all by saying nothing.

My *shōsen* was there. I collected my wits and got aboard.

Spring came—and still no final decision. Terry continued to get up early, but, instead of playing golf, he would admire his curios, or take a walk, or sit in the garden. We had each learned to follow his own habit about arising. Terry arose early all his life; I slept late, or as late as I could, most of mine. My bedroom was on the second floor. When I arose, he would hear me stirring and come to the bottom of the narrow stairway, looking up at me as he had done at my aunt's home so long ago. His face shone with love as he watched me come down. It was cold in the house that time of morning and he would have on a padded *dotera*. He would hold it open and put it around me as I stepped into the room.

"What a big person we are!" he would say.

That was our "good morning." Then, in spite of the doctor's orders, he would proceed to eat an American breakfast to go with the Japanese breakfast he had taken hours earlier.

His long years of training still inhibited him from expressing affection in words. Over the years this was changing slowly but something in his formal nature still recoiled at acknowledging emotion. I often asked him,

"Terry, do you love me?"

Always he was startled at the question.

"Oh, Gwen—don't you know? Again you ask me such a question—have I failed you in any way?"

Then I would feel ashamed and remind myself that I must be content with the way he looked at me and not expect him to tell me. But this did not mean I could avoid voicing adoration and devotion for him most frequently. He demanded expressions of love from me and basked in my breathlessness. Every night I would lay out his clothes for the following morning, suit, shirt, handkerchief, and socks. He loved pretty ties with small figures. The following morning after getting dressed, he would come to me to be told how well he looked. Often, just in fun, I would say,

"Ready to go?"

He would wait and if I said nothing more, he would remark in a very off-hand way,

252

THE BROKEN HEADSTONE

"Do I look all right?"

One morning when I went down to breakfast, Terry seemed especially pale and listless. He had been up early as usual, admiring his curios and waiting for me before having scrambled eggs and dressing in Western clothes for the day. When the meal was over he went to his room to dress. Some time after, while I was in my bedroom, I heard his light tap at the door.

"Come in. Come in. Darling, you look so tired this morning, why don't you stay—!"

I broke off, seeing his face. His eyes were glistening. He had put on a shirt and wore it unbuttoned. The necktie dangled from his trembling hands and in the strangest tone he spoke low to me,

"Gwen, I cannot tie it!"

He insisted that I tie it for him and he refused to stay at home. He called for the car and was driven to the Palace.

He had been a chain smoker but had finally stopped entirely. It was very difficult for him. He controlled his appetite with less success, and though he had become frail and wasted in appearance he still weighed more than he should have. He could not resist Chinese foods or sweets. He and Nomura were alike in respect to the eating of sweets. The Japanese love of the hot bath and the rub down had always been his and now these, his curios, his walks in the garden, and his work were his entire life. He was working too hard for his weakened condition and he knew it and I knew it, but there was nothing to be done. He was expendable. Whatever failure we had in bridging our two countries, as we had dreamed so long ago, was now in the past; now he had his one opportunity to do something for the future. He went about the matters of state charged to him with dispatch and all the energy his fading strength could muster. He was solemn and wan but again at his work. He knew it might soon be over and it was his wish that Mako now live in my country and finish her education there.

We discussed the possibility of sending her back alone—she could live with my parents and enter school. However, America would be very strange to her now and she would scarcely know

253

her grandparents. It seemed very hard to send her off alone after all she had endured. Her education had been so irregular that we did not know what difficulties she might have in gaining entrance to school. She might be forced to enter high school with children several years younger than she. We also considered the possibility that she might be resented for her Japanese blood. Terry thought that in returning to Japan during the war we had done enough for him; now Mako should be in America and I should be with her, for a while, at least. After a year she would be established in school and have friends; then I could rejoin Terry in Tokyo. Hard as the decision was, it seemed the best thing to do.

When the decision was final, Terry remarked, "After all, this child is as much American as Japanese. She has had so much of Japan! She needs to become acquainted with her mother's country."

It would be difficult to find enough money to pay our passage home. Terry had had his basic salary during the prewar years banked for him in Japan and we lived off his overseas allowance. These Japanese deposits had been inflated to the point where they were virtually without value and what little money we now had was in Washington. Terry's account there had been frozen in 1941 but I might succeed in having it released to me. I had deposited a small sum of my own in a Washington bank, in a joint account with an American friend, to avoid its being frozen. Since Mako would only be permitted to enter the United States on a student visa, she would not be permitted to leave school to work. We would have to be very saving until Terry could work something out to send us American money; for the present he had only *yen* and not nearly enough to convert into any substantial number of dollars. He remarked almost casually that if he should die while we were still in Japan we would be left in a very difficult position.

All of his life Terry had been a highly emotional person and now in his illness he could no longer control his tears at all. For many days before we were to leave, Mako and I were often weeping and he had to leave the room when he saw us.

Our last night he announced that he had a date with his daughter; they were going to the movies together, then they were to visit the famous cake shop in our district. They got the freshest cakes there, for Terry had done favors for the proprietress and Mako was her pet. Strangely enough, when they were gone I no longer cried. I sat on the big couch in the living room looking at each piece of furniture: the carved horse we had gotten in Shanghai, the blue and white Ming vase on the Chinese desk, and the other things I had lived with and loved. Later, I went upstairs to fix in my mind how everything there looked. About nine o'clock, friends came to wish us a good voyage. They waited for some time on Terry and Mako, but they did not return until late.

That night was very bad. I was determined not to think about it, but the question persisted, would I ever see him again?

Morning came, and Mako and I got dressed. Joining Terry downstairs, I announced in an effort at gaiety, "Now, there will be no more weeping. Mako and I can't afford to smear our make-up."

Yoshiko came in and informed us that the limousine from the Imperial Household was outside and the formal gate was being opened to make the chamberlain welcome. We went to the *genkan*. The chamberlain had two attendants with him, carrying great bunches of orchids from the Empress. I was overcome at her generosity—she had already presented me with a lacquer jewel box, an exquisite gift. The chamberlain informed us solemnly that the Empress wished to say *go-kigenyo* and *sayōnara*. We bowed and performed the required ritual in grateful acknowledgement of her thoughtfulness. The chamberlain announced that the limousine was at our service to take us to the boat, and suddenly I realized that I would not see Terry alone before leaving. The chamberlain was telling him how often Her Majesty had inquired of us and Terry was obviously moved at her consideration.

Our bags had already been loaded and we began to move slowly out of the door, which opened on the formal gate at the street. There stood the limousine to take us away. The rear door was already held open for Mako and me to enter.

Terry was dressed in his best suit as was customary at farewell. I remembered his telling me how his mother, dying of cancer, had arisen from her bed and dressed herself in her most beautiful kimono—black with a spray of pine trees decorating the sides and the white family crest on the back between the shoulders—to see her son off when he departed for the United States to attend Brown University. The same son now stood there, with both hands crossed on the head of his cane, leaning forward in his characteristic way, the old commanding presence still remaining; he was—himself. I hugged him briefly in the presence of the Imperial Household representatives and got into the car.

As it moved away from the curb, I waved to him standing there with his cane, the tears had begun to stream down his face. Yoshiko stood protectively at his side. I thought again of his mother. She had died three months after seeing him off to America.

The ship did not sail at once and there were terrible moments when Mako begged me to return. At last, when the propellor began to turn over, the ship became alive, and we started to move out into the harbor, she began to gain control of herself and fell silent. Together we watched the land grow smaller on the horizon and disappear from view. It was then that it came to me what a kindness it had been after all that the chamberlain and strangers were present to witness our leave-taking.

We sailed from Yokohama in August of 1949. Mariko was a tall, angular young lady of seventeen. She was a child who had known little childhood; sometimes in conversation she would betray ignorance of simple, everyday things that all girls her age should know; sometimes she quietly announced in a matter of fact tone something which illustrated the insight of one very old and wise who had suffered much. I knew how her father hated to part with her. From the time he had first fainted at her

256

sight in the hospital in Shanghai, she had given him pride and pleasure. He had thrown her in the sea to learn to swim in Cuba and, to the relief of her mother who came near to swooning, she had struck out with a dog paddle to shore. Someone had taught her a few words of Court Japanese and her speech had brought tears to Terry's eyes. He saw in her his hope for the new Japan, the Japan that survived the lesson she would not learn without defeat. His child had known the limits of human suffering, inhumanity, and endurance. It was in her paintings. In the eyes of myriad anguished faces she had done while in bed convalescing from childhood diseases, from the despairing faces she had seen in the streets, the old people that came by our house fleeing the bombers. What strength and power they held! Now from this life in the shadow I was taking her where she might know gladness and hope; where she might have the red velvet gown of my dreams.

We returned to Johnson City and I put Mako in college there. Dr. Fields, the kind and gentle registrar, permitted her to enroll without meeting the formal requirements. We lived at my mother's house where Pechy had lived and now lay in his grave in the backyard.

There was a letter from Terry awaiting me when we first arrived. I was not surprised to see the mistakes in English; Terry's English had become increasingly poor during his illness.

August 15, '49

My Dearest:

On August 12, what a vacant feeling I had when I came back to the drawing room from the gate! It was 10 to 1 p.m. I shall remember this time.

Yoshiko lying on my bed crying for time. I was walking around downstair to upstair. What a change! Just this morning they were here.

I didn't cry but it was worse than crying, because Yoshiko got over with it after some time, I didn't. Both were speechless sometime. When we talked, both of us didn't touch the subject of

257

neither of you and Mariko for a few hours. Both knew what the other party was thinking. I lost pep to go out or do anything, until now (Aug. 15) I didn't go out a step out of my gate.

But today I intend to take a walk near-by....

Forget about Japan, Japanese and me. Enjoy your life in America and think of your future life which is full of *taihen* (troubles).

Love,
Terry

Early in October, as the smell of fall came in the air, and I was reminded of so much of the past, I had a brief note from Japan written in pencil:

Oct. 4, '49

Dear Gwen:

I am missing "morning chat" with you and Mako so badly. I'm so happy to know Mako is receiving a wonderful reception in Johnson City. I am proud that Mako is making a speech at the Hotel. I wish I could hear her. Yoshiko is out going to *panya*. I'm alone thinking of the U.S.A.

Your letters are life-saver for me. Pardon for pencil. As Yoshiko is out I can't use her pen, you know.

Love & Kisses,
Terry

And, written across the margin of one side: "Mako is making up for me what I meant to do."

It was the anniversary of our wedding and I wrote him a long letter, saying we would be together on the next anniversary. He wrote in return a short note that I could scarcely read, so illegible and full of crossed out words and new starts was it:

Nov. 19, '49

Gwen, Darling:

Your Wedding Anniversary card came to me 5 days before 11/14. I'm sending this 5 days ~~before~~ after 11/14. I sent you a short note ~~to you~~ but I couldn't stand to touch on our W. A. because this is first time that you are not with me.

But you must know that you are always close to me and I am the happiest husband and father in the world.

Love,
Terry

Mako had to apply herself diligently to her studies but with the help of her instructors, who were uniformly considerate and helpful, she made rapid progress. How foolish had been our fears that she would not be accepted by her fellow students! She was chosen to ride on one of the homecoming floats, representing the freshman class, in the celebration before the football game.

My father had converted one side of his home into an apartment for Mako and me, and our living expenses were kept to a minimum. Even so, it soon appeared that money would not go as far in postwar America as we had expected, and we had to use every resource to make ends meet. As soon as we got settled, I made efforts at cutting the red tape to release Terry's bank account. I was both pleased and astonished when these efforts succeeded and the account was sent to me in full. It was applied to Mako's schooling and clothes, and we made it go as far as we possibly could.

I began getting letters from Terry saying he was improving— the handwriting was stronger, more like it used to be. He had resigned his post and was resting and working in the garden. He said, "I remember General Petain's famous words, 'My left wing has retired, my right wing has retired, now is the best opportunity to attack.' I decided the hardest thing for me was to give up smoking. I hated to fight in this fight without aid of smoking ... but I must tell you my health is much, much better. My early rising and taking care of the garden must have helped a lot to improve my health. I will be strong and able to make a living again. Wait and see. I have been sick for such a long time. I have decided to oppose my sickness with patience."

Then, in June of 1950—just when I was ready to book passage back to Tokyo—came the outbreak of the Korean War. A letter came telling me to remain in America, as Terry feared the fighting might spread temporarily and did not want me in Japan until the conflict was settled. He wrote that he had full confidence in MacArthur and that it would be over before long. I asked a friend who was going to Japan to urge him to let me return, but Terry wrote again to wait and he wrote Mako explaining why it was better for both of us to be in America for the present.

As we waited our bank account became smaller and smaller, and, without writing Terry of it, I returned to the department store where I had worked—so long ago—in 1930 before my fateful visit to Washington. I had to be patient, also, and the work helped.

One day I had a long letter from Japan in which Terry described our life together,

> Darling:
>
> If I mention the high-lights of our marriage, they are as follows: (1) the Japanese Embassy (2) drive in the Rock Creek Park (3) our wedding (4) Manchurian incident (5) birth of our baby (6) our desire was the rainbow over the Pacific (7) rainbow is falling, our last effort: cablegram to the Emperor (8) war broke out—my talk and your talk at the apt. (9) exchange boat (10) war life in Japan (11) Americans move in (12) my life in the Palace (13) my resignation (14) your going to the USA, etc.
>
> Don't learn to type. You are too good for that and your long suit is not such a thing. (Let Mako learn typing). Someday I hope you write a novel like the above. If you don't, I will....

I caught the bus at 5 P.M. each day to return home from work. Mako would usually be there ahead of me and together we would prepare our supper, chatting of events on the campus and at the department store. One night after she had put away her books and finally come to bed, we lay awake in our twin beds talking back and forth in our tiny room. A Western Union boy knocked at the door and handed me a cablegram. Terry was dead.